THE
SATIN
SLIPPER

THE SATIN SLIPPER

OR

THE WORST IS NOT THE SUREST

BY

PAUL CLAUDEL

TRANSLATED BY THE REV.
FR. JOHN O'CONNOR

WITH THE COLLABORATION OF
THE AUTHOR

NEW YORK
SHEED & WARD
1945

DEDICATION
TO
JOSÉ MARIA SERT
PAINTER

TO THE READERS OF THIS TRANSLATION.*

When the wind blows, the windmills go wheeling round all together.

But there is another Wind, I mean the Spirit, which is sweeping nations with a broom.

When you have it unchained, it sets all the human landscape a-moving.

Ideas from one end of the world to the other are catching fire like stubble!

From Thames to Tiber is heard a great clatter of arms and of hammers in the shipyards.

The sea is at one stroke all covered with white poppies, the night is plastered all over with Greek letters and algebraic signs.

There's dark America yonder like a whale bubbling out of the Ocean! Hark! howling Asia feels a new god leaping in her womb!

And look at that fiery lover, what does he say? I think he has found the right word at last, look at that proud lady whose head droops and who crumbles piecemeal like a wall!

In all those things there is not any logical sequence, but please climb to the top of a tree with me, ladies and gentlemen.

Then you will understand all things, simply by seeing them together, they are all parts of one wide panorama.

All is contrived somehow by that fierce wind blowing without intermission, and the meaning of all——

To find it you need only to look up at that rude horseplay in the clouds, that dishevelled cavalry in the singing sky with that untiring trumpet!

It could not last any longer! it is the same mouth everywhere clamouring for air, it is the same deep heart which says: Open here!

* This Preface was written by M. Claudel in both French and English [*Pub. note.*].

AUX LECTEURS DE LA TRADUCTION ANGLAISE DU "SOULIER DE SATIN."

Quand le vent souffle, tous les moulins tournent à la fois.

Mais il y a un autre vent, c'est l'Esprit qui balaye les peuples devant soi,

Et qui, quand après un long repos le voici déchainé, ça met en mouvement tout notre paysage humain!

Les idées d'un bout à l'autre du monde prennent feu comme du foin!

On entend de la Tamise au Tibre un grand bruit d'armes et de mécaniques.

Toute la mer d'un seul coup s'est couverte de coquelicots blancs, toute la nuit s'est tapissée de lettres grecques et de signes algébriques.

Voici l'Amérique ruisselante qui surgit, l'Asie sent un dieu nouveau s'agiter au fond de ses entrailles.

Et l'amant a trouvé le mot juste enfin, voyez cette femme fière d'un seul coup qui cède et qui s'abat comme un pan de muraille!

Tout cela, vous diriez que, ça n'a pas de rapport, mais celui qui pour mieux voir, il est monté sur un arbre,

Il sait que tout ça, c'est les mêmes cavaleries dans le ciel en chantant et la même trompette infatigable!

C'est la même chose qui ne pouvait plus durer, c'est la même bouche qui demande à respirer, c'est la même poitrine qui étouffe!

The trees all over the World are different but it is the same Wind a-blowing!

I, the painter, have drawn that picture whose subject is everything.

But the *point*, to find it, that's the point for you, my dearest readers.

I mean that vital *punctum* which centres everything.

Look out for it yourselves and please don't be angry if it slips between your fingers like a flea!

The old painter who let loose that living grain of black salt, smiles.

What did he do after all but try to please himself to his own sweet will?

After the manner of Lope de Vega and of all those grand English masters of old, amongst whom he worships with special tenderness and relish.

That funny man in drawers on the Place Malesherbes who grew *Henry the Sixth* and *Hamlet* out of his bulging head like a horse-radish!

Les gestes sont différents, mais c'est le même vent qui souffle!

Et c'est pourquoi j'ai brossé cette toile où il y a toutes sortes de choses.

Mais cet espèce de point vital autour de quoi tout se compose,

Tâchez de l'attraper vous mêmes, chers lecteurs, tant pis s'il fuit entre vos doigts comme une puce!

L'auteur qui a lâché ce grain vivant de sel noir sourit et se réjouit de son astuce.

Et qu'est-ce qu'il a fait, je vous prie? sinon de s'amuser à la façon

De Lope de Vega et de tous les grands vieux dramaturges Anglo-Saxons.

Parmi lesquels celui qui a fait sortir *Henry le Sixième* et *Hamlet* de son crâne en forme de cornichon.

God writes straight with crooked lines.

PORTUGUESE PROVERB.

Even sins.

ST. AUGUSTINE.

THE SATIN SLIPPER

THE ARGUMENT is that all things minister to a Divine Purpose and so to one another, be it events or personalities. Even the falterings of circumstance and the patternings of personality, sin and falsehood, are made to serve truth and justice, and above all, salvation in the long run.

The GENERAL STAGE DIRECTIONS say in effect that the tensity of the action makes the play so arduous that its production had better be as humanly slack as may suit with everyone's convenience. Above all, no pause for scene-shifting.

The author, for his purposes, permits himself to telescope times and places: the battle of the White Mountain happens before Mary of Scotland appears, and she is taken as very much alive after the defeat of the Armada, whereas Lepanto is still in the offing.

FIRST DAY

SCENE I: A Jesuit, dying abandoned on a plundered ship, prays for his brother Rodrigo, the hero of the action, that, since he has refused the directest way to God, he may find the selfsame by whatever winding road his own will may build unto itself; and that his sinful love, bereft of consummation may avail to draw him from self and love of self until he attain to selflessness.

SCENE II: Pelagio, husband of Prouheze (Dona Maravilla) manifests himself as a man of rigid principle just garnished with humanity. Balthazar, consciously very human but strong in military honour, accepts the charge of escorting Dona Prouheze, mildly suggesting his unfitness to take charge of any pretty lady, save in the capacity of husband.

SCENE III: Don Camillo, the villain, discloses a determination to win Prouheze, guessing that she is but lightly attached to her husband. She dallies with him just enough to implicate the whole tragic developments of the drama.

SCENE IV: Dona Isabel makes with Don Luis the secret assignation which leads to the wounding of Rodrigo much later on.

SCENE V: Don Balthazar is setting off in escort to Dona Prouheze, who reveals that she has written to Rodrigo. Account of her passion for him, her forced and loveless marriage of reverential fear with Pelagio. They both look up at the statue of Our Lady, and Prouheze takes off one shoe, which, standing on her mule, she places in the image's hands: " that when I would go headlong into evil it may be with halting foot."

SCENE VI: The Spanish King at Belem, discussing with his Chancellor the need of a strong hand in the new realm of America, asks for a suggestion. The Chancellor suggests Don Rodrigo. With some demur the King accepts and commands him to be brought.

SCENE VII: Rodrigo, avoiding the pursuivants of the King, is resting towards evening, and discussing with his Chinese servant his love of Prouheze; he is interrupted by musket-fire in a distant wood and rushes to the rescue of Saint James, whose image, he thinks, is being set upon by brigands.

SCENE VIII: Jobarbara the negress servant of Prouheze, is distraught from severe vigilance by a Neapolitan Sergeant who has fooled her out of her most precious possessions. The Sergeant mentions that he is rescuing Dona Musica from Don Pelagio's matrimonial disposition of her.

SCENE IX: Dona Isabel (of Scene IV) sees her lover killed by Rodrigo in defence of Saint James' image from the sham attack she had arranged with Don Luis. Rodrigo, badly wounded by Don Luis, borrows a carriage from Isabel's brother and goes off to be nursed in his mother's castle.

SCENE X: Musica and Prouheze, at the fortress inn, discuss their lovers fancifully, but Prouheze's intensity caps the scene.

SCENE XI: The negress is spell-binding to bring back the Sergeant. The Chinese servant of Rodrigo comes instead, looking for the money of which she has cheated him. She tells him Dona Maravilla is within the fortress—he tells her of Rodrigo's mischance and his present lodging, and how Prouheze must be got to him. A band of knights is seeking Musica and he has told them she is quartered at this inn. So they are going to attack next evening, and then the negress must get Prouheze to leave under cover of the tumult.

SCENE XII: Prouheze escapes with great difficulty. Her Guardian Angel looks on, marking and suggesting.

SCENE XIII: Balthazar confesses that he has connived at the escape of Prouheze. He is planning a sham defence for a reason visible in——

SCENE XIV: The Chinaman confesses to Balthazar his responsibility for the attack. The old soldier grimly makes him share his risks, which now are turning into certainties of sudden death. Supper is served.

The attackers ask for Musica. Balthazar compels the Chinaman to sing for them. On the sea a boat sails by with negress, Sergeant and Musica. Balthazar falls across the table shot dead.

SECOND DAY

SCENE I: At Cadiz in a merchant-tailor's shop, Caballeros fitting out for and discussing their coming expedition to America under Don Rodrigo.

SCENE II: The stage factotum, like a circus-clown, tongue-lathering everyone, brings on Prouheze and Dona Honoria, just to wile the time while the real scene (III) is being prepared.

SCENE III: Is the eye of the storm. Don Pelagio as guest of Dona Honoria discusses Prouheze. Honoria insists on discussing her son Rodrigo, unconscious and like to die. Prouheze is in the castle but has not seen the patient. Her presence is favoured by Honoria, since she thinks it will aid her son's recovery. They fall to discussing Pelagio's sad, well-intended marriage with Prouheze. He concludes that all is over between them, and devises a course for Prouheze which he knows will keep her straight. He will give her a task on all fours with her mighty character.

SCENE IV: Pelagio recapitulates with Prouheze their arduous adventures in Africa. He must give up Africa, but she must go in his stead. It is the King's commission. " Give me time to think it over," says Prouheze. "The horses are ready. Attention! Go and change your dress!"

SCENE V: On the Roman Campagna the Viceroy of Naples discussing with his suite the European situation and the Protestant effect thereon.

SCENE VI: Saint James, as the constellation Orion, soliloquizes on Africa and America sundered and joined by the Atlantic. He sees the Two Lovers likewise joined and sundered.

SCENE VII: The King demurs, on second thoughts, to sending Prouheze to such a forlorn hope as Mogador. He will counsel her to give it up and send Rodrigo with the letter. It will test his capacity to go through with his American commission. Pelagio cautiously argues against Rodrigo and Prouheze meeting. But the King stands firm.

SCENE VIII: At sea becalmed off Mogador, Rodrigo chafes and discusses with the captain, Don Camillo, as his rival with Prouheze. She cannot love that half-Moor, yet it was her hand that fired the gun which cut down his main-mast. The currents will drift them to Mogador to-morrow, says the captain, as is shown by the bit of wreckage fished up that very day. It bears the legend Santiago. That is the name of the ship on which Rodrigo's Jesuit brother had sailed for Brazil.

SCENE IX: Inside a battery at Mogador a trial of will and of skill is going on between Prouheze and Camillo. She is drawn by him to look through an opening at Rodrigo's ship in the offing.

SCENE X: The action passes to Sicily, where Dona Musica, shipwrecked on that coast, is entertaining the Viceroy of Naples, who has wandered from his party in the moonlight. They talk of love and delight and of their marriage soon to be.

SCENE XI: Tense conflict of wills again in the torture chamber of Mogador, where Camillo has chosen to receive Rodrigo. He gives him a note from Prouheze: "I stay. You go." Rodrigo, beaten by the note, leaves without sight or speech of Prouheze.

SCENE XII: In the American tropic forest a group of Spanish gentlemen adventurers discuss and reveal the hardships of the campaign, the weirdness of the land, and its relics of strange religions. Their reasons for not going on and against going back. These latter prevail.

SCENE XIII: The Double Shadow, man and woman, protests against the two (Rodrigo and Prouheze) who having one moment made it one, comprising an eternity in one instant, are now by their own act tearing it asunder by a strain which stretches across the world.

SCENE XIV: Now the Moon throws the shadow of a waving palm and speaks of rest and alleviation to all burdened creatures. It sees Prouheze weeping on her wedding night (Outside the action, later on explained, Pelagio dies and Prouheze marries Don Camillo to hamper his power for ill). In words of terrifying beauty the Moon tells her thoughts and then of Rodrigo's despairing resignation as his white sail tacks to the moonlit coast of Brazil. So ends the Second Day.

THIRD DAY

SCENE I: In the Church of Saint Nicholas at Prague Dona Musica, wife of the Viceroy of Naples, who has just won the battle of the White Mountain, kneels at prayer. Enter Saint Nicholas, whose feast it is, and who gives the atmosphere of winter peace. He then mounts to his empty niche. Musica prays for the child she is bearing, and for the wild and wounded people all round. Enter Saint Boniface, giving thanks for the victory, praying for the German people. He mounts his pedestal. Musica goes on praying for the people that she may bring them harmony. Enter Saint Denis of Athens, who modifies the effect of her words with: no world ever can store up happiness, no harmony except what this world's music suspends. The sea of Slavdom with cold, night, mud, snow, wind, unceasing, reminds Europe that activity can be vain and progress interminably postponed. Mankind escapes torture only to suffer boredom. So the East has known. But he came west to the prow of the good ship Europe which steers forever to the western constellations away from the mud and materialism. As if inspired by his unheard soliloquy Musica offers God her child to be a gentle influence to come, to *resolve* humanely these *suspensions* of good accord.

Saint Adlibitum closes the scene. He loves this land of mills and watersheds and most of all the Danube, for it flows towards Paradise. Even if the earthly Paradise is long since dismantled, yet all free spaces are full of its rebuilding. Thither! ah thither!

SCENE II: Don Fernando, on shipboard for the New World, discusses with Don Leopold Augustus on the obscenity of Nature, the sublimity of grammar, and the absurdity of other learned men. It comes out by accident that Fernando is brother to that Dona Isabel whose betrothed was killed by mistake in that skirmish with Don Rodrigo (first day, Scene IX). Isabel is now in America married to Rodrigo's principal lieutenant, Don Ramiro. Fernando is bearing Prouheze's letter to Rodrigo, and tells how he came by it. Leopold Augustus undertakes the risk of delivering the letter. In Scene V, it is plain that he has died of sunstroke, and his landlady beats his clothes and makes the letter fall out, as it is unlucky to handle it.

SCENE III: Is to show the manner of Rodrigo's government. He has just destroyed Almagro's prosperous plantation on the Orinoco, in order to transfer his slaves to the great Panama scheme of transporting galleons overland to the Pacific. (This is a highly important feature to which attention is called repeatedly in the ensuing action.) He compensates Almagro by the offer of all America South of Lima, along with a band of wild young men and desperate veterans gathered in Panama.

SCENE IV: Mogador. Night. Three sentries discuss how Don Sebastian has been tortured to death by Camillo. (Explaining in a few flashes the slow horror of Prouheze's existence in the fortress.)

SCENE V: (Already noted) The letter.

SCENE VI: Ramiro and Isabel discuss the Viceroy, her influence, Ramiro's prospects. No chance while Rodrigo remains. Isabel longs for the letter. It falls at her feet (as though from Scene V). (She presents it in Scene IX.)

SCENE VII: (An introduction to Scene VIII.) Again at Mogador, Don

Camillo puts in the hand of Prouheze asleep a crystal bead of her rosary which he has been seeking all day. He senses innumerable unseen presences.

SCENE VIII: Prouheze in dream sees the Globe. All blue ocean. It turns and Panama is on its rim. More blue beyond. She hears Rodrigo saying her name. She longs for him. The greater Island of Japan looms up. Slowly it takes the form of a warrior in dark armour, and her Guardian Angel speaks. He has her hooked, but he pays out and retracts his line. In many luminous figures he shows her Rodrigo and her own soul wrestling with her attachment by pitting God against Rodrigo, suggesting milder climes than poisonous Mexico or scorching Mogador. He is not using her as a fish to play, but as a bait to catch Rodrigo. His love for her was the only means to make his pride feel the law of altruism, to imagine or allow for any other than self. Prouheze objects that love dis-sacramented is sinful. The angel retorts a famous phrase "Sin, too, serves." He dimly forecasts Prouheze's early death as the appointed way for her to serve Rodrigo and finally to save. He gives her a foretaste of Purgatory, with strength and light to go through her last earthly trials. Then a sketch of Rodrigo's new departures—Japan, shipwreck, (the Globe turns showing the whole Far East from India to China). The long purpose of God towards the Orient races wedded so many ages to nothingness. He vanishes into the land praying Mary for them, and the whole sky glitters into a great image of The Immaculate Conception.

SCENE IX: The Viceroy Rodrigo, in his palace at Panama, is working with his Secretary, Rodilard. Dona Isabel amuses herself with singing and desultory talk. She alludes to the letter to Rodrigo which she has given to the Secretary. Rodrigo takes the letter. "I cannot read."

SCENE X: A terrible duel of wits at Mogador between Don Camillo and Dona Prouheze. It begins with how and why she married him and goes on to a question of the fatherhood of their child. Thence to a diagnosis of Camillo's position and conduct towards Spanish interests and his own. Then to the influence of Rodrigo. Lastly the nature and existence of God. He avows himself Mahometan. But he sees Christ in her and cries out for Him! A tense and poignant encounter, in which Prouheze wins a victory which is left in doubt to the end.

SCENE XI: Rodrigo on the flagship of his fleet sets out for Europe. He takes leave, after his peculiar fashion, of his Secretary and Dona Isabel.

SCENE XII: The fleet is off Mogador two months later. The Viceroy sees through a telescope a stout defence of the fortress against the Moors. He will not go to the aid of Don Camillo. He wants Spain to concentrate on America and give up Africa. Suddenly the fortress signals a parley, and a boat with a woman on board is seen setting off from the port. And

SCENE XIII: The Viceroy on the flagship receives Prouheze in state. She holds a little girl by the hand and presents her credentials. She explains her position at Mogador and how she has used it in the interest of Spain. She makes the child over to Rodrigo. This means that she is returning to her fortress-prison. Camillo's terms are: if you withdraw the fleet I let Prouheze go with it. Rodrigo will take her away, to free her from this preposterous renegade. She says death alone can set her free. Then ensues the terrific struggle between sentiment and principle, love and duty, expedience and austere honour. In the end Rodrigo, broken, weeps. Prouheze is taken on board the dark pinnace and the child screams for her.

FOURTH DAY

All the action of this day takes place at sea, and windward of the Balearic Islands. The sea is the chief actor in the whole drama. This Fourth Day leaves no doubt of it.

SCENE I: Three fishermen are skylarking with a fourth, Mangiacavallo, whose bovine wit makes him fair game. Don Rodrigo's ship, all the battered remnant of his fleet, goes by under one spritsail, and on a line between two masts flutter images of saints. They discuss his pictures, his incongruity with the merry gathering of the Armada against England going on round about them, and his Japanese painter-graver who carries out his suggestions. All through this day, and notable especially in this scene, is a sense of freer breathing, a spiritual lightness of heart, in contrast to the brooding oppressiveness of the Third Day. Prouheze is dead (though 'tis not even hinted) and her tremendous victory over self and circumstance bears visible or tangible fruit.

SCENE II: Rodrigo is in his cabin, working at pictures of saints, dictating them to his Japanese amanuensis. Don Mendez Leal, a lay figure, "a mere silhouette cut out in black cloth," hangs upside down in a corner. They pass from pictures to reminiscence, which tells what has happened since Rodrigo saw Prouheze for the last time. Rodrigo gives some account even of the adventures of his mind. The futile Don Mendez Leal is brought to life by means as entirely artificial as himself, farcical but symbolic. One result of his actualisation by such novel methods is that he is a diplomatist who tells the truth (manifestly absurd like his appearance in the scene). Among other matters he offers his views on "Christian Art." Rodrigo entangles him into a jungle of suggestions for subjects of Sacred Art such as the Earthly Paradise. This stumps the Don, or winds him, and he gives up, by letting fall what he has really come for. He receives a little picture of Saint Gabriel, the patron of ambassadors.

SCENE III: Early morning at sea. In a little boat Dona Sevenswords, aged 16 or so, the daughter of Prouheze and by her entrusted to Rodrigo, is bullying and chaffing a butcher's daughter into an expedition to free the Christian slaves of Barbary. She calls it delivering her mother. She speaks in admiration of the Viceroy, her father; and the Butcher's Daughter disparagingly compares him with Don John of Austria. Sevenswords confesses that she is in love with Don John, whom she has just saved from footpads that very night. She longs to go campaigning with him as his page.

SCENE IV: A Hall in the floating palace of the Spanish King. He is like the King of Spades, whereas in the first Two Days he was like the King of Hearts. Gazing into a skull of rock crystal, he sees the wreck of his Armada. He explains his policy by his religion, and covers the skull as the Chamberlain enters. Glorious news! The Spanish fleet has destroyed the ships of Drake and Frobisher, and is now bombarding the Tower of London. A Jew merchant from Bayonne has brought the news. But Medina Sidonia, somehow, is drowned. The King orders Te Deum for a victory. An Actress begs him to recall Medina Sidonia. She fears he will fall in love with Mary of Scotland. The King promises to recall him on condition that she personates Mary of Scotland to Don Rodrigo, whom he intends to make Viceroy of England. This she undertakes, and with a curtsey she retires. The Hall fills with courtiers and functionaries. Solemn farce about the "victory." Who will go and govern England? All decline. The King tells them that England is Rodrigo's for the asking. But he must ask.

SCENE V: Bidens and Hinnulus, each with their boat-crews, come with our old friends the fishermen, looking for what is not quite evident, even to themselves. They ignore each other's presence except in scornful reference. A boisterous parody of the "scientific spirit." They work in opposite directions until the Whateveritis in the middle gives way and they topple over.

SCENE VI: The Actress and her dresser discuss Rodrigo, and while she makes up and rehearses for Mary of Scotland, the Back-drop goes up suddenly, snatching away the whole outfit and disclosing another actress already made up as Mary of Scotland, but very much half-dressed, painting hard to the directions of Rodrigo. (His Japanese had left him, reasons unsaid.)

They discuss the pictures. She brings the conversation on to herself. She must go back to England. Not at all, says Rodrigo. But her dear Medina Sidonia is there. As Rodrigo shows no jealousy she tells him straight that she would prefer to go with him. Rodrigo flirts with her half in earnest, and not so earnestly, but at greater length, toys with the idea of being England's Viceroy. But he will not touch the thing until he has finished his grand frieze entitled "The Kiss of Peace."

SCENE VII: Diego Rodriguez is coming home on his battered ship from a career of unprofitable ventures. He is sure Dona Austregesila has found his absence too long and is married to some lucky fellow. Don Alcindas comes on board with news of the fair Austregesila. Far from forgetting him she has looked out for his ship every day. Even now she descried it and sent him, Alcindas, with greetings. She has administered so well his patrimony that now he is the richest man in Majorca. Tableau. The lieutenant gets a final kick for daring to doubt the loyalty of such a woman!

SCENE VIII: On Rodrigo's boat, Sevenswords is weaning him from "Mary of Scotland." He frees his soul about Prouheze and their immortal love. Sevenswords tries to enlist him in the crusade for Africa. He counters with vast world-politics too big for her. She pouts, and they patch up a very provisional agreement.

SCENE IX: Again the floating palace. The Throne-room. The sea makes merry with the solemn pomposity of courtiers and King. Rolling and plunging, the floor *will* interfere with the most telling points of the Grand Consult. Meanwhile the courtiers doing their best, lament the personal losses arising from the wreck of the Armada, now certainly known to the chosen. Some material windfalls of legacies and such are bemoaned with greater insincerity. Rodrigo has been sequestrated for two days, and none of the real news has been allowed to reach him. He enters in the superb black of the Court as a grandee of Spain, and simultaneously the King is revealed enthroned. The King makes ironic summary of Rodrigo's achievements, concluding with a critique of his artistry and advancing quite convincing theories of art (they never can keep off it). Rodrigo replies with blasting suavity that the power of majesty to penetrate almost without a glance to the inmost heart and value of what has cost an inferior being so many years of painful study, so much coining of his life-blood, leaves him no choice but to devote his remaining years and energies to the correction of those shortcomings so plain to the royal perception! And so on, till the Viceroyalty of England is passionately urged upon him by the Chancellor. Rodrigo, in all good faith, consents to take office on one condition only: no fleet, no army, no officials, and no taxes. Rodrigo's new views baffle them all and make their sporting appointment into a severe lesson for themselves, but he is still deceived about "Mary of England" the actress, and allows himself to be solemnly charged with a royal match between her and Don Ernest of Spain. But Rodrigo has more disconcerting proposals still. Let not only England, but all Europe, have the freedom of the Americas! There is plenty of space, plenty to develop. The scene ends in a frenzy of play-acting by all the Court, emphasised by the satiric motion of the sea, and the King commands Rodrigo back to close custody, going out with such majesty as the dancing floor-boards allow.

SCENE X: Cinematograph effects are needed. Open sea under the full moon. Sevenswords has induced the poor Butcher's Daughter to swim out with her from Rodrigo's ship. A red lantern on shore was to give the signal of landing where friends with clothes were told to meet them. Sevenswords is done with her "Papa," since he is taken up with this "England" scheme. She will go to Don John of Austria, who is setting off to-morrow. Meanwhile, as her speeches get voluble Butchie's get briefer. After one apology for her bad swimming she drowns quite uncomplaining. Sevenswords, glorying in the sea, swims on, throwing one last encouragement to her comrade. The boat has seen them and is bearing down.

SCENE XI: On a boat making for land Rodrigo in chains with two soldiers and Brother Leo. They torment him by reading and remarking on Sevenswords' parting letter. "Dear Papa he made her think he was her father." "Her father was Camillo the pirate renegade, her mother was his mistress." "No," says Brother Leo, "I married them." Rodrigo forgets his distress. He behaves with wonderful patience under the ingenious devilry of the soldiers. Brother Leo tries to soften or end it, in vain. One says he has just heard a young girl has been fished out of the sea and has died on their hands. Brother Leo tries to comfort him. The letter ends by saying that when she reaches Don John of Austria she will get him to fire a signal-gun. Just here a voice hails them and two nuns come alongside in their trading-boats. While the soldiers go forward Rodrigo asks Brother Leo about Prouheze.

The nuns are dealing in marine-stores to help Saint Teresa's new convents. They come aboard and chaffer. With much ado Rodrigo induces them to take him as part of the "stores." Brother Leo also pleads, and Rodrigo is sold for nothing into the slavery of Teresa of Jesus. As he climbs into the questing-boat a trumpet sounds triumphantly in the distance. The nun explains that it comes from the ship of Don John of Austria. "My child is saved!" In the distance a cannon is fired, and Brother Leo says the final word: *Deliverance to all souls in prison!*

POSTSCRIPT

It will not be out of place to point to a few really amazing subtleties of the plot. They have been hopelessly missed by many smart French critics, who have not given the work the long consideration of the author's. The most casual brief episode of the action is the pivot of all that happens, putting aside the secret springs of Providence, Prayer, and the power of good, weak good, against the strongest evil. Scene IV of the First Day makes the assignation by which Dona Isabel's lover chances to be killed through the mistaken zeal of Rodrigo. His error originates in the over-subtlety of his Chinese servant. Now Dona Isabel it is, married to Ramiro in Panama, that sets Rodrigo on his wild expedition to rescue Prouheze, and so on to Japan and back. It is Don Pelagio's austere and rigid righteousness that sets rolling the ball of inordinate desire, as witness Camillo's daring to make love to Prouheze in the very beginning of the first day. Pelagio seems somehow responsible for Isabel's luckless first love, as also for Musica's wild flight to the Viceroy of Naples. Interesting in the woof of the play is the diplomatic cast of the dialogue, as also of so many situations. Delicately self-revealing is the author, one of France's most trusted agents with foreign nations. Let me express my gratitude for his supervision of my work and my special recognition of exceptionally minute and careful correction and several other kindnesses from Monsieur and from Madame Paul Petit.

JOHN O'CONNOR.

AUTHOR'S FOREWORD

As, after all, it is not entirely impossible that the piece be played some day or other ten or twenty years hence, in whole or in part, it is not amiss to begin by these few stage directions. It is essential that the scenes follow each other without the least interruption. The most carelessly crumpled back-drop, or none at all, will do. The scene-shifters will make the few necessary dispositions under the very eyes of the public while the action is taking its course. At a pinch, nothing need prevent the artists from giving a helping hand. The actors in each scene will appear before those of the preceding scene have finished speaking and will at once have their own share in the small preparatory business. Stage directions will be either clearly posted up or read out by the producer, or by the actors themselves, who will draw the necessary papers from their pockets or hand them on to one another. If they make a mistake, no matter. A rope-end hanging, a back-drop badly drawn and showing a white wall, in front of which the staff goes to and fro, will be most effective. The whole thing must look provisional, developing, disordered, incoherent, improvised in an enthusiastic mood, with happy accidents from time to time; for even in disorder monotony must be eschewed.

Order is the pleasure of the reason; but disorder is the delight of the imagination.

I suppose my piece to be played, let us say, on a Shrove Tuesday—at four o'clock in the afternoon. I imagine a great hall, frowsty from a previous audience, invaded again by the public and filled with the buzz of conversation. Through the folding doors is heard the dull clatter of a well-fed orchestra, performing in the foyer. Another little reedy orchestra in the hall—takes delight in mimicking the noises of the public, leading them and giving them, little by little, a sort of rhythm and a kind of form.

There comes upon the proscenium in front of the lowered curtain the ANNOUNCER. *He is a hefty, bearded fellow, who has borrowed from the best-recognized Velasquez this huge hat and feathers, this cane under his arm and this belt which he manages with difficulty to buckle. He attempts to speak, but every time he opens his mouth—*

*with the public meanwhile making an enormous preparatory tumult—
he is interrupted by a clash of cymbals, a silly bell, a shriek from the
fife, a sarcastic remark from the bassoon, a sly hint from the ocarina,
a belch from the saxophone.   By degrees they settle down and there is
silence.   Nothing is heard now but the big drum, which patiently goes*
poom, poom, poom, *like Madame Bartet's finger of resignation
drumming the table regularly while she endures the reproaches of*
Monsieur le Comte: *underneath all, the side-drum, rolling* pianissimo *with occasional* forte *until the public keeps silence.   The*
ANNOUNCER, *paper in hand, knocking hard on the ground with his cane,
announces:*

THE SATIN SLIPPER

or THE WORST IS NOT THE SUREST

Spanish play in Four Days

THE FIRST DAY

Characters:

THE ANNOUNCER.

THE JESUIT FATHER.

DON PELAGIO.

DON BALTHAZAR.

DONA PROUHEZE (MARAVILLA).

DON CAMILLO.

DONA ISABEL.

DON LUIS.

THE KING OF SPAIN.

THE CHANCELLOR.

DON RODRIGO.

THE CHINESE SERVANT.

THE NEGRESS JOBARBARA.

THE NEAPOLITAN SERGEANT.

DON FERNANDO.

DONA MUSICA (DELICIA).

THE GUARDIAN ANGEL.

THE ALFERES (LIEUTENANT)

SOLDIERS.

FIRST DAY

Short trumpet-call.

The Scene of this play is the world, and more especially Spain at the close of the Sixteenth, unless it be the opening of the Seventeenth, Century. The author has taken the liberty of compendiating countries and periods, just as at a given distance several separate mountain chains make but one horizon.

Another short trumpet-call.
A prolonged whistle or hoot, as though a ship were putting about.
Curtain rises.

THE FIRST DAY

SCENE I

THE ANNOUNCER, THE JESUIT FATHER

THE ANNOUNCER. Let us fix our gaze, I pray you, brethren, on that point of the Atlantic Ocean some degrees below the Line, equidistant from the Old World and the New. There is perfectly well shown here the wreck of a dismasted ship, drifting at the mercy of the waves. All the great constellations of one or other hemisphere—the Great Bear, the Little Bear, Cassiopeia, Orion, the Southern Cross—are hung in good order, like enormous chandeliers and gigantic panoplies, round about the sky. I could touch them with my cane. Round about the sky. And, here below, a painter, wishing to portray the work of pirates—probably English —on this poor Spanish vessel, would have just the notion of this mast, with its yards and rigging fallen right across the bridge, of these tumbled cannon, these open panels, these great splashes of blood and these corpses everywhere, and especially this group of nuns flung down on top of one another. To the stump of the main-mast is fastened a JESUIT FATHER, extremely tall and gaunt, as you may see. His torn cassock shows his bare shoulder. You may hear him speak as follows : *Lord, I thank You for having fastened me so. . . .* But he is going to speak himself. Listen well, do not cough, please, and try to understand a bit. It's what you won't understand that is the finest; it's what is longest that is the most interesting, and it's what you won't find amusing that is the funniest.

(Exit the ANNOUNCER.)

THE JESUIT FATHER. Lord, I thank You for having fastened me so ! And, sometimes, I have chanced to find Your commandments painful.

And my will, at sight of Your rule,
Perplexed, restive.
But, to-day, it is not possible to be closer bound to You than I

am, and, verify each limb as I will, there is not one that can withdraw from You ever so little.

True, also, I am fastened to the cross, but my cross is no longer fast to anything. 'Tis floating on the sea,

The free sea, away to that point where the limit of the known sky melts

And is equally distant from this old world, which I have left,

And from the other world the new.

All has breathed its last around me.

All has been consumed upon this narrow altar, laden with the bodies of my sisters one upon other; doubtless the vintage could not come to pass without some disorder,

But everything, after a little stir, is gone back again into the great paternal peace.

Even though I think myself forsaken, I have but to await the return of that unfailing power beneath, which takes me down and lifts me up with it, as if for the moment I were one with the rapture of the great deep.

Lo! this oncoming wave, the last of them, is carrying me off.

I take over to my use all this unseen work which God has made with a word, and with which I am inmostly amalgamated within His holy will, having given up my own,

All this past which with the future weaves one untearable web, this sea which has been put at my disposal,

The breeze breathing from those two friendly worlds, which I feel upon my face by turns with its surcease, and beyond them in the sky those great unquestionable constellations,—

I take them all to my service for benison upon this land so longed-for, which my heart surmised back there in the night!

Blessings upon her, like that of Abel the shepherd, in the midst of her floods and forests ! May war and dissension pass her by, may Islam never sully her shores, nor that still worse plague which is heresy!

I have given myself to God, and now the day of rest and relaxation is come and I can yield myself to these bonds which fasten me.

They speak of sacrifice, when every choice one makes is but a matter of almost imperceptible movement like a turn of the hand.

In sooth, it is only evil that demands effort, since it is against reality to sunder oneself from those great constant forces which on every side engage and make us their own.

And now, behold the last prayer of this Mass which already in the midst of death I am celebrating by the means of my poor self: my God, I pray You for my brother Rodrigo ! My God, I entreat You for my son Rodrigo !

I have no other child, Oh my God, and well he knows that he shall have no other brother.

You see how first he enlisted in my footsteps under the standard which bears Your monogram, and doubtless, now that he has left Your novitiate, he thinks he is turning his back on You,

His business, as he thinks, not being to stand and wait but to conquer and possess

All he can—as if there were anything that did not belong to You and as if he could be otherwhere than where You are.

But Lord, it is not so easy to escape You, and, if he goes not to You by what he has of light, let him go to You by what he has of darkness ; and if not by what he has of straight, may he go to You by what he has of indirection : and if not by what he has of simple, let him go by what in him is manifold and laborious and entangled,

And if he desire evil, let it be such evil as be compatible only with good,

And if he desire disorder, such disorder as shall involve the rending and the overthrow of those walls about him which bar him from salvation,

I mean him and that multitude with him which he is darkly implicating. For he is of those who cannot be saved except in saving all that mass which takes its impress in their wake.

Even by now You have taught him longing, but he does not yet suspect what it is to be desired.

Teach him that not You alone can be far away. Clog him by the weight of this other lovely being which lacks him and is calling him across the space between.

Make him a wounded man apart, for that once in this life he has seen the face of an angel!

Fill these lovers with such longing as shall involve, in the deprivation of each other's presence through the daily play of circumstance,

Their primal integrity, and their very essences as God conceived them both, long since in imperishable kinship;

And what He shall try to say on earth in wretchedness I am at hand in heaven to construe.

SCENE II

DON PELAGIO, DON BALTHAZAR

The front of a nobleman's house in Spain. First hour of the morning. The garden full of orange trees. A little blue terra-cotta fountain under the trees.

DON PELAGIO.   Don Balthazar, there are two roads going away from this house.

And one, if one could gauge it at a glance, through many towns and villages

Rising, falling, like a neglected skein on a rope-maker's trestle, bears from here straight to the sea, not far from a certain hostelry I know hidden among great trees.

That is the way a knight at arms escorts Dona Prouheze. Yes, I wish that by him Dona Prouheze be taken from my sight.

Meanwhile, by another road among the broom and climbing among the scattered rocks, I will yield to the call come to me from that white spot up there,

This letter from the widow in the mountain,

This letter from my cousin in my hand.

As to Maravilla my lady, there is nothing for it but to watch well the sealine towards the East, in which those sails appear which have to bring her and me to our governorship in Africa.

DON BALTHAZAR.   Eh what, señor, going away so soon?

The home of your childhood, after so many months on savage soil, what! leave it again?

DON PELAGIO.   True, it is the only spot in the world where I feel understood and taken for granted.

Here I used to seek refuge in silence whilst I was His Majesty's dreadful judge, extirpator of robbers and rebels.

A judge is not beloved.

But I found straight away that there was no greater charity than to kill off malefactors.

4

What days I have spent here, with no company from morning
till night but my old gardener,

These orange trees which I watered with my own hands, and
that little nanny-goat which was not afraid of me!

Yes, she used to butt me in play and come and eat vine leaves
from my hand.

DON BALTHAZAR. And now here is Dona Maravilla who is
more to you than the little nanny-goat.

DON PELAGIO. Take care of her, Don Balthazar, on this journey.
I entrust her to your honour.

DON BALTHAZAR. What, it is to me you want to entrust Dona
Prouheze?

DON PELAGIO. Why not? Have you not told me yourself that
your duties are calling you to Catalonia? It will not much lengthen
your road.

DON BALTHAZAR. I beg you to excuse me. Is there no other
knight to whom you can entrust this charge?

DON PELAGIO. Not one other.

DON BALTHAZAR. Don Camillo, for instance, your ensign and
lieutenant over there, who is going to set off at once?

DON PELAGIO, *dourly.* He will go alone.

DON BALTHAZAR. And cannot you let Dona Prouheze wait for
you here?

DON PELAGIO. I shall not have time to come back.

DON BALTHAZAR. What imperious duty calls you?

DON PELAGIO. My cousin, Dona Viriana, who is dying and no
man by her,

No money in the proud and lowly dwelling, hardly bread, add
to that six daughters to marry off—and the eldest only a little short
of twenty.

DON BALTHAZAR. Isn't it she we used to call Dona Musica?—
I lived round there while I was raising the levies for Flanders—

On account of that guitar which she never let go and never played on,
And those big, wide, trustful eyes on you, ready to take in wonder,
And those teeth, like blanched almonds, biting the red lip; and her laughter!

DON PELAGIO.   Why haven't you married her?

DON BALTHAZAR.   I am leaner than an old wolf.

DON PELAGIO.   And all the money that you earn goes to your brother, the head of the house, down in Flanders?

DON BALTHAZAR.   There is no better house between the Escaut and the Meuse.

DON PELAGIO.   I undertake Musica and I give you charge of Prouheze.

DON BALTHAZAR.   Like yourself indeed, señor, despite my age I feel better suited to be a pretty woman's husband than her guardian.

DON PELAGIO.   Neither she nor you, noble friend, I am sure, has anything to dread in these few days' companionship.
And, besides, you will always find my wise servant with her; beware of black Jobarbara!
No better guarded is a peach-tree growing right through a prickly pear.
Then, your sojourn will not be long: in a short time I shall have put everything to rights.

DON BALTHAZAR.   And married the six girls?

DON PELAGIO.   For each of them already I have chosen two husbands, and the order has gone forth summoning my gallants. But who would dare to resist Pelagio, the terrible judge?
They'll only have to choose; else I have chosen for them. The cloister gapes for them.
The Aragonese is no surer of his market when he lands on the place of barter with six new mares. There they are all together quietly in the shade of a big chestnut—

And they do not see the buyer passing from one to the other with delicacy and understanding, hiding the bit behind his back.

DON BALTHAZAR, *with a huge sigh.*   Farewell, Musica!

DON PELAGIO.   And while I have a little time left I will finish explaining you the situation on the African coast. The Sultan Muley . . .

(They withdraw.)

SCENE III

DON CAMILLO, DONA PROUHEZE

Another part of the same garden. Noon. The long wall right across the stage is a kind of hedge, formed of leafy plants. A gloom resulting from the shadow of close-planted trees. However, through some interstices, sunbeams pass which make burning patches on the ground. On the far side of the hedge and letting only flashes of her red gown appear through the leaves while she walks beside Don Camillo, Dona Prouheze. On the near side, Don Camillo.

DON CAMILLO.   I am grateful to Your Ladyship for letting me say farewell.

DONA PROUHEZE.   I granted you nothing and Don Pelagio forbade me nothing.

DON CAMILLO.   This hedge between us is a proof that you don't want to see me.

DONA PROUHEZE.   Is it not enough that I hear you?

DON CAMILLO.   Where I am I shall not often again trouble the Captain-General.

DON PROUHEZE.   Are you going back to Mogador?

DON CAMILLO.   It is the good side of the country, far from Ceuta and its offices, far from that big blue painting where the wake of the galleys is everlastingly writing in white the name of the King of Spain.
What I most appreciate is that forty-foot bar which costs me an old boat or two from time to time and worries visitors a bit.
But as the saying is: those who come to see me do me honour, those who do not come to see me do me pleasure.

DONA PROUHEZE.   It also cuts you off from all reinforcements and supplies.

DON CAMILLO.   I try to do without them.

DONA PROUHEZE.   Fortunate that Morocco just now is split up among three or four sultans who are at war, is it not?

DON CAMILLO.   'Tis true, 'tis my little bit of luck.

DONA PROUHEZE.   And no one better than you to profit by it, is there?

DON CAMILLO.   Yes, I speak all the languages, but I know what you are thinking.
You are thinking of the two years' journey I made into the interior disguised as a Jewish pedlar.
Many folk say that is not the deed of a gentleman or a Christian.

DONA PROUHEZE.   I have not thought so. No one has ever thought that you were a renegade. You see it by this post of honour which the King has entrusted to you.

DON CAMILLO.   Yes, a post of honour—like a dog on a barrel in the middle of the ocean.   But I do not want any other.
And many folk, too, say that there is something of the Moor in my case, because of my rather dusky complexion.

DONA PROUHEZE.   I have not thought so, I know that you are of a very good family.

DON CAMILLO.   Hurrah for the Moor!
Every good gentleman knows that he is only good for knocking on the head, as at quintain.
In theory, because in point of fact we tackle the dirty dog as little as possible.

DONA PROUHEZE.   You know that I feel as you do. I rather like that dangerous race.

DON CAMILLO.   Like them? No, but I do not like Spain.

DONA PROUHEZE.   What is this I hear, Don Camillo?

DON CAMILLO.   There are people who find their place ready made at birth,
Squeezed and embedded like a grain of maize in the compact ear:
Religion, family, country.

DONA PROUHEZE.   And are you detached from all that?

DON CAMILLO.   You'd like to know, wouldn't you? Just like my mother, who wanted me to tell her always the things that she was thinking. That "endearing" smile for only answer, how she used to tax me with it!

Ah! to her other sons and daughters I must say she scarcely gave a thought! She had only my name on her lips when she died. And this Prodigal Son, to change to another subject, a very wicked subject,

Did you think it true that he devoured his substance with gluttons and harlots? Ha! he embarked in transactions of another kind!

Speculations among Carthaginians and Arabs to frizzle the hair on your head! The very *name* was compromised, you think?

Do you believe that Father thought of anything but that darling son? All the livelong days. They hardly left anything else open to him.

DONA PROUHEZE.   What do you mean by that "endearing smile"?

DON CAMILLO.   As if we were agreed under the surface, as if it all were with her connivance. A little sly wink like that! That's what put her beside herself. Poor Mamma!

And still—who the devil made me if not she alone?

DONA PROUHEZE.   It is no business of mine to remake you.

DON CAMILLO.   How do you know? Nay, perhaps it's my business to unmake you.

DONA PROUHEZE.   That will be difficult, Don Camillo.

DON CAMILLO.   It will be difficult, and still there you are listening to me, in spite of your husband's prohibition, through this leafy wall. I can see your tiny ear.

DONA PROUHEZE.   I know that you have need of me.

DON CAMILLO.   You understand that I'm in love with you?

DONA PROUHEZE.   I have said what I have said.

DON CAMILLO.   And that I do not horrify you overmuch?

DONA PROUHEZE. You could not so contrive that all at once.

DON CAMILLO. Tell me, you who listen unseen and walk step by step with me on the other side of this bower, is it not tempting what I offer you?
Others show the woman they love pearls, castles, and how much beside?—forests, a hundred farms, a fleet at sea, mines, a kingdom,
A peaceful and honoured life, a cup of wine to drink together!
But I, nothing of all that sort do I put before you. Listen! I know that I am going to touch your inmost heart,
Show you a thing so precious that, to attain it with me, nothing shall count, and you will weary of your goods, family, country, name, and even honour!
Look! What are we doing here, let us be off, Maravilla.

DONA PROUHEZE. And what is this very precious thing that you offer me?

DON CAMILLO. A place with me where there is absolutely nothing more! *Nada!* There!

DONA PROUHEZE. And that is what you have in store for me?

DON CAMILLO. Is there anything but this nothing which frees us from everything?

DONA PROUHEZE. But I love life, Señor Camillo! I love the world, I love Spain, I love this blue sky, the goodly sun! and I love this lot which God has given me.

DON CAMILLO. I love all that too. Spain is beautiful. My God, how good it would be if one could drop it once and for all!

DONA PROUHEZE. Isn't that what you have done?

DON CAMILLO. One always comes back.

DONA PROUHEZE. But does it exist, this place where there is absolutely nothing any more?

DON CAMILLO. It does exist, Prouheze.

DONA PROUHEZE. Which is it?

DON CAMILLO. A place where there is nothing more, a heart where there is nothing else but you.

DONA PROUHEZE.   You turn away your head when you say that, so that I shall not see the jest upon your lips.

DON CAMILLO.   When I say that love is jealous you pretend that you don't understand.

DONA PROUHEZE.   What woman would not understand?

DON CAMILLO.   She that loves—do not the poets say that she sighs at not being all in all to the being of her choice? He must have no more need but her alone.
She carries death and the desert about with her.

DONA PROUHEZE.   Ah, not death but life would I bring to him whom I love—life, were it at the cost of my own.

DON CAMILLO.   But are not you yourself more than these kingdoms to seize, more than yon America to bring up out of the sea?

DONA PROUHEZE.   I am more.

DON CAMILLO.   And what is it to call up an America beside a soul that sinks?

DONA PROUHEZE.   Must I give my soul to save yours?

DON CAMILLO.   There is no other way.

DONA PROUHEZE.   If I loved you, that would be easy for me.

DON CAMILLO.   If you love not me, love my misfortune.

DONA PROUHEZE.   What misfortune can be so great?

DON CAMILLO.   Save me from being alone.

DONA PROUHEZE.   But isn't it just that you have never left off working for?
Where is the friend that you have not put off, the bond that you have not broken, the duty you did not welcome with that smile of which you spoke just now?

DON CAMILLO.   If I am void of everything it is the better to wait for you.

DONA PROUHEZE.   God alone fills such a void.

DON CAMILLO. And this God—who knows if you alone are not the one to bring me Him?

DONA PROUHEZE. I am not in love with you.

DON CAMILLO. Then I, I am going to be so unhappy and so criminal, yes, I am going to do such things, Dona Prouheze,

That I shall force you outright to come to me, you and that God you keep so jealously to yourself, as if He were come for the righteous.

DONA PROUHEZE. Don't blaspheme!

DON CAMILLO. It is you who are talking to me about God; I don't like the subject. And you think that it was the Prodigal Son who asked forgiveness?

DONA PROUHEZE. The Gospel says so.

DON CAMILLO. I hold that it was the father—yes, while he was washing the wounded feet of that explorer.

DONA PROUHEZE. You will go back too.

DON CAMILLO. Then I don't want any music that day! No guests, no fatted calf! None of the public pomp.

I want him to be blind like Jacob, so that he may not see me.

Do you remember that scene when Joseph sent all his brethren out, that he might be alone with Israel?

No one knows what passed between them in that space, there was agony enough for all the world in those five minutes.

DONA PROUHEZE. Don Camillo, is it then so difficult to be quite simply an honest man? A faithful Christian, a faithful soldier, a faithful servant of His Majesty,

A very faithful spouse to the wife who gets you?

DON CAMILLO. All that is too trammelling and slow and complicated,

The rabble eternally on top of us! I smother! Ah! to be never done with this close prison and all this pile of soggy carcases!

All that keeps us from following our call.

DONA PROUHEZE. What then is this irresistible call?

DON CAMILLO. Tell me, have you never felt it yourself? The gnats are no fitter to resist that ecstasy of light when it sucks up the night.

Than the hearts of men, that call of the fire which may consume them—the call of Africa.

The earth would not at all be what it is, if it had not on its belly that square fire, that gnawing cancer, that ray which eats its liver, that brazier over-glowed with ocean-breathing, that smoking den, that oven where all the filth of animal life comes to be reconditioned!

We are not everything between our four walls.

It is all very fine for you to shut up everything to come to understandings among yourselves. You cannot shut out that greater part of humanity which you have agreed to do without and for which, after all, Christ died.

This breeze breathing on you which makes your leafage rustle and your shutters bang, 'tis Africa that calls it up in throe of her eternal torture!

Others explore the sea—and why should I not away, as far as it is possible, towards that other frontier of Spain, the fire!

DONA PROUHEZE. The captains that the King sends to those new Indies do not labour for themselves but for their master.

DON CAMILLO. I do not need to be thinking of the King of Spain all the time; is he not present everywhere where there is one of his subjects? All the better for him if I make myself at home where his writ cannot run.

It is not a new world that has been given me to mould to my whim,

It is a living book I have to con, and the mastery that I desire is not got except by learning.

A Koran whose lines are written in the ranks of palm trees beyond, with those pearly towns on the edge of the horizon like a running title.

And the letters, those crowds in the shadow of the narrow streets, crowds with burning eyes, those figures who cannot put out a hand without it turning golden.

Just as the Dutch live by the sea, so do those peoples on the very frontiers of mankind (not because the land leaves off but because the fire begins) by the exploitation of those shores beyond the burning lake.

There I will carve me a dominion all my own, an insolent small island to myself, between the two worlds.

DONA PROUHEZE.   For yourself alone?

DON CAMILLO.   For myself alone. A little place where I shall be more lost than a gold piece in a forgotten casket. Such that no one else but you will ever be able to come and find me there.

DONA PROUHEZE.   I will not come to look for you.

DON CAMILLO.   I give you tryst.

SCENE IV

DONA ISABEL, DON LUIS

A street in any town of Spain. A high window guarded with iron bars. Behind the bars Dona Isabel, and in the street Don Luis.

DONA ISABEL. I swear to wed none other than your lordship. To-morrow my brother, that cruel tyrant, is carrying me off from Segovia. I am one of the maids of honour going with our Lady when she goes away to the gate of Castile to receive the homage of Santiago. Be armed, bring a few bold companions. It will be easy for you in some gorge of the mountains to carry me off under favour of the night and the forest. My hand.

(*She gives it him.*)

SCENE V

DONA PROUHEZE, DON BALTHAZAR

Same as Scene II. Evening. A whole caravan ready to set out. Mules, luggage, arms, saddle horses, etc.

DON BALTHAZAR.   Madam, since it has pleased your consort, by a sudden inspiration, to entrust to me the ordering of your deeply respected Ladyship,
I have thought it necessary, before setting out, to make known to you the clauses which should guide our intercourse.

DONA PROUHEZE.   I listen to you with submission.

DON BALTHAZAR.   Oh, I wish this were the retreat from Breda over again! Yes indeed, sooner than order a handsome woman about,
I would lead a disbanded troop of starving mercenaries across a land of brushwood towards a horizon of gallows!

DONA PROUHEZE.   Don't be broken-hearted, señor, and give me that paper which I see ready in your hand.

DON BALTHAZAR.   Read it, I beg you, and be so good as to put your signature at the mark which I have made.
I have felt quite comfortable since I set down my orders so, upon that paper. That is what we shall have to obey from this time on, myself the first.
You will find everything clearly indicated, the stages, the hours of departure and of meals
And those moments, too, when it shall be free to you to converse with me, for I know that women cannot be condemned to silence.
Then I shall tell you about my campaigns, the beginnings of my family, the customs of Flanders, my country.

DONA PROUHEZE.   But I, shall I not have leave to put in a word occasionally?

17

DON BALTHAZAR.   Siren, I have already given you too much hearing.

DONA PROUHEZE.   Is it so unpleasant to think that for some days my fate and my life will not be less to you than your own!
And that in such close companionship you will indeed feel every moment that I have you for sole defender!

DON BALTHAZAR.   I swear it! They shall not snatch you from my hands.

DONA PROUHEZE.   Why should I try to run away, since you are guiding me to the very place where I wanted to go?

DON BALTHAZAR.   And which I refused: it is your consort who commands me!

DONA PROUHEZE.   If you had refused me, then I should have set off alone. Yes indeed, I should have found a way.

DON BALTHAZAR.   Dona Maravilla, I am sorry to hear your father's daughter speak like this.

DONA PROUHEZE.   Was he a man often crossed in his plans?

DON BALTHAZAR.   No, poor count! Ah, what a friend I have lost. I still feel that sword-thrust he gave me through the body, one carnival morning. That is how our brotherhood began.
I seem to see him again when I look at your eyes, you were in them then.

DONA PROUHEZE.   It would be better for me not to tell you that I have sent that letter.

DON BALTHAZAR.   A letter to whom?

DONA PROUHEZE.   To Don Rodrigo; yes, telling him to come and find me in that very inn where you are going to convey me.

DON BALTHAZAR.   Have you really done this foolish thing?

DONA PROUHEZE.   If I had not profited by that amazing opportunity—the gipsy who was making straight for Avila, where I know that knight is living—
Would it not have been a sin, as the Italians say?

DON BALTHAZAR.   Don't be profane and please don't look at me like that, I beg you. Are you not ashamed of your behaviour and have you no fear of Don Pelagio? What would he do if he came to know of it?

DONA PROUHEZE.   No doubt he would kill me without any hurry, and after taking time for consideration, as he does in everything.

DON BALTHAZAR.   Have you no fear of God?

DONA PROUHEZE.   I swear that I do not want to do evil; that is why I have told you all. Oh, it was hard to open you my heart; I fear that you have understood nothing,
Save my real regard for you. So much the worse! Now it is you who are responsible and bound to defend me.

DON BALTHAZAR.   You must help me, Prouheze.

DONA PROUHEZE.   Ah, that would be too easy! I am not watching my chance, I am waiting for it to come to me.
And I have loyally warned you, the campaign is opening.
You are my defender. All that I can do to escape from you and to get back to Rodrigo,
I give you warning, I will do it.

DON BALTHAZAR.   Do you want this detestable thing to come about?

DONA PROUHEZE.   Foreseeing is not wishing, and you see that I so mistrust my liberty that I have put it into your hands.

DON BALTHAZAR.   Do you love your husband not at all?

DONA PROUHEZE.   I love him.

DON BALTHAZAR.   Would you forsake him just now when the King himself forgets him,
Would you leave him all alone on that wild coast in the midst of infidels,
Without troops, without money, without any kind of security?

DONA PROUHEZE.   Ah! That hurts me more than all the rest.
Yes, the thought of so betraying Africa and our charge,

And the honour of my husband's name—I know that he cannot do without me—

Those poor children whom I mother instead of those I have not had of God, those women being nursed, those few and poor retainers who have given themselves to us; to forsake all that—

I confess that the thought of it makes me blench.

DON BALTHAZAR.   Then what is calling you to this knight?

DONA PROUHEZE.   His voice.

DON BALTHAZAR.   You have known him only a few days.

DONA PROUHEZE.   His voice! I am for ever hearing it.

DON BALTHAZAR.   And what does it say to you?

DONA PROUHEZE.   Ah, if you want to stop me from going to him,

Then tie me up; do not leave me this cruel freedom!

Put me in a deep dungeon behind iron bars!

But what prison could hold me in, when even that of my body threatens to break asunder!

Ah me, it is but too solid, and when my master calls me it is more than enough to hold in most obstinately this soul which is his.

My soul which he calls for and which belongs to him!

DON BALTHAZAR.   Soul and body too?

DONA PROUHEZE.   Why do you speak of this body when 'tis that which is my enemy and keeps me from darting in one flight straight to Rodrigo?

DON BALTHAZAR.   And, in Rodrigo's eyes, is this body only— your prison?

DONA PROUHEZE.   Nay, it is but the spoil of war to cast at the feet of the beloved!

DON BALTHAZAR.   You would give it him, then, if you could?

DONA PROUHEZE.   What is there of mine that does not belong to him? I would give him all the world if I could!

DON BALTHAZAR. Be off! Go to him!

DONA PROUHEZE. Señor, I have already told you that I have put myself no longer in my own ward but in yours.

DON BALTHAZAR. Don Pelagio alone is your warden.

DONA PROUHEZE. Speak! Tell him all.

DON BALTHAZAR. Ah, why was I so quick to pledge you my word?

DONA PROUHEZE. What! Are you not touched by the trust I have placed in you? Come, force me to confess that there are things that I could not tell except to you alone.

DON BALTHAZAR. After all I have only obeyed Don Pelagio.

DONA PROUHEZE. Ah, how well you are going to guard me, and how I like you! I have nothing more to do, I leave it all to you,
And even now I am planning in my mind a thousand tricks to get away from you!

DON BALTHAZAR. There is another guardian who will help me and from whom you will not escape so easily.

DONA PROUHEZE. Who, señor?

DON BALTHAZAR. The angel that God has set over you since the day when you were a little innocent child.

DONA PROUHEZE. An angel against the demons! And to defend me against men I must have a tower like friend Balthazar,
The Tower and the Sword riding along in one and that handsome gold beard which marks him out at any distance!

DON BALTHAZAR. You are still French.

DONA PROUHEZE. Just as you are still Flemish. Isn't it pretty, my little Franche-Comté accent?
That's not true! But all these people had great need of us to teach them how to be the real Spanish stuff—they so little know how to set about it!

DON BALTHAZAR. How was it that your husband married you, he already old and you so young?

DONA PROUHEZE.   Doubtless I fitted in with those parts of his nature most severely kept up and most secretly cherished.

So that when I went with my father to Madrid, where the business of his province called him,

Those two grand señors were not long in coming to an agreement,

That I should fall in love with Don Pelagio as soon as he was presented—love him above all things and for all the days of my life as the law and obligation is between husband and wife.

DON BALTHAZAR.   At least you cannot doubt that he fulfils his part of the contract.

DONA PROUHEZE.   If he loves me I was not deaf to hear him tell me so.

Yes, however low he had spoken it—one word—my ear was fine enough to take it in.

I was not deaf to hear the word my heart was listening for.

Very often I thought I caught it in those eyes, whose gaze altered as soon as my own tried to search it.

I interpreted that hand, which lay for one second upon my own.

Alas, I know I am no use to him; what I do I am never certain that he approves;

I have not even been able to give him a son.

Or perhaps what he feels towards me, I try sometimes to believe,

Is a thing so sacred that it must waste its sweetness on the desert air; it must not be disturbed by putting into words:

Yes, he let me hear something of the kind once in his queer wry manner.

Or maybe he is so proud that, to make me love him, he scorns to appeal to anything short of the truth.

I see him so little, and I am so cowed by him!

And yet for a long while I did not think that I could be anywhere except in his shadow.

You see yourself that it is he who takes leave of me to-day, and not I who wanted to leave him.

Nearly all day he leaves me alone, and just like him is this dark forsaken house here, so poor, so proud.

With this murdering sun outside and this delicious fragrance all within!

Yes, one might say that his mother had left him like this in a strict religious order, and had just gone away,

A great lady, unspeakably noble, whom you would hardly dare to look at.

DON BALTHAZAR.   His mother died giving him life.

DONA PROUHEZE (*pointing to the statue above the gate*).   Perhaps that is the mother of whom I speak.

(DON BALTHAZAR *gravely takes off his hat. Both look at the Virgin's statue in silence.*)

DONA PROUHEZE (*as if seized with an inspiration*).   Don Balthazar, would you do me the favour to hold my mule?

(DON BALTHAZAR *holds the mule's head and* DONA PROUHEZE *climbs up on the saddle; taking off her shoe she puts the satin thing between the hands of the Virgin.*)

DONA PROUHEZE.   Virgin, patron and mother of this house, protectress and surety of this man whose heart lies open to you more than to me, and companion of his long loneliness,

If not for my sake then at least for his, since this bond between him and me has not been my doing but your intervening will:

Keep me from being to this house whose door you guard, O mighty extern, a cause of corruption:

Keep me from being false to this name which you have given me to bear, and from ceasing to be honourable in the eyes of them that love me.

I cannot say that I understand this man whom you picked out for me, but you I understand, who are his mother and mine.

See, while there is yet time, holding my heart in one hand and my shoe in the other,

I give myself over to you! Virgin mother, I give you my shoe, Virgin mother, keep in your hand my luckless little foot!

I warn you that presently I shall see you no longer and that I am about to set everything going against you!

But when I try to rush on evil let it be with limping foot! The barrier that you have set up,

When I want to cross it, be it with a crippled wing!

I have done so much as I could; keep you my poor little shoe,

Keep it against your heart, tremendous Mother of mine!

SCENE VI

The King of Spain surrounded by his Court in the great hall of the palace of Belem, commanding the estuary of the Tagus.

THE KING.   Lord-Chancellor, whose hair is white while mine is but beginning to grizzle,
Is it not said that youth is the season of illusion,
Whereas old age, little by little,
Enters into the reality of things as they are?
A very sad reality, a little faded world that goes on shrinking.

THE CHANCELLOR.   That is what the ancients have always taught me to repeat.

THE KING.   They say the world is sad for him who sees clear?

THE CHANCELLOR.   I cannot deny it against everyone.

THE KING.   It is old age that has the clear eye?

THE CHANCELLOR.   It has the practised eye.

THE KING.   Practised to see only what is useful.

THE CHANCELLOR.   To itself and its little kingdom.

THE KING.   My kingdom is great; yea, and great as it is, my heart which holds it all
Refuses to any frontier the right to hold it back—nay, the very sea, this vast ocean at my feet,
Far from setting bounds to it, did but hold in reserve new realms for my laggard longing!
And I should like to find at last what were that thing of which you would have the right to say to the King of Spain that it was not for him.
Sad, is it? How can it be said without impiety that the truth of those things which are the work of a transcendent God

Is sad? And how without absurdity say that the world, which is His likeness and His rival,

Is littler than ourselves and leaves the greater part of our imagination in the void?

Now I maintain that youth is the season of illusion, but that is because it pictures things as infinitely less beautiful and manifold and desirable than they are, and of this delusion we are healed by age.

Thus this sea where the sun is setting—the glittering expanse,

Where the poets every evening saw plunge among the sprats, the impossible trappings of some ridiculous god, Apollo's golden smithy—

The daring eye of my predecessors ranging over that sea, their finger imperiously pointed out the other shore, another world.

Even now one of their servants whips round towards the south, rediscovers Cham, doubles the detested Cape,

Drinks of the Ganges! Through countless crooked straits he lands in China. His is that endless bustle of silks and palms and naked bodies,

All those banks alive with human fry, more populous than the dead, and awaiting baptism;

The other . . .

THE CHANCELLOR.   Our great admiral!—

THE KING.   For him 'tis something absolutely new that comes up under the prow of his vessel, a world of fire and snow, sending forth squadrons of volcanoes to greet Our ensigns!

America, like a huge horn of plenty, I mean that chalice of silence, that fragment of a star, that enormous tract of paradise, its flank leaning across an ocean of delight!

Ah! heaven forgive me, but when at times, as today from the shores of this estuary, I see the sun invite me with a fast unrolling carpet to those regions which are forever sundered from me.

Spain, that spouse whose ring I wear, is little to me beside that dusky slave, that copper-sided female which they are enchaining for me away down under in the realms of night!

Thanks to thee, son of the dove, my kingdom has become like to the heart of man,

Whereas one part here stays along with his bodily presence, the other has found its home beyond the sea:

It has cast anchor for good on that side of the world which is lit by other stars.

That man cannot go wrong who takes the sun for guide!

And that shore of the world which wise men long ago gave up to illusion and madness,—

From that shore now my Exchequer draws the vital gold which here gives life to the whole machinery of State and pushes out on all sides, more thickly than grass in May, the lances of my squadrons!

The sea has lost its terrors for us and keeps only its wonders;

Yes, its moving surges are scarcely enough to break up the broad golden highway which binds the two Castiles,

On which hurry to and fro the double file of my trading ships.

Carrying thither my priests, and my warriors, and bringing back to me those barbaric treasures teemed by the sun,

That sun who at the zenith of his course between two Oceans,

Stands one moment still in solemn hesitation!

THE CHANCELLOR.   The kingdom that your servants of yesterday have gotten to your Majesty

'Tis the task for the men of today to open up and preserve.

THE KING.   True, but for some time past I have been receiving from that quarter none but distressing news:

Pillage, pirate raids, extortion, injustice, extermination of harmless peoples,

And, what is graver still, the fury of my captains—carving each his own share out of my lands, tearing and rending one another,

As if it were for that cloud of blood-stained gnats, and not for the King alone, shadowed by the peaceful Cross,

That God upheaved a world from the bosom of the waters!

THE CHANCELLOR.   When the master is away the muleteers each other slay.

THE KING.   I cannot be in Spain and in the Indies together.

THE CHANCELLOR.   Let there be over there a man to personate Your Majesty, one only over all, invested with the same power.

THE KING.   And whom shall We choose to be Ourselves over yonder?

THE CHANCELLOR. A just and reasonable man.

THE KING. When the volcanoes of my America shall be quenched, when her throbbing sides shall be exhausted, when she shall rest from the mighty endeavour that has brought her up, all burning and boiling, out of nothing,

Then will I give her a just and reasonable man to rule her!

The man in whom I see myself, and who is fit to represent me, is not a wise and just man: I want a jealous and eager man!

What business have I with a just and reasonable man? Is it for him that I shall cut off from myself that America and those wonderful Indies in the setting sun if he does not love it with that unrighteous, jealous love?

Is it in reason and justice that he will wed this wild and cruel land, take her all slippery to his arms, full of reluctance and of venom?

I say that it is in patience and suffering and battle and pure faith! For what man in his senses would not prefer what he knows to what he knows not, and his father's field to that chaotic nursery?

But the man I want, when he has passed that threshold which no man before him has crossed,

In one flash he knows it for his own, and how that blue mountain has long been standing on the horizon of his soul: there is nothing, in this map unrolling at his feet, that he does not recognize and that I have not given him beforehand in writing.

For him the journey has no tedium and the wilderness no weariness, it is already peopled with the towns that he shall found there ;

And war has no perils, and politics are simple; he is merely surprised at all these frivolous resistances.

In like manner, when I took Spain to wife it was not to batten on its fruits and its women like a robber, nor on the fleeces of its sheep, nor the mines in its bowels, nor the bags of gold that the merchants spill at the customs: not like an investor or a landlord,

But to provide her with intelligence and unity, and to feel her entirely living and obedient under my hand, and myself in the fashion of the head, which alone comprehends what the whole person is about.

For 'tis not the mind which is in the body; the mind which contains the body and wraps it round about.

THE CHANCELLOR. I know but one man who answers Your Majesty's wishes. He is called Don Rodrigo of Manacor.

THE KING. I do not like him.

THE CHANCELLOR. I know that obedience sits ill upon him. But the man that you ask of me cannot be woven from other than the stuff of kings.

THE KING. He is still too young.

THE CHANCELLOR. This America which you are going to give him is hardly less young than he.

He was still quite a child when she was already his incredible vision as he went about with his father who told him of Cortez and Balboa.

And, later, his crossings of the Andes, his descent, not like Magellan on the unhindering sea, but from Peru to Para across a leafy ocean, his governing of Granada, ravaged by sedition and plague

Have shown what Rodrigo was, your servant.

THE KING. I consent to Rodrigo. Let him come!

THE CHANCELLOR. Sire, I don't know where he is. I had already given him to understand that America once more was going to call for him.

He listened with a darkening eye and gave no answer.

Next day he had disappeared.

THE KING. Let him be brought to me by force!

SCENE VII

DON RODRIGO, THE CHINESE SERVANT

The Castilian desert. A spot among the low shrubs from which is seen a vast expanse. Romantic mountains in the distance. An evening of crystalline clearness. DON RODRIGO *and the* CHINESE SERVANT *are stretched upon a sloping bluff at the foot of which their horses are grazing unbridled, and they are scanning the horizon.*

DON RODRIGO.   Our horsemen have disappeared.

THE CHINESE SERVANT.   They are down there in the little pine-wood making their horses lie down; one of them is white and shows up all the rest.

DON RODRIGO.   Tonight we will give them the slip.

THE CHINESE SERVANT.   It isn't us they are looking for. We are on the highroad from Galicia to Saragossa. Isn't this the way St. James goes every year, on his feast—
Solemnly to call on Our Lady of the Pillar. (It is to-day, you see that star threading its way?)

DON RODRIGO.   Are they pilgrims going to join the procession?

THE CHINESE SERVANT.   Pilgrims—I have seen arms by the gleam of that phosphorescent blob—
Pilgrims not very wary of showing themselves too soon.

DON RODRIGO.   Very good, very good, this business is none of ours.

THE CHINESE SERVANT.   Still, I am keeping an eye on that little wood of old firs.

DON RODRIGO.   And I am keeping an eye on you, my dear Isidore.

THE CHINESE SERVANT.   Oh! don't be afraid that I shall make off—

So long as you respect our agreement and don't make me spend the night near any running water, well or spring.

DON RODRIGO.   Are you so afraid that I shall baptize you by stealth?

THE CHINESE SERVANT.   And why should I give you thus for nothing the right to make me Christian and to go to heaven with the decoration that I provide? And to make up for other plans that are less pure,
You must first do a little service to my lord your servant.

DON RODRIGO.   That I go with you where a certain black hand is beckoning you?

THE CHINESE SERVANT.   Near by a white hand is beckoning to you.

DON RODRIGO.   It is nothing base that I want.

THE CHINESE SERVANT.   Do you call gold a base thing?

DON RODRIGO.   It is a soul in pain that I am helping.

THE CHINESE SERVANT.   And I my own which is in bondage.

DON RODRIGO.   Imprisoned at the bottom of a purse?

THE CHINESE SERVANT.   Everything that is mine is me.

DON RODRIGO.   Do you grumble because I want to help you?

THE CHINESE SERVANT.   Master, may it humbly please your Worship to take it that I have no confidence in your Worship.
Yes, I would much like to be in other hands than yours; why have I put myself there?

DON RODRIGO.   'Tis I that am in yours.

THE CHINESE SERVANT.   We have captured each other, and here is no way of getting unstuck.
Ah, I was wrong to make you that promise in haste, in the excitement of my disposition!
When all is said and done, what is that water which you want to spill on my head, and why are you so set upon it? What do you get by it, presuming that things are as you say,

And as for this spiritual change you speak of, do you think it will be comfortable? Who would enjoy his kidneys shifting about? My soul is easy as it is, and I don't much care for others to peep into it and mess it about to their fancy.

DON RODRIGO. If you go back upon your word 'tis ill, 'twill be revenged upon you.

THE CHINESE SERVANT *with a sigh*. All right, have it your own way. I give up that gold over there and you give up that parti-coloured idol!

DON RODRIGO. You are wrong, Isidore. I say again that my only anxiety is the help I owe to this soul in peril.

THE CHINESE SERVANT. And you don't want me to be frightened when I hear a man talk like that!

Poor Isidore! What a master have you drawn in the lottery of fate! Into what hands have you fallen by the disagreement between the light and heavy elements of your matter?

You once took me to the comedy at Madrid, but I never saw anything like it there. Hail, saviour of other men's wives!

Pull yourself together, señor, make your heart lesser; open yourself to my soothing reasonable words, let them sink into your sick mind like music.

What is this woman you are in love with, please? Outside that mouth painted as with a brush, those eyes more beautiful than if they were balls of glass, those limbs exactly knitted and fitted,

But within, the vexation of demons, the worm, the fire, the vampire fastened on your substance! The matter of man, which has entirely withdrawn from him and thus remains no more than a limp and shrivelled shape, like the carcase of a cricket. Oh horror!

Am I not in the retinue of your Lordship? How often have I not begged It to think of the salvation of Its own soul and mine?

In a hundred years what will be that hundred pounds of female flesh with which your soul is amalgamated?—

A little filth and dust and bone.

DON RODRIGO. At present she's alive.

THE CHINESE SERVANT. And I will warrant that in a former existence that she-devil made you sign a paper and the promise of carnal commerce!

If you wish, I will undertake to reason with this unbecoming creature, and make her give back by torment and physical entreaty your pre-natal note of hand.

DON RODRIGO. You amaze me, Isidore. Holy Church does not recognize life in any soul anterior to its birth.

THE CHINESE SERVANT, *hurt*. Still, I have studied all the books that you gave me and I could recite them from end to end. Brother Leo pretends that I know as much of them as he does.

DON RODRIGO. From those things which are behind me and hunting me,
And from those things which are in front of me, a white spot on the sea between the dark trees,
I feel I cannot get away.

THE CHINESE SERVANT. What is it that is behind you?

DON RODRIGO. The gallop of horses pursuing me, the command of the King upon his throne, choosing me out of all men to give me half the world,
That half which from all time has been unknown and lost, like an infant in its swathing bands,
That share of the world, all fresh and new like a star that has risen upon me out of the deep and the dark.
And there'll be no need for me to struggle for a footing there and carve myself a tiny province in that land—
I have her whole and entire when still fresh and dewy, she gives herself for ever to my impress and my kiss.

THE CHINESE SERVANT. And what is in front of you?

DON RODRIGO. A flashing point off there, like the vision of death. Is it a waving handkerchief? Is it a wall smitten by the noonday sun?

THE CHINESE SERVANT. I know, it is down there that there is a certain black monster to whom in the cheerfulness of my soul, because even a sage is not exempt from incertitude, and as it were by a slip, if I may say so, *quasi in lubrico*,
I so far forgot myself as to lend money. (*He wrings his hands and rolls his eyes.*)

DON RODRIGO.   Not without interest, I am sure. I know your kind of generosity.

THE CHINESE SERVANT.   What, is it not virtue to give there and then to those who ask?
And how can one tell what is virtue except that it brings immediately its own reward.

DON RODRIGO.   Go on, we will get back your money since you are set on getting it only from your negress.
Devil knows what deal you have been wangling!
And I will baptize you and be quit of you; you can go back to China.

THE CHINESE SERVANT.   It is my dearest wish, 'tis time that I bore fruit among the heathen. For what good is the new wine, save for the innkeeper to put it into old bottles? What good the bushel, save to measure those pearls which we are commanded to cast before swine,
Instead of storing up therein the futile glimmer of our personal wick?

DON RODRIGO.   You use the scriptures like a Lutheran grocer.

THE CHINESE SERVANT.   Only bring me back to Barcelona.

DON RODRIGO.   Isn't it there that you implored me not to go?

THE CHINESE SERVANT.   If I cannot hold you off from this madness, at least I may as well profit by it.

DON RODRIGO.   Madness anyone would call it, but I am madly right!

THE CHINESE SERVANT.   Is it right to want to save a soul by drowning it?

DON RODRIGO.   There is one thing that just now I alone can bring her.

THE CHINESE SERVANT.   And what is this unique thing?

DON RODRIGO.   Joy!

THE CHINESE SERVANT.   Have you not made me read fifty times over that for you, a Christian, it is sacrifice that saves?

DON RODRIGO. Joy alone is the mother of sacrifice.

THE CHINESE SERVANT. What joy?

DON RODRIGO. The vision of the joy she gives me.

THE CHINESE SERVANT. Call you joy the torment of desire?

DON RODRIGO. It is not desire that she has read upon my lips. It is recognition.

THE CHINESE SERVANT. Recognition? Tell me even the colour of her eyes.

DON RODRIGO. I do not know. Ah, I admire her so much that I have forgotten to look at her!

THE CHINESE SERVANT. Excellent! I have seen big ugly blue eyes!

DON RODRIGO. It is not her eyes, it is her whole self that is my star!

Long ago on the Caribbean Sea, when at the first hour of morning I came out of my stifling box to take the watch,

When for an instant I was shown that queenly star, that resplendent gem all alone in the diadem of clear-browed heaven,

Ah, it was the same sudden thrill, the same wild unmeasured joy!

No man can live without admiration. There is within us the soul which shudders at ourselves,

There is this prison of which we tire, there are those eyes which have a right to see to the end, there is a heart which craves to be filled!

Too soon I found in the firmament nothing but this accustomed leaden flame,

The dim, secure ship-lantern, the seaman's sorry guide over the inappeasable waters.

But now there is quite another star for me, that point of light in the live sands of the night,

Someone human like myself, whose presence and whose countenance, beyond the ugliness and misery of this world, are compatible with a state of bliss alone.

THE CHINESE SERVANT. A treat for every sense.

DON RODRIGO. The senses! I liken them to the camp followers that come after the army
To plunder the dead and batten on the captured towns.
I will not so easily accept this ransom paid by the body for the soul which has gone thence;
Or that there is anything in her which I cease to crave.
But I am saying ill; I will not slander these senses which God has made.
For they are not base acolytes; they are our servants ranging the whole world through
Till they find at last Beauty, before whose face we are so glad to disappear.
All that we ask of her is that we evermore have only to open our eyes to see her again.

THE CHINESE SERVANT. Nothing else really? It was not worth putting ourselves about. I fear that our conversation is not of very much profit to this lady.

DON RODRIGO. Is it nothing that I have found her out, who was so well hidden?

THE CHINESE SERVANT. Plague take that storm which cast us on the coast of Africa and that fever which kept us there!

DON RODRIGO. It was her face that I saw when I woke again.
Say, do you think that I recognize her without her knowing?

THE CHINESE SERVANT. You would have to know all that happened before our birth. Just then I saw nothing; yes, I remember well that I had not yet come to the use of eyesight:
So that nothing occurred to disturb my preparation of the butterfly Isidore.

DON RODRIGO. Drop your pre-natal life, save that in the thought of Him who made us we were in some queer way together.

THE CHINESE SERVANT. Truly, truly! We were already together, all three.

DON RODRIGO. Already was she the single boundary of this heart which brooks none.

THE CHINESE SERVANT. Already, my dear godfather, you were thinking of giving me her for godmother.

DON RODRIGO. Already she held this joy which is mine by right and which I am on the way to ask her to give back.

Already she looked upon me with that face which destroys death.

For what is it that they call dying except ceasing to be needful? When has she been able to do without me? When shall I cease to be that, which lacking, she could not have been herself?

You ask what joy she brings me? Ah, if you knew the words that she says to me while I am sleeping,

Those words which she does not know she is saying, which I have but to shut my eyes to hear!

THE CHINESE SERVANT. Words that shut your eyes and shut my mouth.

DON RODRIGO. Those words which poison death, those words which stop the heart and say time shall be no more.

THE CHINESE SERVANT. It is no more! Look, already one of those stars of yours which are no longer any use, look at it going

Away and across the skiey page, making a great scrape of fire.

DON RODRIGO. How I love these millions getting on together! There is no soul so broken that the sight of this immeasurable concert does not wake to thin melody!

Lo, while the earth, like a wounded man that is out of the fight, is drawing solemn breath,

The peopled heavens without any discomposure, as if bent upon a sum, all thronging to their mysterious task!

THE CHINESE SERVANT. In the middle the three stars, the staff of that huge pilgrim who visits the two hemispheres by turns,

What you call Saint James's Staff.

DON RODRIGO *in a half whisper and as if to himself.* " Look, beloved! All that is thine, and 'tis I who will give it thee."

THE CHINESE SERVANT. Queer light, those million drops of milk!

DON RODRIGO. Below there, under the leaves, it shines upon a woman who weeps for joy and is kissing her bare shoulder.

THE CHINESE SERVANT. What means that shoulder, I pray you, Mr. Saviour of souls?

DON RODRIGO.   That too is a part of those things which I shall
not possess in this life.

Did I say it was her soul alone I loved? It is her whole self.

And I know that her soul is immortal, but the body is not less so.

And the two together make the seed which is destined to flower
in another garden.

THE CHINESE SERVANT.   A shoulder which is part of a soul, and
all that together is a flower—poor Isidore, do you understand?
Oh, my head, my head!

DON RODRIGO.   Ah, Isidore! If you but knew how I love her
and long for her!

THE CHINESE SERVANT.   Now I understand you, and you are not
talking Chinese any more.

DON RODRIGO.   And do you think that her body alone could
enkindle in mine such longing?

What I love in her is not at all what can be dissolved and escape
me and be far away, and some time cease to love me; it is what
causes herself to be herself and brings forth life to my kisses and not
death!

If I teach her that she was not born to die, if I ask of her her
immortality, that star in the deeps of her which she is without
knowing,

Ah, how could she refuse me?

It is not what in her is troubled and mingled and unsure that I
ask of her, not what is inert and neutral and perishable,

It is the naked essence, the pure life,

It is that love as strong as me, burning under my longing like
a great naked flame, like laughter in my face!

Ah, if she gave it me (I am failing, and night is coming on my
eyes)

If she gave it me (and she must not give it me),

It is not her beloved body that would ever content me!

Never, save through each other, should we contrive to get rid of
death,

Just as violet melting into orange sets free pure red.

THE CHINESE SERVANT.   *Tse gu! Tse gu! Tse gu!* We know
what hides under those fine words.

DON RODRIGO.   I know that this union of my being with hers is impossible in this life, and I will have no other.
Only the star that is herself
Can slake this dreadful thirst of mine.

THE CHINESE SERVANT.   Why then are we presently making for Barcelona?

DON RODRIGO.   Did I never tell you that I have received a letter from her?

THE CHINESE SERVANT.   Things are clearing up bit by bit.

DON RODRIGO *reciting as if he were reading*.   "Come, I shall be at X . . . I am setting out for Africa. There is much to reproach you with."
A gipsy woman brought me this paper. I set off, yielding to your importunity, while the King's people were on my track.

THE CHINESE SERVANT.   Oh yes, it's me! Blame me, I pray you! The business of my soul and my purse—that is all you had at heart!

DON RODRIGO.   It was all weighed in the same scale. The drop of water gathering.
And all Spain to me like a table tilted.

THE CHINESE SERVANT.   Ah, that black image over there and that money of mine. Oh! Oh!
Oh, that purse I gave her in the impetuosity of my intestinal emotion!
I did hope that under that exotic bosom it would swell slowly, melodiously, like a fruit!

DON RODRIGO.   "Reproach" said she—How wrong I was! Yes, I shall hear nothing from her but reproach.
I must not go on existing. I must be given to understand those things which kill her love for me.

THE CHINESE SERVANT.   I on my side can provide some.

DON RODRIGO.   I shall have to see that she is quite right and that I approve! I must hear her pass sentence on this heart which beats for her alone!
I thirst for those devastating words! More! More! I am hungry for this nothingness that she wants to plant in me.

For I know that it is only in the absolute void of all things that I shall meet her.

Is it because I am handsome or noble or virtuous that I want her to love me? Or have I other reason than this desperate need I have of her soul?

Or when I think of her do I ask nothing of her but that sudden sacred transport of her heart towards me? Does not her whole self then disappear, yes, even those matchless eyes?

I want to confront her as witness of this separation between us so wide, that the other one, caused by that man who took her before me, is only the painted semblance.

This abyss going down to the roots of nature,

To be bridged without motive or merit by the act of faith alone that we are to make in each other, that oath in the eternal—

I know that she cannot be mine save by her free self-giving.

THE CHINESE SERVANT. Nothing is got for nothing except that precious elixir, caked at the bottom of the tiny phial, which liquefies at the blessing of Our Lady of Compassion.

And look you, the drops that escape from it take fire as soon as they touch our gross air.

DON RODRIGO. It is not Our Lady that you have in mind, but that Chinese idol on a lotus which you found and which you cannot take your eyes from.

THE CHINESE SERVANT. One single drop of perfume is more precious than a great deal of spilt water.

DON RODRIGO. Do you say that of your own or where did you get it?

THE CHINESE SERVANT. When I shut my eyes on a night like this, many things come back to my thoughts from no one knows where.

I hear a deep sound like that of a brazen gong, and that is bound up with an idea of the wilderness and great sun and a nameless town behind battlemented walls.

I see a canal mirroring the crescent moon, and can hear an unseen boat rustle in the reeds.

DON RODRIGO. Still you were very small as yet, you told me,

when you left China, after the Jesuits by purchase had saved you from death.

THE CHINESE SERVANT. From death of body and of soul, thanks be to the heaven above!—
Whose starry substance I see like a stream of molten ore gaining
On this bridge which the Earth makes between the two Houses of the Night.

DON RODRIGO *raising himself on his elbows*. Just so! What's this? Away down in the west I see coming on in good order a number of little lights.

THE CHINESE SERVANT. And away down in the east, on the crest of that hill, appears another procession.

DON RODRIGO. It is James, who, every year on his feast day, comes over to call on the Mother of his God.

THE CHINESE SERVANT. And she, mother-wise, goes a third of the way to meet him.
As has been solemnly stipulated before notary after long disputes.

DON RODRIGO. Look! I see the little lights in the west scattering; all is quenched! Nay it is the red flash of muskets! Hark! there are cries!

THE CHINESE SERVANT. I am afraid it may be our pilgrims of just now, those whom we saw hiding behind the pine wood.

DON RODRIGO. Do you think they are making for Saint James?

THE CHINESE SERVANT. Doubtless they are heretics or Moors and the statue is all solid silver.

DON RODRIGO *starting up*. My sword! To the help of our lord Saint James!

THE CHINESE SERVANT *also standing up*. And when we have rescued him from the miscreants we will not give him back without a goodly ransom.

(*They go out.*)

SCENE VIII

THE NEGRESS JOBARBARA, THE NEAPOLITAN SERGEANT

The inn at X . . . on the seashore.

THE NEGRESS *rushing at the sergeant shrieking.* Oh you cheat! I must kill you. Fie! Shame! Shame! Tell me what you've done with my nice bingle-bangle you took o' me?

THE SERGEANT. How do you do, ma'am!

THE NEGRESS. Bad man, I couldn't forget you in a hurry.

THE SERGEANT And I don't want to listen to you. (*He takes his nose in two fingers of his right hand, with the left arm imitating Punch's big stick.*)

THE NEGRESS *panting for breath.* In gold, I gave you, my nice bracelet all of gold—I gave you, it was worth more than two hundred pistoles!
And there was a hand hanging on it, and a guitar, and a key, and a guava, and a halfpenny, and a little fish, and twenty other nice things, and they all bring luck together.
But take care, I've prayed over it, yes, I've sung over it, I've danced over it and I've drowned it in the blood of a black hen!
So that it is all right for me, but him that takes it from me goes sick, he croaks!

THE SERGEANT. I am glad to be rid of it.

THE NEGRESS. What, is it true you sold it, you mongrel?

THE SERGEANT. Didn't you give it to me?

THE NEGRESS. I had lent it to you; you said it would bring you luck, villain,
In a certain job you had to do in hell!
And after that you left here by a crack in the wall, pulling up your leg

Like lizards, scorpions, crickets, daddy-longlegs, and the other dusty animals.

THE SERGEANT. Tell me, the captain that is setting off for India, the first thing he does, isn't it to go to the banker, who gets him arms and foodstuff,
Money to pay his soldiers and his sailors?
The next year he comes back with ten bags of gold.

THE NEGRESS. But you haven't brought back one.

THE SERGEANT. I haven't brought back one bag? And it won't be nice if I give you a big piece of green and red silk, enough to make fifteen handkerchiefs, and a gold necklace that will go four times round your neck?
And a gold bracelet? And another gold bracelet? And ditto another gold bracelet and over and above that another three, four, five gold bracelets?

THE NEGRESS *examining him all over.* Where have you put all that?

THE SERGEANT. Where have I put all that? Why, where he put your mammy—
After hiding behind a clump of banana trees he got her, as all the women of the village were stacking the grain by moonlight, that brave Portingale of Portugal, when he took her to Brazil to teach her good manners and the taste of sugar cane, nothing to beat it
If he had not had that happy thought, instead of being to-day that respectable matron, the oracle of the Judge's house,
All dressed up in a bit of paper and your hair done up in palm oil,
You'd still be dancing like a ninny on the banks of the river Zaire, trying to snap the moon in your teeth.

THE NEGRESS *dazed.* Matron . . . moonlight . . . cane-oil . . . you make my head swim. Now I do not know where I was—(*with a screech*)—I was at the money you took, you thief!

THE SERGEANT. The money I took? And isn't it much better than money, this star that I have been to the mountain to pick with my fingers?

This firefly that I caught in my hand and put in a little cage,
Just when he was trying to embrace a jasmine flower with the
cockles of his heart?

THE NEGRESS.   You are talking of that poor girl you brought
with you the other day—
Both of you hidden at the bottom of that cart-load of rushes?

THE SERGEANT.   Now the boat is ready—this evening, if the
wind is too,
We weigh for the Latin shore.

THE NEGRESS.   And what about the bracelet you took and the
chain you have to give me instead?

THE SERGEANT.   Follow them! Stick close to me! What is to
keep you from going with us?

THE NEGRESS.   What do you want to do with that poor girl?

THE SERGEANT.   I have promised to give her the King of Naples
—why not? That's a brain-wave that I got all of a sudden; I am
sure there is a King at Naples!
I told her that the King of Naples had seen her in a dream, ah,
what a scrumptious young man I made up for her—double-quick—
him sending me to rummage the world to find her.
I am to know her by the sign of a dove-shaped mark under the
shoulder.

THE NEGRESS.   And had she really that sign?

THE SERGEANT *hitting one hand with the other*.   There is the queer
thing; she had! She told me so, but she would never let me see it.

THE NEGRESS.   What is her name?

THE SERGEANT.   They call her Dona Musica on account of a
guitar which fortunately she never plays. Her real name is Dona
Delicia.

THE NEGRESS.   Didn't anyone see her go?

THE SERGEANT.   They wanted to marry her by force to a big
specimen of an ugly cattle drover, all dressed in leather, a solemn
mug come down to them from the Goths!

The poor little sweetheart said that she wanted to go into a neighbouring convent to pray for light and guidance, and we set off to pray for light and guidance, both on the same horse.

THE NEGRESS.   Were you followed?

THE SERGEANT.   They won't catch us.   (*He wets his finger and holds it up.*) Already I feel the first puffs of this blessed wind from Castile; soon it will take our fairy barque away.

THE NEGRESS.   What are you going to do with the poor girl?

THE SERGEANT.   Do you think that I am going to hurt her? It would be like a pastry-cook eating his own tarts.
I fade away at her feet with respect and tender feeling!
I blow on her to remove the dust! I sprinkle a little water on her with the end of my fingers! I polish her every morning with a feather-mop of the down of the humming bird!
Mother, keep your eye on that road that goes twisting away there,
As far as that mountain that looks like a lion crouching,
Till there is a sign of that thing that makes me sick to think of,
A certain cloud of dust with the flash of arms and stirrups!
—Ah, what a fine trade mine is! It never brings me so much wages that I wouldn't like some more.

THE NEGRESS.   The rope will be your salary, you big ugly blackguard.

THE SERGEANT.   Never a rope for me! I retreat in good order! I shut my eyes and suddenly you cannot tell me from a pomegranate stump.
Cheer up, darling girls! Your love, the golden Sergeant, is still here to find you, at the bottom of those holes where you are mouldering, with a fishing rod.
When your little innocent hearts begin to swell, when your souls sigh daintily at the sound of the unknown beloved down there,
When you feel that you are like those seeds that nature has provided with down and feathers to fly away on the breath of April,
Then I turn up on your window-sill, flapping my wings and painted all yellow.

SCENE IX

DON FERNANDO, DON RODRIGO, DONA ISABEL, THE CHINESE
SERVANT

*Another part of the desert of Castile. A gully among reeds and ever-
green oak. There has been a battle. On the ground corpses, among
which is that of* DON LUIS, *masked. Here and there carts and baggage-
waggons, grooms holding horses by the bridle.* DON RODRIGO *wounded,
sitting against a tree trunk.*

DON FERNANDO *to Don Rodrigo.*   Sir knight, I thank you.

DON RODRIGO.   I am glad to have been able to save my lord
Saint James.

DON FERNANDO *pointing to Don Luis.*   It was not at all Saint
James that the gentleman had in mind.

DON RODRIGO.   He fought like a gentleman and I thought I
should never come through.

THE CHINESE SERVANT.   Yes, but your doublet is the worse
for it.

DON FERNANDO.   Do you feel seriously wounded?

DON RODRIGO.   Not much. Give me one of those carriages.
My servant will take care of me.

DON FERNANDO *to Dona Isabel.*   And you, dear sister, pull
yourself together. Do not stay like that, all white and aghast.
And give thanks to this knight who has saved us all.

DONA ISABEL.   I thank you.

SCENE X

DONA PROUHEZE, DONA MUSICA

The garden of the inn at X . . .

DONA MUSICA.   You know so many things, I do so love to talk with you!

DONA PROUHEZE.   Only let us take care, little sister, that Don Balthazar does not see us.

DONA MUSICA.   The day is waning. It is the hour when the lord relieves his sentries,
Lest his captive get away.

DONA PROUHEZE.   I am glad to be so well guarded. I have made sure of all the outlets. There is no means of getting away even if I would. What luck!

DONA MUSICA.   And yet I got in here without anyone's leave.

DONA PROUHEZE.   Who would have thought to look for you, coiled up like a snake in that great heap of rushes? Now it is I that have you captive and will keep you from running away.

DONA MUSICA.   Is it you that keep me from running away, or rather isn't it I that have taken you to myself so sweetly
That now you don't know how to get loose? Oh, how lovely you are and how I love you! If I were your husband I should want to keep you always in a bag; I should be dreadful with you!

DONA PROUHEZE.   As soon as he comes back I will settle that business.

DONA MUSICA. You will settle nothing of the kind, for I have never had the notion of marrying that cattle drover and I will hop on to the edge of the roof and snap my fingers at him. It is the bonny King of Naples that I will marry!

46

DONA PROUHEZE.   There is no king at Naples.

DONA MUSICA.   There is a King of Naples for Musica. Don't try
to hurt me, or I shall break your little finger.

And it isn't true either, perhaps, that I have that mark on the
shoulder like a dove? I have shown it to you.

DONA PROUHEZE.   'Tis you that are the dove.

DONA MUSICA.   My goodness, how happy he will be when he has
me in his arms!

Ah, how long the time has been!

"Why did you make me look for you so far away,
Musica?" he will say. I fancy I hear him.

How glad I shall be to hear him say my name!

Only he knows it now.

DONA PROUHEZE.   You have never seen him, silly.

DONA MUSICA.   I do not need to see him to know his heart.
Why, who was calling me so loud? Do you think that it was not
hard to leave home like that and trample on all my people?

He is calling me and I am answering quick.

DONA PROUHEZE.   Yes, Musica, I know the man your heart is
waiting for; I am sure he cannot play you false.

DONA MUSICA.   Isn't yours still waiting for someone? But who
would dare to threaten your peace when it is under the guardian-
ship of such beauty?

Ah, you were made to run in harness, you and that dreadful man
who just now tried to catch me and whose business it is to deal out
death.

DONA PROUHEZE.   Still you see that Señor Balthazar does not
rely on my beauty alone for my defence, but has multiplied the
guards around this old castle; I myself asked him to.

DONA MUSICA.   Are you so much in love with your prison that
you thus take delight in making it more secure?

DONA PROUHEZE.   Its bars have to be very strong.

DONA MUSICA.   What can the world do against you?

DONA PROUHEZE.   No doubt 'tis I that can do much against it.

DONA MUSICA.   I don't want any prison.

DONA PROUHEZE.   Somebody says that for him prison is where I am not.

DONA MUSICA.   I have a prison, and no one can get me out of it.

DONA PROUHEZE.   What, Musica?

DONA MUSICA.   The arms of the man I love; she is caught, wild Musica!

DONA PROUHEZE.   She has escaped! She is only there a moment: who could keep her for ever with a heart like hers?

DONA MUSICA.   Already I am with him and he knows it not. It is for my sake, before he knows me,
That, leading his men, he endures as much; it is for me that he feeds the poor and forgives his enemies.
Ah, 'twill not take long to understand that I am joy and that 'tis joy alone, and not the acceptance of sadness, that brings peace.
Yes, I want to mix in every feeling of his like some pleasant sparkling salt to transform and re-pure them. I want to know how he will henceforward set about being sad and doing evil—even when he wants.
I want to be both rare and common to him, like water, like sunshine; water to the thirsting mouth—never the same, when you come to think of it. I want to fill him suddenly and leave him in an instant, and I want him then to have no way of getting me back, neither eyes nor hands, but only the core and that ear within us opening,
Rare and common to him like the rose we inhale from day to day while summer lasts, and yet once only!
That heart that has been waiting for me, ah, what joy for me to fill it!
And if sometimes of a morning the note of a single bird is enough to quench in us the burning of revenge or of jealousy,
What will my soul be to the soul within him, made one with those ineffable chords, in a concert that no one but he has drunk in? His very silence will make me sing!
Where he is I am always with him. And while he works I am the babble of the enamoured fountain!

I am the drowsy turmoil of the great harbour under the noonday
sun;
  I am the thousand villages on all sides, with the harvests that have
no more to fear from the robber or the tax-gatherer;
  I, little I, yes, I, am that silly joy on his ugly countenance,
  The justice in his heart, that rapture on his face.

DONA PROUHEZE. There is nothing man is less fit for than happiness, nothing he sickens of so soon.

DONA MUSICA. Is he made for suffering?

DONA PROUHEZE. If he asks for it, why refuse him?

DONA MUSICA. How suffer when you are there? Whoever looks
at you forgets to live or die.

DONA PROUHEZE. He is not there.

DONA MUSICA. Then there is someone, dearest sister, whose
absence is your perpetual company.

DONA PROUHEZE. Little sister, you are over-bold; be quiet!
Who would dare to lift his eyes to Prouheze?

DONA MUSICA. Who could tear them away again?

DONA PROUHEZE. Who would trouble her heart?

DONA MUSICA. One voice only in the world, a single voice
speaking soft and low.

DONA PROUHEZE, *as if speaking to herself*. . . . inward to this
indissoluble sacrament.

DONA MUSICA. Would you have it silent?

DONA PROUHEZE. Ah, by that alone I live!

DONA MUSICA. Do you love him so?

DONA PROUHEZE. How dare you say it? No, I do not love him
at all.

DONA MUSICA. Do you regret the time when you did not know
him?

DONA PROUHEZE. Now I live for him.

DONA MUSICA.   How, when your face is for ever forbidden him?

DONA PROUHEZE.   My suffering is not.

DONA MUSICA.   Don't you want his happiness?

DONA PROUHEZE.   I want him to suffer, too.

DONA MUSICA.   He does suffer now.

DONA PROUHEZE.   Never enough.

DONA MUSICA.   He is calling; will you not answer?

DONA PROUHEZE.   To him I am not a voice.

DONA MUSICA.   What are you, then?

DONA PROUHEZE.   A sword, right through his heart.

SCENE XI

THE NEGRESS and afterwards THE CHINAMAN

Near the inn. A region of fantastic rocks and white sand. The negress naked, dancing and whirling in the moonlight.

THE NEGRESS. Hurrah, lovely mammy made me black and shiny.

I'm the little fish of night, the little tom-tom twirling, I'm the pot bobbing, bouncing in the cold, cold water, bustling, boiling. (*She rises starkly on tiptoe.*)

Sing hi to you, daddy mammy crocodile,

Sing hee to you, daddy hippo potam horse.

—while the river turn to me, while all the forest turn to me, while all the villages turn, turn, turn, to me, while all the boats turn to me,

Because the hole I make, because the boil I make,

Because the knot I make in the water bubbling, troubling,

I've water to wash me, oil to smoothe me, grass to rub me down!

I'm not black, I shine like lookin'-glass, I buck like pig, I duck like fish, I roll like little cannon!

Hi! Hi! Hi!

Here I am, here I am,

Come, come, come, come, little Mister Italian!

Yes, yes, yes, yes, my little yellow canary,

I put a halfpenny in your pocket.

All that kept you from loving me I killed; I broke it with the blood of a cut chicken!

I need only turn about, turn about; come to me, you cannot go against me.

(*Enter* THE CHINAMAN.)

All the threads that tie me to you I roll 'em up, wind 'em on me like on a reel. You come, I come to you, I bring you near, twisting round about like a little cannon, turning like a rope on the windlass that drags the anchor from among the roots.

51

Hi! Hi! Hi! Hi! Here! Here! Here! Here! (*She falls, quite done, into the arms of the* CHINAMAN, *who catches her from behind. She rolls a white eye, then screeching bounces away and wraps herself in her clothes.*)

THE CHINAMAN.   Beardless creature, vain for thee to plaster on thy black hide this parti-coloured integument; I can pierce thee to the soul.

THE NEGRESS.   Hey!

THE CHINAMAN.   I see your heart quite smothered by the dug, like a clot of blackness shedding an evil ray.

THE NEGRESS.   Hi!

THE CHINAMAN.   I see your liver, like an anvil which the demons use to forge untruth, and the two lungs above, like frightful bellows.

THE NEGRESS.   Ho!

THE CHINAMAN.   I see your guts, like a bag of reptiles letting off their pestilential and balsamic vapour.

THE NEGRESS.   And what more do you see?

THE CHINAMAN, *gnashing his teeth*.   I see my money all cluttered up on each side of the spinal column, like the grain in a head of maize!
And I am going to get it back on the spot. (*He draws his knife.*)

THE NEGRESS, *screaming*.   Stop, stop, ducky dear, if you kill me I shan't be able to show you the devil!

THE CHINAMAN.   You promised me before, and that's how you got that money out of me.

THE NEGRESS.   Never again shall your master set eyes on Dona Prouheze.

THE CHINAMAN.   Unclean alligator! Musky child of mud and fat worm of low tide!
We will take up this conversation adulteriously, I warrant you.

THE NEGRESS. Dona Maravilla is in this stronghold and Don Balthazar is defending her, and Don Pelagio is coming back to-morrow, or day after, and he is taking away Dona Maravilla, to Africa. Don Rodrigo will never see her again. Tra-la-la! He will never see her again, tra-la-la.

THE CHINAMAN. Listen, Señor Rodrigo has been cut up and knocked over while, sword in hand, he was desperately defending James against the robbers.

THE NEGRESS. What James?

THE CHINAMAN. Saint James in silver. We have brought him here (I mean Rodrigo) into the castle of my lady his mother, which is four leagues from this inn.

THE NEGRESS. Sweet Mother!

THE CHINAMAN. Tell her he is going to croak, tell her he wants to see her; tell her to come and meet him soon, and be hanged to good form.

As for me, since my exhortations, together with my profound groanings, have not contrived to give him back his bodily substance,

There is nothing left for me but to withdraw in silence, having planted him in the middle of his vomit, giving modesty a free hand.

As for thee I will not let thee go until thou hast shown me the devil.

THE NEGRESS. And why are you so set on seeing the accursed?

THE CHINAMAN. The handsomer dealings I have on that side the more precious will my soul be in the eyes of those who want to water me.

THE NEGRESS. But how do you expect Dona Prouheze to leave this inn, which is guarded on every side?

THE CHINAMAN. Listen, this morning I met a band of knights. They were looking for a lady called Musica, whom a certain blackguard from Naples has carried off.

THE NEGRESS. Musica? Heavens!

THE CHINAMAN. You know her?

THE NEGRESS.   Go on.

THE CHINAMAN.   Very soon, by force and threats, they wrung from me the confession that the said Musica is at this seaside inn full of dreadful pirates.

THE NEGRESS.   But that's not true.

THE CHINAMAN.   I know; what does it matter? To-morrow evening they attack Balthazar and his men.

THE NEGRESS.   But they'll find nothing at all.

THE CHINAMAN.   They will at least find a certain witch whom I have described,
Who is the most dangerous accomplice of the thief with the velvet eyes.

THE NEGRESS.   I won't go back to the inn.

THE CHINAMAN.   Then I will kill you on the spot.

THE NEGRESS.   Dona Prouheze is there, and will know how to settle everything.

THE CHINAMAN.   Tell her to get away with you under cover of the tumult.

THE NEGRESS.   How so?

THE CHINAMAN.   A hundred yards from the inn, down there behind the prickly pears, I will wait for her, with my groom and with horses for her and you.

SCENE XII

THE GUARDIAN ANGEL, DONA PROUHEZE

A deep ravine surrounding the inn, full of briars, creepers and shrubs ntertangled. On the brink the GUARDIAN ANGEL *in costume of the period, sword at side.*

THE GUARDIAN ANGEL.   See her, making her way right through the tangled thorns and creepers, slipping, scrambling, recovering, with knees and nails trying to scale that steep ascent! Ah, what that desperate heart can hold!

Who says the angels cannot weep?

Am I not a creature like her? Are God's creatures not bound together by any bond?

What they call suffering—does that go on in a world apart, shut out from all the rest? Does it escape an Angel's vision? Is suffering a pleasant thing to countenance for one who has charge even of its object?

Is it quite separate from that love and justice whose ministers we are? What use were it to be a Guardian Angel if we did not understand it?

One who sees good in its fulness—only he fully understands what evil is. *They* know not what they do.

And should I have been chosen to guard her, without a secret kinship with her?

—At last! She has, in spite of all, come to the end of those briars and charitable thorns that try to hold her back. Here she is, showing on the brink of the ditch.

(DONA PROUHEZE *comes out of the ditch. She is in man's clothes, all torn, her hands and face disfigured.*)

Yes, thou art beautiful, poor child, with that disordered hair, ıhat unseemly costume.

Those cheeks dabbled in blood and clay, and that look, which hurts me, in thine eyes, of resolution and madness!

55

Ah, thou dost me honour and I am pleased to show my little sister thus. If only there were none to see us!

DONA PROUHEZE, *looking round her, dazed.* I am alone.

THE GUARDIAN ANGEL. She says she is alone.

DONA PROUHEZE. I am free.

THE GUARDIAN ANGEL. Ah me!

DONA PROUHEZE. Nothing has kept me back.

THE GUARDIAN ANGEL. We wanted no other prison for you but honour.

DONA PROUHEZE. I should have been better guarded. I have been loyal. I gave full warning to Don Balthazar.

THE GUARDIAN ANGEL. He is going to pay for thy escape with his life.

DONA PROUHEZE. Rodrigo is going to die.

THE GUARDIAN ANGEL. There is yet time to lose his soul.

DONA PROUHEZE. Rodrigo is going to die.

THE GUARDIAN ANGEL. He lives.

DONA PROUHEZE. He lives, someone tells me he still lives! There is still time to give him the sight of me and so keep him from dying.

THE GUARDIAN ANGEL. 'Tis not Prouheze's love that will keep him from dying.

DONA PROUHEZE. At least I can die with him.

THE GUARDIAN ANGEL. Hark how glibly she speaks of putting away that soul which does not belong to her—which has cost so much to make and to redeem!

DONA PROUHEZE. There is no one but Rodrigo in the world.

THE GUARDIAN ANGEL. Try then to go to him.

(*She falls fainting on the ground.*)

DONA PROUHEZE, *panting.* Oh, this effort has been too much for me! I am dying! I thought I should never manage to get out of that horrible ditch!

THE GUARDIAN ANGEL, *setting his foot on her heart.* It would be easy for me to keep thee here if I would.

DONA PROUHEZE, *very low.* Rodrigo is calling me.

THE GUARDIAN ANGEL. Bring him that heart, then, on which my foot is planted.

DONA PROUHEZE, *as before.* I must.

THE GUARDIAN ANGEL, *removing his foot.* See where thou art going to lead me.

DONA PROUHEZE, *in a low voice.* Up, Prouheze. (*She gets up, staggering.*)

THE GUARDIAN ANGEL. I am looking on our God.

DONA PROUHEZE. Rodrigo!

THE GUARDIAN ANGEL. Ah me, I hear another voice in the fire, saying:
"Prouheze."

DONA PROUHEZE. How far the way is to that bush yonder!

THE GUARDIAN ANGEL. It was still longer up to Calvary.

DONA PROUHEZE. Rodrigo, I am thine.

THE GUARDIAN ANGEL. Thou art his? Is it thou that shalt fulfil him with thine outlawed body?

DONA PROUHEZE. I know I am his treasure.

THE GUARDIAN ANGEL. One cannot get this idea out of her silly little head.

DONA PROUHEZE, *stepping out.* March!

THE GUARDIAN ANGEL, *stepping at her side.* March!

DONA PROUHEZE, *taking a few tottering steps.*　Rodrigo, I am thine! Thou seest how I have broken this bitter bond!
Rodrigo, I am thine! Rodrigo, I come to thee!

THE GUARDIAN ANGEL.　And I—I am coming with thee.

(*Exeunt.*)

SCENE XIII

DON BALTHAZAR, the ALFERES (lieutenant)

The inn. In one corner the fortified porch with a heavy door, studded with nails and bolts and fastened with iron bars. At the back of the stage, framed in by pine trees, the sealine. Evening.

DON BALTHAZAR.   That is understood. As soon as those black-guards attack, order all to get together at once and man the doors and the covered ways that I have got ready on both sides of the gate. Absolutely forbidden to fire before I lift my hat.

ALFERES.   Shall I not leave a few sentinels along the ravine?

DON BALTHAZAR, *stroking his beard.* Must not divide our forces. On that side the inn is sufficiently defended by that quite impracticable ditch. I have tested it myself.

ALFERES, *gauging his chief's girth.*   Hm!

DON BALTHAZAR.   What are you saying, Alferes?

ALFERES.   What I say is, do you believe all the Chinaman's tale?

DON BALTHAZAR.   His presence is enough; I know him,
'Tis luck that I was making my round last night and heard the cries of our poor Jobarbara,
She had fastened on him tooth and claw, but if I had not got there I believe he would have split her like a fig.

ALFERES.   Rely on me to defend the King's money against these robbers.

DON BALTHAZAR.   We have more than money to defend.

ALFERES.   Dona Prouheze . . .

DON BALTHAZAR.   I said nothing. But the Chinaman pretends

59

that it is the god of love and not of thieves you will see capering about presently through the smoke of your muskets.

ALFERES, *going through the motion of present.*   One top-knot or another, bang!

DON BALTHAZAR.   That's right, bring him down, Señor Alferes, it will be a service to us all.

I am not speaking for myself, but why must I always be mixed up in other people's love-affairs when nobody is ever interested in mine?

Supposing you had been ordered to guard anyone, yes, let us say a great criminal,

And she learns that her loved one is dying and asking to see her,

Would you find it pleasant to listen to her tears and her entreaties? What good is that?

Is it fair to torment me like this, as if I were free myself not to do what is written, and what I have been ordered?

ALFERES.   Are you talking of a man or a woman?

DON BALTHAZAR.   A man, naturally. Pray, what are you thinking of ? A certain prisoner, I tell you, who was handed over to me to keep . . .

ALFERES.   You are all red and upset as if you were just getting clear of a fight.

DON BALTHAZAR.   Twenty years of that, Alferes, twenty years of that and it is as if it were just now.

Kissing my hands, as if that were any good!

—"What harm is there in my going to see her—him, I mean—now that he is going to die?"—"No harm, except that it is forbidden."

"But I tell you he is calling me"—"I do not hear him."

"By the Mother of God I swear to come back."

"No."

What would you have done had you been in my place?

ALFERES.   Nothing other than what your worship did.

DON BALTHAZAR.   I know you are a man of discretion and good judgment. The only thing wrong about you is your wearing your moustache that way, which is not Army orders.

Anyone who in my place would have acted otherwise, anyone who by silly soft-heartedness let himself be turned aside or play underhand tricks with duty,

I say that he would be a man without honour. Nothing for him but to get killed; life is no longer pleasant for an old man, what?

ALFERES.   I say you are not an old man.

DON BALTHAZAR.   What hurt me most was not those prayers and those complaints—there was no crying—

But those words they say to you in a low, balanced voice that goes right through your heart.

No, when they saw that everything was useless—that silence afterwards, and that kind of smile.

You know that kind of slackening, when we know there is nothing more to do; there are mothers then that start singing over their children's corpses.

All the same I could not have expected those lips on my hand, and that voice thanking me.

(*Enter* a SOLDIER.)

SOLDIER.   Captain, there is a group of knights down below, halted near the big stone. One of them is leaving the rest, and makes towards us, waving a handkerchief.

DON BALTHAZAR.   Very good; tell everyone to rally to the bridge.

ALFERES.   Even the sentry guarding the ravine?

DON BALTHAZAR.   Even him; and go and get me the Chinaman.

SCENE XIV

DON BALTHAZAR, ALFERES, THE CHINAMAN, A SERGEANT, SOLDIERS,
SERVANTS

Same place.

A SOLDIER, *bringing in the Chinaman.*   Here is the fellow.

DON BALTHAZAR.   Good day, Master Chinaman. I am sorry to
hear the news that you bring from Don Rodrigo.

THE CHINAMAN.   There is nothing in this to do with Don
Rodrigo.

DON BALTHAZAR.   Were not you his servant?

THE CHINAMAN.   I am the man whom Providence has put near
him, to give him the chance to save his soul.

DON BALTHAZAR.   How's that?

THE CHINAMAN.   If he procures me holy baptism will it not be
an immense joy to heaven, to whom a Chinese catechized
Gives more honour than ninety-nine Spaniards who persevere?

DON BALTHAZAR.   No doubt.

THE CHINAMAN.   Such merit, which depends on me alone to
earn for him when I like,
Is worth much care and sedulity on his part. I will not give up
my soul to him so easily and for a song.
So that, properly speaking, he is rather my servant than I his.

DON BALTHAZAR.   Still it seems to me, my son, that you do him
very good service.
But that is not the question just now; and since you speak of
song, why, just all I want is to know if you can sing.

THE CHINAMAN.   What, sing?

DON BALTHAZAR. Why, yes. (*He lilts coaxingly.*) Tra-la-la! Sing, what? I have no guitar. But you need only take this plate and beat time with a knife, whatever you like. Something pretty!

THE CHINAMAN, *shaking all over.* And you don't want to know what I was doing last night talking to that negress of the devil?

DON BALTHAZAR. My only desire in the world is to hear your sweet voice.

THE CHINAMAN, *falling on his knees.* Señor, spare me, I will tell you all!

DON BALTHAZAR, *to Alferes.* There is nothing that frightens people more than things they don't understand.

    (*To* THE CHINAMAN). Come along!

> "A song that rises to the lips
> Is like a swelling honey-drop
> That overflows the heart."

THE CHINAMAN. The truth is that, prowling round the castle in the interest of Don Rodrigo,
 I blundered on to a party of knights-at-arms who asked me if I had heard tell of a certain Dona Musica.

DON BALTHAZAR. Musica, did you say?

THE CHINAMAN. They told me that you knew her—
Of a certain Dona Musica, who may have gone away with an Italian sergeant and whom they are looking for.
Then it was that I had the idea of pointing out to them this castle as filled with pirates so that I could myself, under cover of the attack and the noise,
Carry off the persons that you are guarding.

DON BALTHAZAR. You would do better not to talk of Musica, and to sing as I asked you. (*He draws his sword.*)

THE CHINAMAN. Mercy, señor!

    (*Enter a* SERGEANT.)

SERGEANT. Señor, there is at the gate a man who, without removing his hat and in very eurt terms, demands that we forthwith let him look for Dona Musica whom we are guarding in this place.

DON BALTHAZAR. Tell him, without removing your hat and in very curt terms, that we are keeping our music to ourselves.

THE CHINAMAN. You see I did not lie.

DON BALTHAZAR. Dona Musica will never be so well guarded, wherever she is, as Dona Prouheze shall be by me to-day.

THE CHINAMAN. I see! You think that we are all secretly agreed and that it is Dona Prouheze we are after. Oh! Oh!

DON BALTHAZAR. Oh! Oh!

> "I dreamt I was in heaven
> And woke up in your arms."

(*He pricks the* CHINAMAN, *who gets up screeching.*)

On, I pray you, carry on.

(*Enter* SERVANTS *carrying covered dishes of everything needed for supper.*)

DON BALTHAZAR. What is that?

THE SERVANTS. Your supper, which we have brought you hither as you commanded.

DON BALTHAZAR. Good! We can take it easy here eating in the shade, while those gentlemen will see about making a show for us.

ALFERES. You will be very uncomfortable. All the shots they fire through this door will be for you.

DON BALTHAZAR. Not at all; it is the Chinaman that will get them. Look you, Chinaman, if your friends fire 'tis you they will kill.

THE CHINAMAN. I am not afraid of anything at all. So long as I am not baptized a bullet cannot hurt me.

DON BALTHAZAR. Meanwhile look at this table covered for us with the finest fruits of land and sea,
Sweet stuff and salt stuff; these shells, blue like the night; this

fine pink trout under its silver skin, like an eatable nymph; this scarlet crayfish;

This honeycomb; these pellucid grapes; these over-ripe figs a-bursting; these peaches like globes of nectar—

(Enter a SOLDIER.)

SOLDIER.   Captain, there is a group of armed men making for the gate with a ladder and axes. What must we do?

DON BALTHAZAR.   Why, let them come on. I have given my orders.

(Exit SOLDIER.)

Where was I?—these peaches like globes of nectar—(*Above the gate appears a man in black cloak and great plumed felt hat, taking aim at* DON BALTHAZAR *with a carbine.* DON BALTHAZAR *flings a peach at him, hits him full in the face—he tumbles down.*)— this ham ready carved; this wine of delicious bouquet in a glittering decanter; this pasty like a sepulchre of meats embalmed with powerful spices to rise again in the stomach with a glow of well-being.

The earth could not get together for us on this table-cloth anything more pleasant.

Let us look it over for the last time, for we shall never again taste any of that, my comrade.

(Violent knocking at the door.)

DON BALTHAZAR.   What do you want?

VOICE OUTSIDE.   We want Dona Musica.

DON BALTHAZAR.   You want music? Sing, Chinaman.

THE CHINAMAN.   I cannot sing.

DON BALTHAZAR, *threatening him.*   Sing, I tell you.

THE CHINAMAN, *singing.*   If a man should hear me sing
        He would think me very gay
        I am like the little bird
        Singing with his death on him.

VOICE OUTSIDE.   We want Dona Musica.

DON BALTHAZAR. No use, she has just set sail for Barbary. Sing, Chinaman; that'll cheer them up.

THE CHINAMAN, *singing.* I took ship in a little shell
　　　　To go to Barbaree-ee
　　　　To try to find the hair of a frog
　　　　Because there's none in Spain.

VOICE OUTSIDE. If you don't open we are going to fire.

DON BALTHAZAR. Sing, Chinaman.

THE CHINAMAN, *singing.* I went into the meadows
　　　　To ask the violet
　　　　If there was anything could stop
　　　　The bitter pain of love.
　　　　She answered me . . .

(*Through a split in the door a musket barrel is seen to come which swivels right and left.*)

THE CHINAMAN, *jumping right and left to avoid the musket.*
And what she said was this . . .
　　　　And what she said was this.

DON BALTHAZAR. Well, well, what did she say?

(*On the sea at the back of the scene a boat appears with a red sail on which are* MUSICA, *the* NEGRESS *and the* NEAPOLITAN SERGEANT. *The musket withdraws.*)

THE NEGRESS, *singing in a sharp voice.*
　　　　That for the pain of love
　　　　There never was no salve.

THE CHINAMAN, *looking towards the sea.* Heavens, what do I see?

DON BALTHAZAR. What do you see?

THE CHINAMAN. Look yourself.

DON BALTHAZAR, *singing.* Don't look at me!
　　　　They are looking at us
　　　　To see if you are looking at me.

　　　　　　　　　　(*Hatchet blows on the door.*)

A SOLDIER.   Captain, captain, must we fire?

DON BALTHAZAR.   Not till I order. What do you see, China-man?

THE CHINAMAN.   I see a boat putting out to sea
And in it there is that negress of calamity with her yellow devil.
But look yourself.

DON BALTHAZAR.   It is too tiring to look round.

THE CHINAMAN.   Señor, make away, those people are getting
ready to fire.

DON BALTHAZAR.   No.

> (*The barrel of the musket again passes through the hole in the
> door, aiming at* DON BALTHAZAR. *The boat has dis-
> appeared.*)

THE VOICE OF MUSICA, *unseen.*   A tear! a tear!
> A tear from the brim of your eyes!
> A tear from your lovely eyes.

DON BALTHAZAR.   Ah, what a charming voice! I have never
heard anything so beautiful.

THE VOICE, *supported by those of the* NEGRESS *and the* SERGEANT
in parts.   . . . it runs down your face
> It falls to the deep of your heart,
> To the deep deep heart, it falls!

> (*Shots.* DON BALTHAZAR *falls dead face downwards among the
> fruit, holding the table in his arms.*)

THE VOICE, *farther away and farther.*   A tear! a tear!
> A tear from the brim of your eyes!
> A tear from the bottom of the sea!

END OF FIRST DAY

THE SECOND DAY

Characters

DON GIL

THE IRREPRESSIBLE

DONA PROUHEZE

DONA HONORIA

DON PELAGIO

THE VICEROY

THE ARCHÆOLOGIST

THE CHAPLAIN

SAINT JAMES

THE KING

DON RODRIGO

THE CAPTAIN

DON CAMILLO

DONA MUSICA

DON GUSMAN

RUIS PERALDO

OZORIO

REMEDIOS

THE DOUBLE SHADOW

THE MOON

THE APPRENTICE

CABALLEROS

THE MERCHANT TAILOR

GENTLEMEN

SCENE I

DON GIL, THE MERCHANT TAILOR, CABALLEROS

A merchant tailor's shop at Cadiz. Shelves and counters filled to overflowing with red cloth of every shade, rolled and unrolled. Seen through the door a workshop of needlewomen. The room is full of busy clerks, valets coming for parcels, caballeros talking or coming to place orders. One of them is fencing with the wall, using the draper's yard-stick. Another is munching olives. A third is trickling water into his mouth from a ewer. A very fat caballero is in the middle of the room in shirt-sleeves while an apprentice takes his measure.

THE APPRENTICE, *measuring the waist and shouting.* Thirty-five!

> *(Shouts of laughter from the bystanders.)*

A SAILOR, *coming in.* Are the standards ready?

THE MERCHANT TAILOR. There are two completed. You can take them. What a life! The others will be ready in a week. The needlewomen are working on them at this moment.

FIRST CABALLERO, *to the fat man.* Flanders has prospered you, Don Gil.

SECOND CABALLERO. The Panama crossing will melt you down.

DON GIL. Bah! I have to make room in my belly for all America.

THIRD CABALLERO. What are the winds doing to-day?

ANOTHER. Just the same, for the century and a half that we have been here, fattening the money-lenders:
Relentless Neptune, with untiring lung, blowing on this little basin where Europe washes her feet
And driving his folk in hustling waves through the gate of Hercules.

But what will his second wind be like, gentlemen, to swamp us as soon as the mighty bellows fills again!

In not less than a month, I swear, our squadron will heave to, stripped of rigging in that pouch and haven of the world over there, dotted all over with isles at anchor like buoys ready-made,

That smoking sea-cauldron that God with golden hands has set up between the two Americas.

FIRST CABALLERO.   And still no news of our Achilles?

SECOND CABALLERO.   He is Achilles in Scyros, not hiding in a woman's lap, but running after her, so they say, sword in hand! No news of the fellow.

DON GIL.   I swear I will not set off without Señor Rodrigo.

SECOND CABALLERO.   The same here.

DON GIL.   Even if my lodgings here for over a year cost more than a rabbi's inheritance.

FIRST CABALLERO.   Rodrigo is a just man to everyone—

SECOND CABALLERO.   With his eyes open when they should be—

THIRD CABALLERO.   And shut when need be. He knows the soldier, gentlemen.

DON GIL.   Enough said! He is my personal friend.

FOURTH CABALLERO, *to the merchant tailor*.   None of your red getting on for purple, none of your mulberry juice, none of your sour wine that gives me the belly-ache! I want a frank open red like what runs in the veins of a gentleman.

THE MERCHANT TAILOR.   I have recruited all the bugs that browse the monkey-puzzle of the Hesperides!

My workmen from morning till night are floundering in a swill of fire and slaughter, pulling out of their vats pieces all dripping with a vermilion gravy ruddier than the sea that swallowed up Pharaoh!

And that is not enough! I am looted, gentlemen! All these gentlemen from the four corners of Spain coming to take the colours of our crusade.

FIRST CABALLERO.   Down to our attorney! The modest man, finding the red sold out, has made shift with a suit of pink satin.

SECOND CABALLERO.   What I want is three big black spots on the back, like ladybirds.

THIRD CABALLERO.   And a big Blessed Sacrament in gold braid on the middle of the chest.

DON GIL.   It's we fellows in red that are carrying faith and food and sunshine to those human worms, to all those famishing lizards, to those weather-beaten images swarming in the steamy shade, or ranging the frozen uplands.

FIRST CABALLERO.   It is just like the Corrida! On our terrestrial ball, there is one side in the sun and another in the shadow.

SECOND CABALLERO.   I will complete your idea: one part real and one not quite real. Yes, that is just the idea that I bring back from my expeditions.

FOURTH CABALLERO, *between his teeth*.   Hark at them, the mouldy elders! The gold you get there is real.

SECOND CABALLERO.   I am not so sure. What was in my pocket melted away quick.

DON GIL, *sanctimoniously*.   It isn't shadows of souls that we are going out to save.

FIRST CABALLERO.   Nor shadows that are working on our plantations.

SECOND CABALLERO.   Nor the shadow of a stick to warm their shadow behind if they do not go hard at the job.

DON GIL.   We have to wake up all those sleepy-heads. So much the worse if their skin catches it a bit! Have we spared our own?

All the same, life is worth more than the shades below!

Behold us across the sea; and to that land, which had no right to be without us, we have opened the gates of morn. It has taken all the ages since the creation of the world to get to them, along roads strewn with hot coals and broken glass. It is their turn now to suffer a trifle.

Eyes right! Here we are!

FIRST CABALLERO.   In red!

SECOND CABALLERO.   That is the colour of our Lord on the cross.

FIRST CABALLERO.   There's folk we are going to bring the cross to in every sort of way.

SECOND CABALLERO.   Haven't we got it on our back ourselves, poor adventurers?
Well and truly strapped on among the rest of the outfit.

DON GIL.   In red, in red! We are all going off in red! That is a vow we took in the hands of Friar Lopez.
In red! Under the orders of Master Don Rodrigo! We shall wait while we must. It is five months yet to the month of the Precious Blood.

SCENE II

THE IRREPRESSIBLE, DONA HONORIA, DONA PROUHEZE

General break-up of the last set. The music imitates the noise of a carpet being beaten, making a fearful dust. While they are dragging off the properties of the previous scene, enter among the scene-shifters THE IRREPRESSIBLE, *giving orders and tumbling them about like a circus clown.*

THE IRREPRESSIBLE, *whirling the tailor's measure and waving the red cloth like a toreador.*   Come along, caitiffs, the public is getting restive; get a move on for the love of Mike. Whoo! Wow! Pst! Look alive, shift that away, clear the floor!

Caitiffs is nice and stagey. I ought to have waited for my costume, but I hadn't the patience to go on mouldering in that box where the author keeps me huddled. Twenty times the dresser popped in at the door, but it was always for someone else. And there I stuck, straddling my chair in front of the glass!

They are nervous of my push. I bring things on too quick; in two ticks we should get to the end, and the public would be more than happy.

That is why the author keeps me in reserve, an odd man, if you see what I mean, with a whole crowd of characters that make a great noise tramping through the empty barns of his imagination, and whose faces you will never see.

But I am not so easy to keep down; I escape like gas under the door and explode in the middle of the play. Look out, things are going to move. I am off on my magic steed! (*He makes believe to pedal very fast on an invisible bicycle.*)

We are no longer at Cadiz; we are in the Sierra What's-its-name, in the middle of all those great forests which have made the fame of Catalonia.

A peak! Yonder is the castle of Don Rodrigo. Don Rodrigo is here very ill, when all's said and done; his wound is tickling him; I should think he is going to croak; that's a mistake—he will get better, or the play would be over. Allow me to introduce to you Don Rodrigo's mamma.

(*Enter* DONA HONORIA.)

THE IRREPRESSIBLE, *bellowing.* Stay where you are! Wait till I come for you,
What the—? Who told you to come? Be off, be off!

(*Exit* DONA HONORIA.)

—Don Rodrigo's mamma, Dona What-is-it? Will Honoria suit you?

Of course, just like her to come! I was just going to do you her portrait.

It's annoying, the way things turn out with me. That's why I have never been able to be a painter. My characters begin to exist all of a sudden before I have so much as cut out their eyes.

Look here, I am drawing Dona Honoria. (*He draws with a piece of chalk on the back of the stage manager.*)

Well I shan't have got her ear-rings in before she begins to put her tongue out at me, and she comes unstuck off the back of this underling, like Marguerite from the skull of Jupiter.

When I do a dog I haven't finished the backside when he begins to wag his tail and trots off on three legs without waiting for his head.

Now then, what about it? You will see her all right for yourselves presently. (*He throws the chalk into the middle of the audience.*)

And now it's no longer the morning sun. It's getting late; there is lovely moonlight. (*He hums the beginning of the sonata.*)

I say, up there, let down the sky-cloths, the main floodlight, the front spot-light, garden side.

Now that we have the desired atmosphere I crave your leave to bring on Dona Prouheze. What a name! How it makes her kind of real!

Dona Prouheze got here in the costume that you have seen some days ago, as many days ago as you like, for you know that on the stage we handle time like an accordion at our pleasure; the hours spin out, and the days get pinched. Nothing easier than to set several times going together in all directions.

As a matter of fact, I am afraid that Madam's nerves have broken down under the strain. Not that she is exactly off her head—but she has had a stroke, she is inhibited, her ideas won't move.

Has she yet got to seeing her lover? Not a bit. Rodrigo is at his mother's and she is taking care of him; she is taking care of them both.

Both of them, separated by thick walls, are vainly running up and down the stairways of delirium, trying to get together.

I am going to fetch them.

(*Exit, and re-enter with* DONA PROUHEZE, *whose hand is laid upon his wrist. He looks like a mesmerist bringing on his subject. She has resumed her woman's dress.*)

THE IRREPRESSIBLE. Speak, Prouheze. Let this crowd which surrounds you unbeknown hear your voice. Speak and tell us what weighs down your guilty heart.

DONA PROUHEZE. Rodrigo!

THE IRREPRESSIBLE. Rodrigo? He is out hunting. What I mean is, his body is there all right, there on the other side of those flushed window-panes that you can see across the courtyard,

But now for hours in dream he has been trying to get out of that tangled thicket which he hears crackling and rustling in front of him under the weight of an invisible presence.

"Is it you?" In vain he is trying to say your name, all softly, as you said his just now. There is no answer.

And presently he will break out into this glade in among dead trees covered with immemorial moss.

Everything is strangely white against the black background of the plantation—even to that butterfly which opened up for a moment in a ghastly ray of daylight; there is no one there.

DONA PROUHEZE. Rodrigo!

THE IRREPRESSIBLE, *walking backwards towards the wings, still keeping his eyes on* DONA PROUHEZE). Come on now, Honoria. Here's your cue.

(*Enter* DONA HONORIA.)

THE IRREPRESSIBLE. Let this soul in pain feel her suffering love caught up and enfolded in your own maternal love,

And let your mother-heart reason with her lover-heart.

> (*The two women embrace.*)

The hour of trial draws nigh! I have only to set up in front of you a window-frame . . .

> (*He signs to the scene-shifters, who place in position a window-frame, on which the two women come and lean a moment.*)

. . . And look you what a fatal mouthful of Spain comes in to fill it:

These mountains, covered with wild forest, more matted than the buffalo's fur; the moonlit night; the wings of that great mill to our right, which every second cut across the rays of the moon;

And away down there up the shaded ways, Don Pelagio with his body-servant in front, is climbing ponderously towards us.

> (*By this time the setting of Scene III is complete.*)

All is ready; come along.

> (*Exit, taking with him* DONA PROUHEZE. DONA HONORIA *remains in the set near* DON PELAGIO, *who is already on.*)

SCENE III

DONA HONORIA, DON PELAGIO

A room in the castle of Asyoulikeit . . . DON PELAGIO *and* DONA HONORIA. *Both are standing. The impression is that the noonday Angelus has just been rung. They sign themselves and sit down. It is a day in early autumn. Long silence.* DON PELAGIO *lifts his finger with a listening gesture. Silence.*

DONA HONORIA. 'Tis a belated tree-cricket; this sunshine deceives him. He begins with the glowing faith of bygone times. But quite soon he notices he is alone; there is no reply. He closes with that long stroke of the bow that you have noticed, *diminuendo.*
To give time to the general silence to flow all round again.

DON PELAGIO. It is so sad, so sacred, so solemn! You understand what that thin voice is saying to us, Dona Honoria,
To you and to me and to every living creature.

DONA HONORIA, *half aloud, as if she had not heard.* The bees are buzzing all round the door of the hive. There are roses still.

DON PELAGIO. I have tried to cause no bustle here. Only your horses in the stable do not get on with mine.

DONA HONORIA. There has been no need for you to speak loud. Every living thing in this castle knew at once that you were here.

DON PELAGIO. Say that I was expected.

DONA HONORIA. It is true. At this banquet of sorrow your place was set. (*Pause.*)

DON PELAGIO. How is she?

DONA HONORIA. Things are ill. The doctor was quite gloomy this morning. It is not so much the sword-wound at one side of the breast . . . do not mind if I weep; it is my son, you know, . . .

But that sort of dreadful internal inflammation. It is two weeks since he was conscious.

Tonight will decide everything.

DON PELAGIO.   But 'tis of her I am speaking.

DONA HONORIA.   And how do you want us to be when he is dying?

DON PELAGIO.   Am I to understand that she takes turns with you at the caballero's pillow?

DONA HONORIA.   No, she has not seen him. She has not asked to. Her chamber is in the great courtyard just opposite ours.

DON PELAGIO.   Time was when my lady would have been provided for just a little lower down—

A very good strong prison that your father showed me.

DONA HONORIA.   The great thing is for my son to live.

DON PELAGIO.   Is it this guilty love that will heal him?

DONA HONORIA.   While she is there he cannot die.

DON PELAGIO.   Nor get well, maybe.

DONA HONORIA.   I know not. It is her name and not mine that he keeps muttering in his dream. 'Twas her that he was on the way to join. I was not at all surprised to see her land here.

DON PELAGIO.   And I suppose I had better go away again.

DONA HONORIA.   Perhaps your arrival also was necessary.

DON PELAGIO.   All the same there was one event that would have been still happier: my horse should have shied just now on the road hither and flung His Majesty's Judge into one of those convenient ravines which beckoned him.

DONA HONORIA.   There are things it is not right for chance to end.

DON PELAGIO.   "Rodrigo," she would say, if in that case you had let her come near him. I can see her putting her hand on his forehead:

"Live on, the old man is dead."

DONA HONORIA.   Not for a moment did that thought sully our hearts.

DON PELAGIO.   Do you think that my soul was not great enough to set her free had it been my part to do so without crime?

Yes, but what God has joined together man cannot put asunder.

(*Silence.*)

Not love makes marriage but consent.

Not the child I never had, nor the good of society, but consent in God's presence—in faith:

To the very end of me, to the last particle of that consent which two beings are capable of yielding to each other,

For better, for worse.

What she has given to me I cannot give her back, even if I would.

DONA HONORIA.   She asks nothing; she does not complain; she has explained me nothing; she keeps silence; she is here with me far from the sight of all men.

DON PELAGIO.   That is my fault. Yes, naturally you say it is I that have done ill

To marry her, already old and she so young, not knowing what she was consenting to.

DONA HONORIA.   I am not thinking of you.

DON PELAGIO.   But I am thinking of her, and every word I say meseems she hears in her silence, one by one.

I loved her. When I saw her, I was as if flooded with sunshine; in a little while my whole soul came out of the mist to meet her like a palace undreamed before.

And why could I not wait for my palace to be finished before love made entrance?

I was full of works and ways. It was all awaiting her. Where would she have found such a home to harbour her?

The architrave was set upon the column.

DONA HONORIA.   Grand as another's roof may be, we love better what we ourselves have helped to build.

DON PELAGIO.   There is sense in what you say. But did I not

know better than she what would make her happy? Was I so
ignorant of that life which she knew not at all?

Who knows a plant best? Itself that is sprung by chance, or the
gardener who knows the right place to set it?

I saw her so young in that Madrid so strange to her, motherless,
a legendary father, surrounded by fortune-hunters.

In taking her to wife, was it love or understanding that was
wanting to me?

Besides, I prayed; I received guidance.

You know that from my childhood I have put myself under the
protection of the Mother of God, giving up to her the keys of my
soul and of my house.

It is she that taught me "in all things to seek peace."

It was that very peace that I would have liked to give her, young
creature who seemed made for it, if only she had willed to open to
it her petals.

To carry her off with me a little way beneath that coarse, brutal,
and killing surface of things which is not truth.

What matters it whether she love me? What I felt for her 'twas
not to my dignity to tell her. It was this world of God's wisdom
that was to speak for me in my stead.

What matters it whether she love me if I can manage to teach one
single being what I know, and fill one single heart with joy and
understanding?

DONA HONORIA.   All that just amounts to a crazy creature who
escapes from prison on all fours like a beast across the ditch and the
tanglewood.

DON PELAGIO.   Why did she make off like that? Had I not set
her in paradise in the midst of things excelling?

DONA HONORIA.   Paradise is not meant for sinners.

DON PELAGIO.   As a fact the only time I have seen her smile
quite freely was those hard months in Africa that she spent with me.

DONA HONORIA.   You gave her no children.

DON PELAGIO.   God refused them to me.

DONA HONORIA.   At least you could not refuse her suffering.

DON PELAGIO.   Was not mine enough for her?

DONA HONORIA.   You are not in her shoes. She had to have something to open her soul and this body that stifles us.

You were saying that you wanted to teach her to understand—but how contrive to understand under this shell, which hardens and thickens every day?

This forest round about me, which only now have I begun to understand

Since I began to watch this dying child:

A falling bough; that bell behind the mountains which the wind carries to us once a year;

That bird taking sudden flight—what long reverberations they make in my heart!

DON PELAGIO.   As for me, think you she understands the thought I am forming this moment?

DONA HONORIA.   Yes, I know that for the first time now your soul has gone right through to hers.

DON PELAGIO.   What thought can she have beside that window before her, in her eyes?

DONA HONORIA.   You are not absent; she is still your captive.

DON PELAGIO.   Am I causing the death of him she loves?

DONA HONORIA.   'Tis you that have tied the hands of her prayer. It is you that cut her off from God, and close her mouth, and shut her like a damned soul in a prison of helplessness and despair.

DON PELAGIO.   It was high time I came.

DONA HONORIA.   What are you going to do?

DON PELAGIO.   Know you not that I am a judge, bound to give sentence in every lawsuit that comes before him?

DONA HONORIA.   Señor, don't hurt us.

DON PELAGIO.   Do you think I want to do her ill?

DONA HONORIA.   It is your good that I am afraid of.

DON PELAGIO.   Take my word, the guilty man's best friend is none of your comforters, nor his confederates, nor even his confessor,

But only the judge who has power to give him acquittal and freedom.

DONA HONORIA. By no other means than death, mutilation, slavery, banishment.

DON PELAGIO. With a little of all that. Not with honey and soft touches do you cure a wounded soul. Mingled with all those methods I know some stronger and more subtle.

DONA HONORIA. Is it those you have come to bring us?

DON PELAGIO. Am I not her husband? Is it not my mission to stand by her? Shall I forsake her in her agony?
I know what will suit that generous soul.
All that you told me just now I meant to make you say, and I have quite understood.
'Tis not flowers and fruit that she expected of me; 'tis a burden.

DONA HONORIA. What are you bringing her?

DON PELAGIO. Instead of one temptation another greater still. Show me to her chamber.

(DONA HONORIA *hesitates*.)

Show me to her chamber.

SCENE IV

DON PELAGIO, DONA PROUHEZE

Another room in the castle of Asyoulikeit. (In point of fact, there is no change of scene.) DONA HONORIA goes off. DON PELAGIO passes behind a curtain, then comes back and stands at the back of the stage. The scene-shifters have come on, carrying to the front of the stage a tapestry-frame on which is spread a chasuble, part rolled up, part showing the head of a crucifix. DONA PROUHEZE enters from the wings and works at the tapestry, her back to DON PELAGIO.

DON PELAGIO. Nothing more natural. That wretched misunderstanding,
That stupid attack on the inn where poor Balthazar defending you—for he thought he was defending you—
Found his death . . .

> (*She starts and seems about to speak, but says nothing and relapses into her apathy.*)

It is to your credit that you escaped.
We may call equally providential your falling in with those helpful caballeros who made it easy for you to flee right to this safe abode,
Where under the wing of our respected relative Dona Honoria—yes, she is slightly related to us through the ancient kings of Leon from whom I descend; you remembered it very aptly—

DONA PROUHEZE, *very low.* I was awaiting you.

DON PELAGIO. Quite so.
Besides at the thought of Africa once more, which you have tasted a bit in my company . . .
What wonder if your heart failed you?

> (*Slight movement from* PROUHEZE.)

The continual and hopeless war, Islam, like an expedition into
a country accursed against people bewitched; water rationed;
Below us treason; above us slander; with us the ill-favour of
people always asking money; the means for everything lacking;
Jealousy at court; hatred from the people whom we cost so dear;
boredom of the King,
You and I have relished all that drop by drop.

DONA PROUHEZE. I remember that boat which with endless
trouble we managed to get in during the siege.

DON PELAGIO. And instead of flour or coin brought us only
reprimands. I was a thief called upon to clear himself.

DONA PROUHEZE. Next day the tribes, taken in rear—thanks to
that marabout whom we had won over—scattered. I charged by
your side sword in hand.

DON PELAGIO. Of all that you had enough.

DONA PROUHEZE. Why say this thing to me? You know it is
unjust.

DON PELAGIO. Still, I am going to go back there alone.

DONA PROUHEZE. Is it so urgent that you set off?

DON PELAGIO. The news recalling us from Spain is no better.
I have lost too much time as it is.
And honour bids me follow to the death a task I no longer believe
in.

DONA PROUHEZE. What, you no longer believe in Africa?

DON PELAGIO. I have seen the truth in a flash. Africa is one of
those things in which I have faith no more.

(*Silence.*)

DONA PROUHEZE. Still, not so faithless as others; she had not
deceived you. You knew what shores you were landing on.

DON PELAGIO. Yes, I loved her; I longed for her disconsolate
face.
'Twas for her, since the King allowed, that I left my pedestal
of judge errant.
As my ancestors thought of Granada . . . (*more softly*) as my

ancestors thought of Granada . . . (*he keeps silent a long time, thinking the following*):

As my ancestors thought of Granada, so also I think of the iron ramparts of that other Araby closed up and empty, which the legions of Satan tried to keep us out of as if the damned alone could dwell in flame!

There, in the greatest light that this flesh can bear, to proclaim that there is another God than Allah and that Mahomet is not his prophet.

For me the crusade is not over. God has not made man to live alone.

Failing that wife, I must not let go that enemy He has given me. Moor and Spaniard must not forget that they were made for one another;

Nor those two hearts slacken their grip who so long have fought in fierce withstanding.

(*Aloud:*) The wind!

(*Silence. A gust of wind makes the window rattle. Whispering, raising his finger.*) But I hear the great noise of autumn wind sweeping the earth and the sea.

Suddenly 'tis silent and then it is—isn't it?—that tree-cricket thinly trying to resume his song of summer days . . .

Easy to see it will not be for long.

DONA PROUHEZE. You no longer believe in your vocation.

DON PELAGIO. I have been the builder of a dream.

DONA PROUHEZE. Only woman then is not a dream? For ever that! What is woman, feeble creature? 'Tis not because of woman that life loses its savour.

Ah, if I were a man, no woman would make me give up Africa! There is something worthy of our steel! Enough for a lifetime!

DON PELAGIO. Do you hope to overcome it?

DONA PROUHEZE. It is not hoping for anything that is splendid —it is knowing that one has it for good and all!

Just to grip one's enemy by the throat, isn't that enough? He is held! And not only does he compel us to give all the strength that is in us,

But we feel that he has it in him to compel it three or four times over. Always something new to look for.

DON PELAGIO.   "What good is all this useless labour?" the Lord Chancellor said to me.
"Spain is poor. All the money that you make me pour out on barren sand
"Would blossom here in roads, canals, and droves of merry children."

DONA PROUHEZE.   That is the way the Protestants talk, who look to feed themselves and to get rich, and want their reward on the spot.
But you have taught me to think: "Woe to him who looks to himself!"

DON PELAGIO.   What must one look to, then?

DONA PROUHEZE.   Say it yourself.

DON PELAGIO.   This enemy whom God has given me.

DONA PROUHEZE.   That is your portion upon earth.

DON PELAGIO.   It is not my enemy that I am looking at just now.

(Silence.)

DONA PROUHEZE, *slowly turning round to him.*   Look at me, then. Why should your eyes, too, not be apt to see impossible things?
Is it really for ever me? Look! There is no motion of my body but says I am no longer yours.

DON PELAGIO.   You are mine so long as you can serve me.

DONA PROUHEZE.   What service, when even him (*she raises her hand feebly towards the window*)
I see dying before my eyes.

DON PELAGIO.   Do you deem it a service to keep him from dying?

DONA PROUHEZE.   I do not want him to die.

DON PELAGIO.   What alternative do you propose? What kind of happiness could you bring him were he to live?

DONA PROUHEZE.   I bring but a single word.

DON PELAGIO.   What word?

DONA PROUHEZE.   One that will keep him evermore from hearing any other.

DON PELAGIO.   Will not death do as much?

DONA PROUHEZE.   My soul, if he possessed it, I know would keep him from dying. For when shall I cease to have need of him?

DON PELAGIO.   Your soul, for him to take it, must be yours to give.

DONA PROUHEZE.   If I give myself, is it other than wholly and entirely?

DON PELAGIO.   Not entirely.

DONA PROUHEZE, *slowly*.   Not entirely! Not entirely!
Ah, piercing truth—hard veracious word.

DON PELAGIO.   You cannot give to another what you have given up once for all
To God, from Whom I have my orders in what concerns your person.

DONA PROUHEZE, *in a whisper*.   God . . . God . . . once for all . . . once for all . . .

DON PELAGIO.   What you give over to him is yourself no more.
Is no more the child of God, no more the creature of God.
Instead of salvation you can give him but pleasure.
It is no more yourself: it is that thing instead which is the work of yourself—that idol of quick flesh.
You will not suffice him. You can but give him things within limits.

DONA PROUHEZE.   The longing I have for him is not so.

DON PELAGIO.   Now, yourself, what do you ask of him? And what can you give him in return?

DONA PROUHEZE.   Nothing that can suffice for him—that he may never cease to crave me!

DON PELAGIO.   That is the longing of the damned.

DONA PROUHEZE.   Has such longing been given me for ill? A thing so fundamental—how can it be evil?

DON PELAGIO.   What does no good at all must needs be evil.

DONA PROUHEZE.   Is it true that I was made for his ruin only?

DON PELAGIO.   No, Prouheze, why should you not be fit to do him good?

DONA PROUHEZE.   What good?

DON PELAGIO.   What is good in itself is what will do him good.

DONA PROUHEZE.   It is better to do evil than to be useless
In that garden where you have shut me up.

DON PELAGIO.   That is true.
There is only one certain castle known to me where it is good to be shut up.

DONA PROUHEZE.   What castle?

DON PELAGIO.   A castle that the King has given you to hold to the death.
That is what I have come to tell you, Prouheze—a task the size of your soul:
You must sooner die than give up the keys.

DONA PROUHEZE.   Die, do you say, Señor?

DON PELAGIO.   I thought with that word to reach the ear of your heart. But to live will be harder still.

DONA PROUHEZE.   Is it to me that the King gives this castle?

DON PELAGIO.   I am giving it to you in his name.

DONA PROUHEZE.   Which is it?

DON PELAGIO.   Mogador in Africa.

DONA PROUHEZE.   That place which Don Camillo won and is now holding?

DON PELAGIO.   Yes; I mistrust that officer. You will have to take his place and make him your lieutenant.

DONA PROUHEZE.   You are not coming with me?

DON PELAGIO.   I cannot; I must keep the strongholds of the north.

DONA PROUHEZE.   What will you give me to help me in my task?

DON PELAGIO.   Not a man and not a halfpenny.

DONA PROUHEZE.   Do you know what things Don Camillo said to me and I listened to on the day before his departure?

DON PELAGIO.   I can imagine them.

DONA PROUHEZE.   How long have I to keep your castle?

DON PELAGIO.   As long as needs must.

DONA PROUHEZE.   Have you such confidence in me?

DON PELAGIO.   Yes.

DONA PROUHEZE.   I am a woman. Have I to be warden of that place lost between sea and sand?
And at the side of a traitor who wants nothing better than to flout you?

DON PELAGIO.   I have nobody else.

DONA PROUHEZE.   I cannot take up this charge.

DON PELAGIO.   I know you have already taken it.

DONA PROUHEZE.   Leave me time to think it over.

DON PELAGIO.   The horses are ready. Up! Go and change your dress.

SCENE V

The Roman Campagna. On the Appian Way. A group of gentle-
men; among them the VICEROY OF NAPLES. *They are seated on the*
scattered remains of a temple of which a few columns only remain
standing. In the tall grass bas-reliefs and inscriptions may be dis-
cerned. It is sunset; all the air is full of golden light. In the distance,
the Basilica of Saint Peter in course of construction, surrounded with
scaffolding. Horses and baggage here and there, in charge of grooms.

FIRST LORD.   And meanwhile the Chancellor of France with
his company is going back pitter-patter along the Nomentan way.

SECOND LORD.   Having gone north just the same length of road
as we have measured southwards.

THE VICEROY.   I told him to think of us the last time he looked
at Saint Peter's; our eyes would then keep company with his.

FIRST LORD.   He has no need of Saint Peter's to keep Your
Highness in mind.

THE VICEROY.   Do you think that I got the better of him? Bah!
It is one of those little treaties that leave both sides hot and dis-
satisfied,
So that one has to be made over again every two and a half
years with a great show of our ironmongery
So as to bring back a little order into our tangled inheritance.

FIRST LORD.   The inheritance of the Bold!

SECOND LORD.   Have we not added a few small bits to it?

THE VICEROY.   The tailors who have pieced them together for us
are falling out. I have bad news from the Indies.

FIRST LORD.   Really? Why couldn't they send Your Highness

there instead of that elusive Rodrigo whom the King insists on hunting after?

THE VICEROY.   My place is here at the foot of this column in the sea which upholds all Europe and is the handle of the universe.

And Islam will not prevail to pull it down nor will the stirring up of the raging races of the north, to snatch this Italy where all roads meet across the ring of the Alps, and which gathers up in one handful every thread and every fibre.

The strong man of Europe is the man who most needs Italy and whom Italy needs.

SECOND LORD.   Once more, thanks to Your Highness, peace is coming back to Rome,

The Frenchman has withdrawn his opposition grumbling, and whilst upon the steps of the Vatican the furry ambassadors of Russia are mingling with those of Japan and the Indies,

The legates of the new Pontiff are getting ready to set out for Trent.

FIRST LORD.   And presently the new dome of Saint Peter, like a great stack of corn, will raise its head over an indivisible Europe.

THE ARCHÆOLOGIST.   Rome is all right where she is. As for me I am glad to see Naples again

And that sonorous people whom Apollo and Neptune keep brewing and stirring like a niggard fumbling with both hands in a bag of pistoles.

SECOND LORD.   But your business, Learned Man, isn't it rather with the dead than with the living?

THE ARCHÆOLOGIST.   Call you the dead those living metals and marbles that I brought out of the lava—more than living, immortal?

Our title-deeds, in God's image, for centuries reposing in the archives of a volcano: those superb Ideas of which we are but the spongy translation!

Ah, 'tis those dead that have taught me to watch the living as they go.

THE VICEROY.   It is true. In that human eruption of Naples too our friend has cunningly discovered some statues.

THE ARCHÆOLOGIST.   The loveliest of all. Ah, how sorry I am, my lord, that you have not thought fit to keep it for yourself!

THE CHAPLAIN.   I am going to stop my ears.

THE VICEROY.   A splendid female, I cannot deny.

THE ARCHÆOLOGIST.   Fisherman's daughter do you call her? I call her a daughter of the sea, fit for a god and a king!

THE VICEROY.   That is why I made a present of her to my friend Peter Paul Rubens.

SECOND LORD.   Is it she that we saw going off on that boat laden with statues, pictures and curios of all kinds that you were sending to the Duke of Alva?

THE VICEROY.   Exactly; her mother along with her, like a plant with its root.

SECOND LORD.   So many beautiful things for the north? Like spilling wine into beer! What I love I like to keep all to myself.

THE VICEROY.   And what should I have got out of that beautiful girl, a little selfish pleasure, a small dilettante thrill. Beauty is made for other use than pleasure.

SECOND LORD.   Peter Paul Rubens has no eyes but for his big iridescent blondes.

THE VICEROY.   Gentlemen, do you take me for a fool? Our friend Rubens is too proud. It isn't as a model that I am sending him this daughter of the sun; it is as a challenge!
With a beautiful work there is something else to do than copy it: you put it into competition. 'Tis not its results that it teaches us, 'tis its means. It teems us joy, heart-searching and wrath! It puts a sacred madness into the artist's heart.
Therefore I do not want to leave that prince of painters easy among his roses and lilies. Here is this living Italy with her marble sisters that I am sending to bring him to earth.

FIRST LORD.   I would rather send gunpowder and cannon to the Duke of Alva. It isn't Rubens who will keep Flanders for the King of Spain.

THE VICEROY. It is Rubens who will keep Flanders for Christendom against heresy. What is beautiful brings union; what is beautiful comes of God; I cannot call it other than Catholic.
Isn't that damned good theology, Master Chaplain?

THE CHAPLAIN. My lord, you are a theologian, as that greybeard gentleman who just spoke
Is an archæologist, among the Naples girls.

THE VICEROY. What did those sour-faced reformers want except to act the part of God, reducing the alchemy of salvation between God and man to that feeling of faith—

THE CHAPLAIN. Say rather consciousness or illusion of faith—

THE VICEROY. To that personal and furtive transaction in a narrow closet,
Blaspheming that works are no use, God's works doubtless no more than man's,
Sundering the believer from his laicized body,
Sundering heaven from an earth evermore hireling, secularized, enslaved, tied down to the manufacture of the useful!
And the Church does not defend herself merely by her doctors, her saints, her martyrs, by glorious Ignatius, by the sword of her faithful children;
She appeals to the universe! Attacked by robbers in a corner the Catholic Church defends herself with the universe!
This world is grown too narrow for her. She has brought another up from the bosom of the Waters. From end to end of creation all that are children of God she has called to witness—every race and every age!
She has brought out of the ground the stones of antiquity, and on the Seven Hills, upon the basis of the five empires, lo, she lifts for ever the dome of the new faith.

THE CHAPLAIN. I should never have thought that Rubens was a preacher of the Gospel.

THE VICEROY. And who then better than Rubens has glorified Flesh and Blood, the very flesh and blood that God willed to put on, the instrument of our redemption?
'Tis said that the very stones will cry out! Is it to the human body alone that you will refuse a tongue?

Rubens changes tasteless and fugitive water into everlasting generous wine.

Shall all this beauty be in vain? Come of God, is it not meant to return to Him? You must have poet and painter to offer it to God, to join word to word and from all together make thanksgiving and acknowledgment and prayer outside of time.

As the meaning has need of words, so the words have need of our voice.

'Tis with His entire work that we shall pray to God! Nothing that He has made is vain, nothing alien from our salvation. It is that entire work, leaving out no part, that we shall raise in our cunning lowly hands,

For the Protestant prays alone, but the Catholic prays in the commonalty of the Church.

(Bells of Rome in the distance.)

FIRST LORD, *to the* CHAPLAIN.   Are you answered, heretic?

THE CHAPLAIN.   I hear the bells of Rome, which forbid me to answer; and among them those of my convent of Santa Sabina saying me *farewell* and *Alleluia.*

THE VICEROY, *to the* SECOND LORD.   And you, Lucio, do you believe me?

SECOND LORD, *looking at him tenderly.*   All that you say is true.

THIRD LORD.   We are proud of our captain.

THE VICEROY.   'Tis not because you love me that I am right.

FIRST LORD.   'Tis because you tell the truth that we love you, And 'tis by loving you that we have learned to be aware of one another.

SECOND LORD.   And to form this band of little brothers at your side.

THE VICEROY.   Why should you want me to take a wife, when I have such friends about me?

THE ARCHÆOLOGIST.   You have nothing but praise for everything, but it vexes me to see that you make use of none and so easily do without all.

THE VICEROY.   If I made use of any I must needs destroy it, and then you and I should be very well sped!

I am not given to destruction; everything I touch I would like to make immortal, a treasure without end!

But no, I need but you, the joy in those manly eyes which tell me they are glad I'm here!

To horse! We must make the stage before nightfall.

SCENE VI

Night. The stage is taken up in its whole height by a gigantic figure, all studded with lights, of SAINT JAMES (Santiago) *with the pilgrim shells and the diagonal staff. It is known that the name of Saint James has sometimes been given to the constellation of Orion, which visits both hemispheres by turns.*

SAINT JAMES.　Pilgrim of the west, long while a sea deeper than my staff held me on this donjon-keep on four blocks of massive earth,

On this Atlantic rose which at the far end of the primal continent closes up Europe's inland basin, and every evening, sovereign vestal, bathes in the blood of the slaughtered sun.

And there, on that half-sunken mole, fourteen centuries I slept in Christ,

Until the day when I took the road again in front of Columbus's caravel.

'Tis I drew him with a thread of light while mysterious winds night and day breathed upon his sails,

Till in the black wave he saw the long russet tresses of those hidden nymphs the sailor calls tropic grapes.

And now in the skies, yet never leaving Spain, I pace my circular beat,

Whether the shepherd of the tableland of Castile looks me up in the Bible of the Night, between the Virgin and the Dragon,

Or the look-out man sights me behind Teneriffe, already steeped in sea up to the shoulders.

I am the lighthouse between both worlds; those who are sundered by the abyss need but to look at me to come together.

I take up too much room in the sky for any eye to be mistaken,

And yet as near to nothingness as the beating heart, as a thought in the darkness going out and in.

On the bosom of the Great Water at my feet, which gives back my scallop-shells, and whose timeless sleep feels itself throbbing simultaneously against Africa and America,

I see the white wake of two souls at once fleeing and pursuing:

One ship drives straight towards America;

The other, breasting unknown current and adverse swell, with labour hardly keeps its direction.

A man, a woman, both look on me and weep.

I will not fail you.

Happy folk and the well-contented do not look at me.

It is sorrow that makes through the world that great hole across which my semaphore is planted.

When earth does but uproot you, 'tis in the sky that you will take root again.

All the walls that keep your hearts asunder cannot prevent your existing at the one time.

You find me like a trysting-place. In me your double restlessness unites with my eternal motion.

When I disappear from your eyes it is to go to the other side of the world to bring you back news, and soon again I am with you for the whole winter.

For though I seem motionless I never miss a moment of this ecstatic roundabout in which I am caught up.

Lift to me your eyes, my children, to me, the Great Apostle of the Firmament, abiding and delighting in this ecstasy.

SCENE VII

A hall in the Escurial.

THE KING.   Señor, your proposition, which you made me accept with reluctance, no longer pleases me at all.

I cannot thus leave a woman at the head of a band of robbers in a castle half-abandoned between sand and sea, between treason and Islam.

DON PELAGIO.   The alternative is to send troops and money.

THE KING.   I have no troops or money for Africa.

DON PELAGIO.   Then let Your Majesty be resigned to lose Mogador.

THE KING.   I would rather lose Mogador than the soul of one of my daughters.

DON PELAGIO.   God be praised, Dona Prouheze's soul will not be lost! She is in safe keeping. Not for ever shall the soul of Dona Prouheze be lost!

THE KING.   What is Mogador, after all?

DON PELAGIO.   A great thing to me and to many of your ancestors who coveted it.

THE KING.   A burnt-up corner of the earth.

DON PELAGIO.   Just what Christians need to do their purgatory in.

THE KING.   Between that and America I have no hesitation.

DON PELAGIO.   You have seen Don Rodrigo?

THE KING.   I have seen him.

DON PELAGIO.   Ready at last to set out for America?

THE KING.   He is ready if I give orders to Dona Prouheze to return.

DON PELAGIO.   The counsel is enough. Leave Dona Prouheze the merit of deciding.

THE KING.   I will. And Don Rodrigo himself on the way to his Government shall be charged to bear my letter and that which you shall add.

DON PELAGIO.   Why Rodrigo?

THE KING.   Are you afraid for your wife's virtue?

DON PELAGIO.   Why this useless torture?

THE KING.   Why useless? Why should I try to spare him?
I want him to see the face of the woman he loves once more in this life! Let him look upon her and get drunk with it, and carry it away with him!
Let them look each other in the face once for all!
Let him know that she loves him, let him have her entirely in his will, and part from her by his own unaided will,
For ever, and never again to see her!

DON PELAGIO.   If you plunge him into hell, have you no fear that he will stay there?

THE KING.   So much the worse! He himself has wished it; I see no way to spare him. I want to stuff his heart in a single stroke with so much fuel as shall last him all his life!
Above that world over there which is preyed upon by the other, above a world in boiling chaos, in the midst of that huge heap of matter all crumbling and unsure,
I must have a soul absolutely incapable of being stifled; I must have such a fire lit as shall burn up in an instant every temptation, like so much straw,
Cleansed for evermore of cupidity and luxury.
I like to think of that burning heart, that devouring spirit, that eternal grievance which leaves the spirit no rest at all. Yes, if he had not had that love I should have had to put in its place some great injustice of my own devising.

DON PELAGIO.   Another man than I could say to you: "But how if he gives in?"

THE KING.   If he gives in, why, certainly, he was not the man I needed, and I shall find another.

DON PELAGIO.   For so much toil and suffering what will be the reward that you keep in store for him?

THE KING.   My son, the only one he expects, the only one worthy of him: ingratitude.

DON PELAGIO.   Well, let Rodrigo set off, then: and, as Your Majesty suggests, I will presume to add my letter to Yours.

THE KING.   Forgive me for this trial to which I am compelled to put Dona Prouheze.

DON PELAGIO.   Sire, I have no fear for her.

THE KING.   At least you will go and see your wife again?

DON PELAGIO.   I shall not see Dona Prouheze any more in this life.

THE KING.   What, do you think she will not follow this counsel that ourselves and you with us are giving her, and Rodrigo is bearing to her?

DON PELAGIO.   I think she will not.

THE KING.   Does this exile hold so many charms for her?

DON PELAGIO.   It is at least a kind of exile that takes her far from me.

THE KING.   But Rodrigo on his part is going far away.

DON PELAGIO.   So much the worse! She has found her destiny and her destiny has found her.

Who once has known it does not easily free himself
From that winnowing of the wings of Fate upon our secret longing.

SCENE VIII

DON RODRIGO, THE CAPTAIN

Night. DON RODRIGO'S *ship motionless on the open sea. One of her masts is cut off mid-way.*

DON RODRIGO. Better steer through the sand a cart harnessed to unshod cows, better drive a herd of asses across a scree,

Than be passenger on this sump-tank, to travel the length of one's shadow by arrangement with the four cardinal points!

Better do ten leagues a day on my own legs

Than get on like this by zigzag, essay, stratagem, inspiration,

And at last dump myself to bake while you wait till a drowsy angel wakes!

THE CAPTAIN. My lord, 'tis seen you are no sailor.

For us the fun is not in driving silly before a following wind,

It's in tricky wrestling with adverse gusts, by means of that helping sail, the rudder,

Till in the end they bring us in spite of themselves where we want to be.

That's why they say of our father Ulysses that he was the cunningest of mortals.

DON RODRIGO. You call it tricky to offer everlastingly first one broadside then the other?

And all to pocket occasionally a sort of flabby puff that brings us two cables' length along?

And every night, starboard, larboard,

That red light to madden us, showing the entry to the kingdom of Don Camillo!

THE CAPTAIN. Of your friend Don Camillo to whom you are bearing such good news.

DON RODRIGO. I reckon to settle with him. 'Tis I who am

giving him back his command, but 'tis to that worthy gentleman that I owe my life.

THE CAPTAIN. How's that, I pray you?

DON RODRIGO. Not even my mother's prayers would have sufficed to pull me round. I was already nearing the dark shore.
Don Camillo's name went through me suddenly like a spike. (*Declaiming*) "He gave me back at once
Both suffering and life."

THE CAPTAIN, *striking palm with fist.* I see your drift! One's rival's name is better than a quick-fire on the sole of the foot.
Almost the same thing happened to me ten years ago at Valencia with one Dolores, for whom my rival was a salt-meat merchant.

DON RODRIGO. That's it, my comrade, you understand me perfectly; tell me again your adventure with the salt-pork merchant. It does me good to talk to you and take myself down.
With Master Camillo for *rival*, as you say, and better rival to all appearance,
And, for brothers in distress, all the half-salted victims of the villainy of a tripe-seller, here am I tingling in the general pickle!
How simply it all works out! You see me refreshed, reasonable and easy in my mind.
In troth you would not have done otherwise, and I am sure you agree with me. The great thing is that they must not be alone. When a man has not contrived to win love by his own good points, there is nothing for it but call in the police.
I have the King's command enjoining her to come back. Yes, I will take her back with me on this boat.
And after that I have promised to go away for good. But I shall be alone with her on this boat.
She has yielded herself to that Camillo; why should she not give in to me?
A fig for her soul! It's her body I want; nothing but her body, the rascal complicity of her body,
To enjoy and be rid of! Else I shall never be rid.
Then cast her off. She shall drag herself to my feet, and I will trample on her with my boots.
What do you say of the scoundrel husband who gave her over like that to that Camillo?

THE CAPTAIN.   'Tis thought he found no one else who would guard him better than she against that half-bred Moor.

DON RODRIGO.   Ah, he is a great politician! His wife guarantees him against Don Camillo, and Don Camillo guarantees him against me. He himself is gone away to the Presidios.
I have put him out in his reckoning.

THE CAPTAIN.   Why then, drop this old world that will have nothing of you—Europe, Africa—seeing that another is calling you!

DON RODRIGO.   No, no, I will not leave her like that; all shall be cleared up. It will be enough to see her for a minute. I cannot believe that she is in love with that son of a bitch! Ah, I know it is me that she loves and avoids! Let me but speak to her and I know that all will be explained in a second, and there will be no need of explanation!

THE CAPTAIN.   Still, if she had wanted, she only had to let herself be taken the other day.

DON RODRIGO.   Do you say that you saw her lift an arm?

THE CAPTAIN.   You saw her as I did; our ships tacking against the wind on opposite courses were not more than a cable's length asunder.

DON RODRIGO.   It was she! Yes, I saw her lift her arm, I was looking at her and she at me.

THE CAPTAIN.   And then at once a red flash—bang!—and that ball that mowed down our main-mast.

DON RODRIGO.   . . . Fire! Fire! Fire! Why did you not obey me?
She ought to have been sent to the bottom! You ought to have let go your whole broadside as I ordered you!

THE CAPTAIN.   I had enough to do to keep our own ship from sinking. It is no joke to get your main-mast by the board.

DON RODRIGO.   And while you were getting unstuck she escaped us. Next day the wind had changed.
And now these three days we have been taking our ease like this

under Don Camillo's balcony. There are the two of them looking on at us and laughing.

THE CAPTAIN. Bah! The currents have come on, and even to-morrow perhaps with a bit of luck we shall anchor under Mogador.

DON RODRIGO. You say the currents have taken up?

THE CAPTAIN. Yes, and you can see in the sky that the stars are not blinking now quite the same way. Did you not notice at sunset those long filmy clouds like a handful of reeds?
That is the south wind gradually petering out of the African breath.
To-morrow you will hear our sails stretching and straining in the great trooping of the sea, and the will of God will blow upon us.
Whereof doubtless the herald-sign is this old bit of wreckage that we fished up this very day.

DON RODRIGO. Of wreckage? Where is it?

THE CAPTAIN, *lifting the lantern*. Here. It is the stern-board of a barque that's been lost.

DON RODRIGO. I cannot read.

THE CAPTAIN, *going near it and spelling*. . . . TIA . . . Tiago.

DON RODRIGO. Santiago?

THE CAPTAIN. Santiago. You seem astonished.

DON RODRIGO. It is the name of a boat that was going to Brazil; my brother, a Jesuit father, was aboard her.

(He uncovers.)

SCENE IX

DON CAMILLO, DONA PROUHEZE

Inside a battery in the fortress of Mogador.

DON CAMILLO. I have finished showing you over my little outfit. This is a battery which I built commanding the bar. Armed with a few good big lads that I took the liberty of borrowing from a warship of my lord the King,
Unfortunately lost on the coast. She mistook the meaning of my lights
Altered by mischance two days before without warning.

DONA PROUHEZE. I have listened to you with interest. I like my new establishment. But I ought to tell you that I have already seen it all.

DON CAMILLO. And who took the liberty of showing you the house before me?

DONA PROUHEZE. Your lieutenant, Don Sebastian, at my orders.

DON CAMILLO. Very good. Excellent discipline, to resort to the lieutenant over the captain's head.

DONA PROUHEZE. In the King's name there is no other captain here nor governor but myself.

DON CAMILLO. It tickles me to death to hear you talk like that, my lord Governor,
When I think how you are in the hollow of my hand.

DONA PROUHEZE. Did I put myself there? Have I shown any fear of you? Have I brought with me a single musket, a single man-at-arms? Nothing but my maid.

DON CAMILLO. That's true; you have been faithful to our tryst.

DONA PROUHEZE. Don Pelagio and His Majesty have clearly shown that to get the better of Don Camillo it needed but a woman.

DON CAMILLO. All the same I will shut my hand when I want to.

DONA PROUHEZE. You won't want to before I do.

DON CAMILLO. I can put you back on your little boat.

DONA PROUHEZE. And show that you are afraid of me?
Declare against your sovereign? Show your cards and throw away every trump in the little hucksterings and negotiations that I know of?
Give me up to Don Rodrigo there at sea, awaiting me?

DON CAMILLO. I can put you in prison.

DONA PROUHEZE. You cannot.

DON CAMILLO, *violently.* Are you not in my power?

DONA PROUHEZE. 'Tis you that are in mine.

DON CAMILLO. What is the joke?

DONA PROUHEZE. I say that it rests but with me to make you spend the night at the bottom of your deepest den.

DON CAMILLO. You have got yourself all this power in two days?

DONA PROUHEZE. Two days are a lot for a woman among all these silly men.

DON CAMILLO. I will give you up to them.

DONA PROUHEZE. Each of them is my defender against all the rest.

DON CAMILLO. I have friends outside this stronghold.

DONA PROUHEZE. Giving me up you would hand yourself over too.

DON CAMILLO. Where is my den?

DONA PROUHEZE. Take it easy. I have need of you just now. And it amuses me to do what I like with you.

DON CAMILLO, *looking through an opening.* It amuses me too.

And to complete my happiness I need only look at faithful Rodrigo mounting guard out at sea.

DONA PROUHEZE, *also looking out.* How small his ship seems. A tiny white dot.

DON CAMILLO, *pulling her back.* Come. You cannot look long without danger at that fiery gulf.

DONA PROUHEZE. A tiny white dot!

SCENE X

THE VICEROY OF NAPLES, DONA MUSICA

A virgin forest in Sicily. A lofty and deep cave, down the front of which falls a thick armful of green creepers flowering pink. A streamlet flows out of it over the stones. A murmur of many running waters. Dazzling moonlight. Through the sparkling leaves the sea is suggested in the distance. As these directions are impossible to realize, they may with advantage be substituted by DONA MUSICA *making them known to the audience.*

DONA MUSICA, *supposed to be coming back from the stream with a pailful.* Here is the water! You have put a whole armful of green wood on the fire; you are going to kill it entirely! To say nothing of the black smoke it makes, which can be seen thirty miles away in this moonlight!

I never make but a tiny fire. You do not want them to find you, I suppose? (*She trims the fire and puts a pot on it.*)

THE VICEROY. There is no need for fire at all.

DONA MUSICA. We cannot stay like this together through the night, like beasts.

And you shall see the tisane that I can make with certain herbs I know and lemon flowers.

THE VICEROY. Do you live on tisane?

DONA MUSICA. Me? I want for nothing.

THE VICEROY. Who supplies you?

DONA MUSICA. Down there on that sort of headland in the sea where this sort of forest ends,

There is a sort of hut or chapel, half-tumbled, like those the pagans used long ago, I suppose, with columns in front,

And inside an old headless stone statue so indecent that I hardly dare to look at it.

There the country folk bring every sort of food by way of offering . . . You understand, my little king? . . . Don't look at me like that . . .

Fruit, bread, cakes, honey, eggs, I don't know what else; even bits of roast goat;

And all that I take and make no bones about it.

THE VICEROY.   Does no one hinder you?

DONA MUSICA.   They are much too afraid! Not one of them now would enter this forest for an empire.

It is the headless beldam that pouches the provender, you understand, nothing more natural! She has a hefty appetite.

THE VICEROY.   I will send a missionary to those poor people.

DONA MUSICA.   And police to stuff me into prison?

THE VICEROY.   What do you mean by making your way into my lands like this without papers?

DONA MUSICA.   It isn't my fault! The ship refused to go on.

I have told you about it already! There was not a breath of air, and the boat went suddenly to the bottom as if it had just got where it wanted to be.

No doubt something opened; I only had time to jump into the water—

No one but me could swim—with the pot and those other useful things.

My poor sergeant floated a bit; not long; enough to wave me good-bye with his hand.

Fortunately the land was not far off, and the current carried me.

(*Trumpet sounds in the distance.*)

THE VICEROY.   Those fools still looking for me! No doubt my horse mentioned me to them.

What a good idea it was suddenly to leave them! I didn't know what I should find at the end of this inviting little road.

DONA MUSICA.   Silence, sir king! . . . That's it, take my hand and think about me so hard that no one ever will be able to find you.

THE VICEROY.   How do you presume to be sure that I am the King, or the Viceroy in his stead?

DONA MUSICA.   Did you not send your servants to look for me?
That sergeant who was your sergeant? And I, since I arrived, had
only to wait for you
Here. Why be surprised that I recognized you at once?

THE VICEROY.   All that is true. I had forgotten. By dint of
having forgotten I see that there was never a time when I did not
know it.

DONA MUSICA.   Have you also forgotten that mark on my
shoulder like a dove—I will show it to you some other time—by
which you were to recognize me?

THE VICEROY.   I have never thought of anything else.

DONA MUSICA.   That's a lie you are telling. I can feel everything
that passes in your mind; yes, I move with it
And I know that my face merely pops up a moment there like a
misty little moon in the hollow of a troubled sea.
Hold on, now, what precisely are you thinking of? Bang!
Answer me without thinking.

THE VICEROY.   I am thinking of this fire burning, this ever-
flowing stream going by,
Answering itself further and further away in voices three and
four.
It should not be hard to know what it is telling, to put words to
that long, long strain. Ah, what sour remembrance!

DONA MUSICA, *squeezing his hand.*   Where is it, that sour
remembrance?

THE VICEROY.   Vainly I try to bring it back. It is like the stream;
I do not know whether it is before me or behind me.

DONA MUSICA.   Why then, what hinders you from recalling it,
master King?

THE VICEROY.   This little hand in mine.

DONA MUSICA.   It isn't true, for at once I feel again someone
diving down and getting away. Where are you? And what are
you thinking off?

THE VICEROY.   Of this breathing wind,

Of all those suppliants who beset me, justice to be done on weeping women,
All the evil I have done unwitting or half-willing.

DONA MUSICA.   What more?

THE VICEROY.   Of this expedition I have been told to get ready against the Turks.

DONA MUSICA.   And what more?

THE VICEROY.   The French, the pirates, the Pope in Rome, those gold tassels they can never find for my robe of state,
Those relief measures for the famine in Calabria, which have turned out so ill, the money-lenders I have had to borrow from, my enemies in Madrid.

DONA MUSICA.   All this, does it worry you at present?

THE VICEROY.   Not a bit. Only noise.

DONA MUSICA.   Does it hinder you from attending to anything else?

THE VICEROY.   Indeed there is something else . . .

DONA MUSICA.   What else?

THE VICEROY.   Something fitful beneath it all, something that I want to hear better.

DONA MUSICA.   When I command you silence, what happens? You hear then?
I do not mean the wind or the sea or this running stream. What do you hear?

THE VICEROY.   Faint music.

DONA MUSICA.   Sing a little of that music, dear heart, to see whether I know what it is like.

THE VICEROY.   I cannot, though I would.

DONA MUSICA.   Do you want *me* to sing?
I was able to rescue my guitar, but now it has no strings.

THE VICEROY.   There is no need of strings.

DONA MUSICA. Then look at me a little, till I know just where to take up the music. (*With a faint cry*) Ah-h!

THE VICEROY. Have I hurt you?

DONA MUSICA. My heart is standing still!

THE VICEROY. Is it forbidden to look in your direction?

DONA MUSICA. Hurt me again like that.

THE VICEROY. What is that frightened face I see in the moonlight?

DONA MUSICA. It is my soul trying to defend itself and fleeing with broken cries.

THE VICEROY. Is that all the song that you said you had ready?

DONA MUSICA. My song is the one that I awaken.

THE VICEROY. It is no song; it is a tempest carrying off the sky and the wood and the water and all the land.

DONA MUSICA. From all that is Music absent?

THE VICEROY. Look at me before I answer.

DONA MUSICA. I am absent.

THE VICEROY. Divine Music is within me.

DONA MUSICA. Promise that it shall never fail.

THE VICEROY. What can I promise? I am not singing: it is my ears that have suddenly come open.
And who knows if to-morrow I shall not be deaf again?

DONA MUSICA. True it is. Poor Musica!
To-morrow will be the forest no longer, the moonlight no longer. To-morrow there will be that dreadful suit to settle, that suppliant to satisfy, those bad men at Madrid slandering you,
Those troops to get together, that money to pay back, that robe that doesn't fit.

THE VICEROY. Listen, Musica, I am beginning to understand something.
Do you know what?

Yes, only for my deafness, even those things you are saying
Might be found to fit in with that heavenly gush of tuneful words that I hear a moment and then another moment between whiles;
Not so much words at all as their delicious pulp!
'Tis that ineffably harmonious order which is truth; it is that long ocean swell against which nothing can stand,
And I know that all those frightful gnashings, all that untuned disorder, are my fault, because I have no docile ear.

DONA MUSICA.   And if I live with you, what then? Will you ever be so deaf as to hear me not at all?

THE VICEROY.   You were singing under a stone in Spain, and even then I was listening at the bottom of my garden in Palermo.
Yes, it is you I was listening to and not another;
Not this play of waters, not this bird, still heard when he is mute!

DONA MUSICA.   Tell me again! This vast harmony which gives you much joy—say that it is none the less I who set it going.
It's I at the bottom of your heart, that single note, so pure, so melting.

THE VICEROY.   You.

DONA MUSICA.   Say that you will always listen for it. Do not set anything between you and me. Do not hinder my dear life.

THE VICEROY.   Say rather how did you manage to exist before I knew you?

DONA MUSICA.   Perhaps you knew me then indeed unawares.

THE VICEROY.   No, I know that it is not for me that you exist, any more than that bird I took unawares, heart beating, in the night,
For me and not for me.

DONA MUSICA.   Without you the bird would be dead, head under wing, in his cage.

THE VICEROY.   Do you think that I alone was meet to hear you and revel in you?

DONA MUSICA.   Without you I should never have begun to sing.

THE VICEROY.   Can it be true that I have given happiness to someone?

DONA MUSICA.   This happiness that makes you love so much,
My voice speaking with you, this joy, O my love,
That I am shy to give you.

THE VICEROY.   And do you believe that joy is a thing that can be given and got back just as it was?
What you give me you will see on the face of others.
For you alone, Musica, my exaction and my rigour.
Yes, I will not give up teaching you your place, your tiny place.

DONA MUSICA.   Go on! Swagger as if you knew all about it! That place I have found myself below your heart—do you know that?
It is mine, and if you could find me out there I should not feel so cosy.

THE VICEROY.   You shall explain me that presently. Come, we are not cosy like this. Let us take counsel of the night and all the earth. Come with me to this deep bed of rushes and bracken which you have made ready.

DONA MUSICA.   If you try to put your arms round me you will never hear the music again!

THE VICEROY.   All I want is to sleep near you, hand in hand, listening to the forest, the sea, the running water and that other thing for ever returning,
That hallowed joy, that sadness unbounded, mingling in this unspeakable happiness.
Later on when God has joined us, other mysteries are in store.

SCENE XI

DON CAMILLO, DON RODRIGO

In the fortress of Mogador. A narrow vaulted room, lit by an unseen window. At the back a great curtain of black cloth like those which veil the grille in the parlour of enclosed convents. From the ceiling hangs a pulley with a piece of rope. In a corner a heap of rusty irons. DON RODRIGO *standing motionless in the middle of the room watching the square of black cloth. The shadow of* DON CAMILLO *behind him moves outlined on the wall beside his own.*

DON CAMILLO.   I am saying, what hinders you from drawing that curtain and easing your mind about it?

DON RODRIGO.   Don Camillo, I am glad to have found you at last. I believed you hidden in some hole.

DON CAMILLO.   I thought it better not to show myself all at once, and to leave you in free possession of these places,

Giving order that all doors should open and no useless presence irk you.

Nothing showed save that black officer to whom you had entrusted your letter. I suppose you await the answer with some impatience. Your steps have nowhere met anything but silence and vacancy.

It is like that fine Persian story that you know: "The stone-king's castle."

Only perhaps at times that subtle scent of woman, the light rustle of a gown. . . .

And you had to end up here just where I wanted to guide you, this little torture chamber, this boudoir kept for urgent interviews—one might call them "gripping conversations"—

Behind that curtain you are looking at sat the judge, the unknown onlooker, concerned to watch both the victim and the good functionary who had to work the same—

What's the matter? you are not in a hurry to see me.

DON RODRIGO.   I am looking at my shadow on the wall.

DON CAMILLO, *mingling his shadow with that of* DON RODRIGO.
Allow me to bear it company.
See, we two now form but one person with several heads and
three arms.
Wheresoever you go henceforward you can never help the
remembrance of me being mixed with your reflections.

DON RODRIGO.   You are accustomed to mixtures.
My shadow added to that of a Moorish dog merely increases its
blackness.

DON CAMILLO.   When your courteous shadow is gone by,
evermore to haunt a different shore,
The Moor's will still live in this castle
Familiar of another, covering and protecting with its blackness
another;
Yes, 'twill but have to go about a little to uncover another.

DON RODRIGO.   I am wondering why I do not make you a
shadow altogether.

DON CAMILLO.   Quite, I am not armed. You have only to kill
me, if you reckon there is no other way of settling with me.
However, I will beg you as preliminary to take cognizance of
this note which Madam has kindly given me for you.

DON RODRIGO.   *She* gave it *you* for *me?*

DON CAMILLO.   Herself to myself for yourself. Her Excellency
was at her dressing table (you know that my high functions with
Her Excellency give me access at any time to Her Excellency),
My colleague (I mean the chamber-maid) was busy in a corner
with Her Excellency's wimple.
I read your letters and I have been entrusted with the answer,
Required to deliver it without delay into your own hands.
                    (*He hands him a letter.*)

DON RODRIGO.   But this note is none other than that very one
which I was commissioned to put in her hands.

DON CAMILLO.   I think there is something written on the back.

DON RODRIGO, *reading.* "I stay, you go." (*He repeats in undertone.*) "I stay, you go."

DON CAMILLO.   'Tis plain. She is staying, and you have but to go.

DON RODRIGO.   Have the goodness to tell Dona Prouheze that I desire to see her at once.

DON CAMILLO.   To order me about like that you must think me blacker than I am painted. And did not that comrade just now, on the request for audience you formulated, bring you back a refusal meant to speed you?

Besides, who knows? this room is not so remote that your voice may not reach straight to the ears of Her Excellency.

DON RODRIGO.   Will she disobey those orders which the King himself has charged me to convey to her?

DON CAMILLO.   Not orders, if I have read aright; counsel—

DON RODRIGO.   Even that very order which, together with the King, her husband before God gives her?

DON CAMILLO.   Her choice is to remain here.

DON RODRIGO, *shouting.* Prouheze, do you hear me?

(*Silence.*)

DON RODRIGO, *shouting again.* Prouheze, Prouheze, do you hear me?

DON CAMILLO.   Perhaps she isn't there after all. Impossible to tell.

(*Pause.*)

Curious errand you have taken upon yourself.

(*Pause.*)

You do not answer, but your shadow on the wall is there telling me that it thinks as I do.

You love her, and all that you have to proffer is this letter from the greybeard offering her to come back. How enticing!

As for yourself (yes, I have read your letter too; it was given me with the rest of the packet);

You propose to disappear for good; well, you have but to begin on the spot.

(Pause.)

What was expected was a whole pennoned fleet thundering at our tiny Mogador and we replying our best.

Then yourself, red feather in hat, at the head of fifty fellows, pike in hand, delivering the assault.

Don Camillo cowed and cut to pieces, and Madam carried off panting; what avails against superior force?

Instead of all that you want to make her little head ache. There is nothing that a woman hates like deciding anything by herself.

"Come, Madam, tell me if it is really true you love me, and then come back to your husband for love of me! Don't you admire the splendid immolation I am ready to make

"Of you?" *(Pause.)*

Your shadow does not budge. There it is, stuck to this sorry wall,

Where more than once another shadow lonelier still

Swung gently—at the end of a rope—by the light of a little dying charcoal fire. *(Pause.)*

Myself, even with that crippled boat, would have tried to do something. Even lamed as you are, I mean your boat,

By a woman's hand.

I am very happy to tell you I have taken my precautions. (*A pause. Stepping towards* RODRIGO *and raising his voice.*) You have not enough? You want to hear more?

I think this at least will prove to you that you both have limed yourselves.

She does not love you, you say;

She does not love you and I see you quite amazed at it; but **did** you love her? All you had to do was to take her.

You wanted to satisfy at once your soul and your flesh, **your** conscience and your inclination, your love, as you call it, and your ambition.

For there is all the time at the bottom of you that America—older than that woman's face, which works on you and which it would be such a pity to give up. How well I understand you!

Archly you wanted to put yourself into such a state of temptation that there would have hardly been any fault in yielding! Only a refreshing little fault!

Besides, such magnanimity well deserves some reward.

What more virtuous than to obey the King? To give back a lady to her husband, and steal her from a ruffian? And all that while sacrificing oneself!

Love, honour, vanity, interest, ambition, jealousy, lechery, the King, the husband, Peter, Paul, James and the Devil,

Everyone would have had his share; that was all discharged in one deal.

DON RODRIGO, *in an undertone*. It were good and wholesome that I heard all these things.

DON CAMILLO. Have I said true?

DON RODRIGO. There lacks but the one essential.

DON CAMILLO. Answer me then. You are overheard. By my faith I think I saw that curtain move!

DON RODRIGO Wherever she is, I know that she cannot help hearing the words I say to her,

And I know that she is there, by the sound my soul makes speaking to her,

As a blind man singing knows whether he is in front of a wall or a shrubbery or the void.

DON CAMILLO. I am sure that virtue will borrow irresistible tones from your lordship's voice.

DON RODRIGO. For a saint or a man of the sort that you were describing

All is simple. The spirit speaks, the longing speaks, 'tis well. Forward! Nothing more but instant obedience.

DON CAMILLO. There is no other way of winning salvation in the other world or woman in this.

DON RODRIGO. The choice is made, and I ask nothing better than to leave the women to you.

DON CAMILLO. What then are you doing here?

DON RODRIGO. It does not depend on a healthy man whether the plague attack him, or colic, or leprosy, or any other devouring malady.

DON CAMILLO.   Is it to such amiable accidents that you compare
our Prouheze?   (*Pause*.)

DON RODRIGO.   I do not like to hear you say that name.

DON CAMILLO.   Pardon me, I crave.

DON RODRIGO.   My soul is stricken.

DON CAMILLO.   We are trying to cure it in here.

DON RODRIGO.   It is like this grain of corn whose cure is the
full ear alone.

DON CAMILLO.   The full ear is waiting for you in that other world
over there which the King hands over to you.

DON RODRIGO.   But first I thought to have from her that thing
she alone can give me.

DON CAMILLO.   What thing?

DON RODRIGO.   How should I know it save in the receiving?

DON CAMILLO.   This mysterious thing; why not say that it is
one and the same with her body?

DON RODRIGO.   'Tis true. How make it clear?
The good my soul is craving is bound up with that forbidden
body.

DON CAMILLO.   Speak; you have but to say the word.
Twice already you have called her. I feel she is only waiting for
your third call: "Prouheze, come." She is there; you have but to
utter her name,
And she will be before you at once.

DON RODRIGO.   Presently, when I have taken ship; then will I
call her.

DON CAMILLO.   Don't say that she is driving you away.

DON RODRIGO.   Was it I that wrote on stone that great Law
which sunders us?

DON CAMILLO.   Love laughs at laws.

DON RODRIGO.   That does not hinder them from being; were I to shut my eyes it would not put out the sun.

DON CAMILLO.   Love is sufficient to itself!

DON RODRIGO.   And I, I think that nothing is sufficient to love! Ah, I have found a very great thing! Love is to give me the keys of the world and not to filch them from me!

DON CAMILLO.   Isn't it a funny thing to see you asking at once and in one word
The fulfilment of the body and of the soul?

DON RODRIGO.   Is it my fault that the two natures in me are so strongly welded as to make but one?

DON CAMILLO.   What can the poor woman do?

DON RODRIGO.   All I had—ah, the weight is so heavy that it seems like the whole world—
All that I had I have brought with me here to her. Has she nothing to give me in exchange?

DON CAMILLO.   What can she give you in exchange?

DON RODRIGO.   If I knew it I would not ask it.

DON CAMILLO.   Well, there is no other answer for you than this denial, and this order to set off.

DON RODRIGO.   I accept.

DON CAMILLO.   I stay.

DON RODRIGO, *in an undertone.* "I stay." (*He looks at the paper.*)
Yes, those are the two very words that she gave me to read on this paper.
'Tis written. No room for doubt. Yes, 'tis exactly you that she has chosen.

DON CAMILLO.   I understand her better than you. There is something of the woman in me; I shall know better than you how to settle down with her, whatever you think.
She can do me good, and to you she can do nothing but harm.

DON RODRIGO.   She has already dispossessed you of your command.

DON CAMILLO.   I have given up my place to her. Yes, that's already something of mine I have given her and she has taken.

DON RODRIGO.   The rest will come by degrees.

DON CAMILLO.   I called her, and she came. But I won't conceal from you that the good she can do me seems more formidable than the ill.

DON RODRIGO.   Send her back, then.

DON CAMILLO.   Your lordship is pleased to jest, but—believe me or not—yes, I would have sent her back already if I could.

DON RODRIGO.   I can lend you a helping hand.

DON CAMILLO.   Reason and chance, ambition and adventure, I wanted no other masters.
Here is she intervening against me like destiny, a thing on which I have no grip.

DON RODRIGO.   Such of old was Helen.

DON CAMILLO.   As soon as you are gone, your sail hardly out of sight,
You think, no doubt, she will fall into my arms.

DON RODRIGO.   I do not say so soon. But count upon time and on this hell which is about you.
She will not with impunity live long all alone on the brink of your desire . . .
May I beg of you, Sir, to show me to this room which you have kept for me?

DON CAMILLO.   My tradesmen are already busy repairing your ship.

SCENE XII

DON GUSMAN, RUIS PERALDO, OZORIO, REMEDIOS,
Indian porters

A glade in a virgin forest in America on the bank of a river encumbered with islands and tree trunks. A camp of bandeirantes *among brakes of yellow cane lined with green.*

DON GUSMAN.   And you say that on one of those blocks you recognized the outline of the Holy Cross?

RUIS PERALDO.   Not on one only but on plenty others; a cross with equal arms all coiled about with spirals like serpents.

DON GUSMAN.   So on the tomb of this buried people, whose very name is perished, there is the Cross. From the bottom of their grave they stretch out the Cross to those living men who from the world's end have taken the road to find them.

RUIS PERALDO.   There is not only the Cross, there are those monsters or bottles that I described to you,
Those giants like the fallen Cherubim of Scripture who through the creepers half eaten by the trees accursed, turn their Ethiop faces towards the four points of the compass.
One of them taller than the rest, and all white with parrot dung, was quite wrapped round when I saw it, in the coils of a huge serpent.

DON GUSMAN.   These words redouble my desire; I want, sword in hand, to pit myself against these wardens of hell.

RUIS PERALDO.   As for me, I'm off; I have my bill. I have felt the rottenness of that plague-stricken place taking me by the inwards.
God forgive me for having penetrated into that place, which was meant to remain hidden from every human eye, abominable burial ground!

I have now but one thought, and that is to get to the sea again before I die, to hear the noise of the surf on the white sand!

All my comrades are dead; I have none left but these famished Indians.

DON GUSMAN. Ozorio, give them a few fistfuls of maize.

OZORIO. And ourselves, Señor Captain, with what shall we finish the journey?

DON GUSMAN. You can go back, if you wish, with Señor Peraldo.

OZORIO. Oh, and find in Santarem my creditors, waiting, and ready to throw me into the bug-hole!

No, I will go on to the end which is the far end! I will put my hand on those blasted emeralds!

Those crosses the Señor was talking about just now—I recognized them, as the very ones Sergeant Castro spoke to me about. I know what they mean; it is all marked down on my paper.

DON GUSMAN. And you, Remedios?

REMEDIOS. If I go back to Santarem my wife number one is watching for me. Your Excellency knows quite well that my case is a hanging matter and perhaps a burning.

DON GUSMAN. Forward, by the grace of God.

RUIS PERALDO. As for yourself, Señor Gusman, it is not the emeralds that are drawing you on to the accursed place, nor the hangman that bars your retreat.

DON GUSMAN. I want to give back to humanity that people doubly dead; I want to raise the Cross above their tomb; I want to drive the devil from his pestilential lair, so that in no part of the world is he safe!

Columbus discovered the living, and I, I want to possess all those peoples that death has filched from the King of Spain.

I want to propitiate with the true Cross the ancient masters of the land. Whatever was our conquest I want this ancient world to be our heritage.

OZORIO. Forward!

RUIS PERALDO. Farewell. Neither for you nor for me is there any chance of turning back.

SCENE XIII

THE DOUBLE SHADOW

THE DOUBLE SHADOW *of a man with a woman, standing, is seen cast upon a screen at the back of the stage.*

THE DOUBLE SHADOW.   I charge this man and this woman with leaving me a masterless shadow in the land of shadows.

For of all these images which pass upon the wall, lit by the sun of day or the sun of night, there is not one but knows his author and faithfully reproduces his outline.

But I, whose shadow can they say I am? Not of this man nor of this woman singly,

But of them both at once, who have sunk each other in me.

In this new being made of formless blackness.

For as this man—upholder and matrix of myself—passed along the walk the length of this wall, hard smitten by the moon, going to his appointed home

The other part of me and its scanty covering,

This woman, suddenly began to go before him without his being aware.

And the mutual recognition of him and her was not prompter than the shock and fusion of body and soul without a word, nor more immediate than my existence on the wall.

Now I charge this man and this woman—by whom I have existed a single second—never to end again, and by whom I have been stamped on the page of eternity,

For what has once existed is for ever part of the imperishable archives—

Why have they written on the wall, at their risk and peril, this sign which God forbade them?

And why, having created me, have they thus cruelly severed me, me who am but one? Why have they carried off to the far ends of this world my two quivering halves,

As if in me on one side of themselves they had not ceased to know their limits?

As if it were not I only that exist, that word one instant legible outside the earth amid that whirring of bewildered wings.

SCENE XIV

THE MOON

The shadow disappears, and the screen is taken up during the whole of this scene by a palm tree growing more and more indistinct and waving weakly.

THE MOON.   The Double Shadow is gone asunder on the wall which, in the depths of this prison, corresponds to my presence in the height of the sky,

And instead of this solitary palm-branch that broke off from the shadow, that woman's bare arm with the hand waving faint and slow,

There is only this palm which the sea-breeze in gusts after long pauses keeps moving and a-tremble,

Free and still in bondage, real yet imponderable.

Poor plant! Has she not had enough to do all day to defend herself against the sun?

It was time for me to come. 'Tis well! Ah, how sweet it is to sleep with me!

I am all over her, within and without, but how well the creature I love knows that my light is only peculiar to her darkness!

She has no more to do, she is not perpetually busy putting back what life takes from her,

She yields, she is fain, I am at hand to uphold her, she knows, she trusts, she is sped,

She is full, she floats, she sleeps.

All creatures together, all beings good and bad, are drowned in the compassion of Adonai.

How should they know nothing of this light which is not meant for the eye of the body?

A light not to be seen but to be drunken-in, for the living soul to drink of, for every soul to bathe and drench in the hour of its repose.

How still it is! Scarcely a faint cry, now and then, that bird unable to awake.

The hour of the milky sea is ours; if you see me so white 'tis because I am Midnight, the Mere of Milk, the Waters.

Them that weep I touch with wonder-working hands.

Sister, why weepest thou? Is not this thy wedding-night? See how sky and earth are shining; why, where then didst thou think to spend it with Rodrigo if not upon the Cross?

Look at her, you who listen; not as, on this screen, she might interrupt my light with her body, nor like the dead proof which at any time I could draw of her soul on this magic surface,

There is no question of her body! But this sacred throbbing by which the commingling souls know each other without go-between, like father and mother at the moment of conception—that is what I serve to manifest.

I outline her with my waters in which she is bathing.

That spasm, that desperate outbreak suddenly,

And suddenly that frightful slacking, the abyss, the void she was in and leaves for me!

See her on her knees, that woman of sorrow, lost in the light! It would never have begun if I had not kissed her on the very heart.

It began with those big tears like the sick spasms of agony springing from behind the thought, from the depths of a being cut to the quick,

The soul wanting to vomit and the iron entering in!

No, perhaps she would have given up the ghost in my arms at that first onslaught if while her heart stood still

(While a great tract of sea was sparkling down below and a little sail was tacking towards that Pool of Death)

I had not offered her the word: "Never—

"Never, Prouheze."

"Never" she cries, "There at last is the thing that he and I can share, it is 'never' that he learned from my lips in that kiss just now wherein we were made one!

"Never, there at least is a kind of eternity for us which may begin forthwith.

"Nevermore can I cease to lack him, nevermore can he cease to lack me.

"There is for ever someone from God's side forbidding him my bodily presence

"Because he would have loved it too well. Ah, I want to give him much more!

"What would he have if I gave it him? As if what I read in his craving eyes could have any end!

"Ah, I have wherewith to grant him what he asks!

"Yes, it is not enough to play him false; I will betray him.

"That is what he learned of me in that kiss where our souls conjoined.

"Why should I refuse him his heart's desire? Why should anything lack to that death at least that I can give him, since he expects not joy from me? Has he spared me? Why should I spare what is deeper down in him? Why should I refuse him the stroke I see his eyes awaiting, that I read even now in the depth of his hopeless eyes?

"Yes, I know he will not wed me save upon the Cross, and our souls each to each in death and night, beyond all human motive!

"If I cannot be his Paradise at least I can be his cross! To rend him soul and body, I am quite as good as those two cross-pieces of wood!

"Since I cannot give him Heaven at least I can tear him away from earth. I alone can provide him with a need on all fours with his longing!

"I alone had power to bereave him of self.

"No district of his soul, no fibre of his body but I feel made to fasten to me, nothing in his body, nothing in that soul which made it, but I have power to keep for ever with me in grieving slumber.

"As Adam, when he slept, dreamt the first woman.

"When I thus hold him by every confine of his body, by the whole texture of his flesh and person, with those nails driven deep into me,

"When he has no more means of escape, fastened to me for ever in that impossible marriage-bed, when he has no more way of rending himself from that winch of my prevailing flesh, or this unpitying void, when I have proved him his nothingness by my own, when his nothingness holds no more secrets that mine is unable to verify,

"Then will I give him to God all bared and mangled, to be fulfilled in a lightning-flash; then shall I have a spouse and hold in my arms a god!

"My God, I shall see his joy! I shall see him with You and I shall be the reason why!

"He asked God of a woman and she had power to give Him to

him, for there is nothing in heaven or on earth that love has not power to give."

Such are the raving things she says, and she does not notice that they are even now past and that she herself, in a moment and for ever,

Will pass to that place where they are gone—

Naught remains but peace

The hour is midnight—and now brims that chalice of delight which God offers to all His creatures.

She is speaking and I am kissing her on the heart.

And as for that voyager whose burning shuttle, in haste to lay a thread between the two worlds, the promiscuous straining of the hurricane has so often failed to withhold,

He sleeps under furled sails, he tosses at the bottom of my most forlorn silt,

In the fathomless slumber of Adam and of Noah.

For since Adam slept when the woman was taken from his heart, is it not right that once more he

Sleep on this his wedding-day when she is given back to him and swoons to her fulfilment?

Why be otherwise evermore?

No, not slumber, his sleep is the first-fruits of another state of things.

When his cup is full—and have I not filled it?—should he not be drunken? No second cup is needed, that one was enough!

You cannot die without touching the other side of life.

And when his soul is severed from him in that kiss; when, bodiless, it went to meet another; who could say that he abode in life?

When and how the thing came to pass he knows no more: before and after, past and future alike are done away. All that could be given is given. One of the sides on which being is bounded has disappeared. Into a place whence there is no returning.

Rodrigo, and do you hear it still, that voice saying to you: "*Rodrigo*"?

Now do you know that man and woman could not love other-where than Paradise?

"That Paradise which God has not thrown open to me and that your arms have built for me one brief moment, ah, woman, you gave it me only to make me understand how I am shut out.

"Every kiss of yours gives me a paradise from which I know I am outlawed.

"Where you are I am powerless ever more to escape from that paradise of torment, from that native land encompassing all, which, with each heart-beat, penetrates and shuts me out.

"O woman, you have found it out, that spot in me that you cannot touch save with closed eyes. There in the depths of me is that wound you cannot deal except with closed eyes!

" 'Tis you that throw open Paradise to me and you that hinder me from resting there. How should I be with all when you deny me to be elsewhere than with you?

"Each pulsation of your heart renews my punishment, that impotence to escape from the Paradise you contrive to keep me out of.

"Ah, 'tis in that wounding that I have you back! It is through that I feed on you as the lamp feeds on the oil,

"On that oil eternally burnt by this lamp which never avails to give light."

Thus doth he speak, and I do kiss him on the heart.

END OF THE SECOND DAY.

THE THIRD DAY

Characters

SAINT NICHOLAS

DONA MUSICA

SAINT BONIFACE

SAINT DENIS OF ATHENS

SAINT ADLIBITUM

ACOLYTES

DON LEOPOLD AUGUSTUS

DON FERNANDO

THE VICEROY

ALMAGRO

SOLDIERS

THE LANDLADY

DON RAMIRO

DONA ISABEL

DON CAMILLO

THE MAIDSERVANT

DONA PROUHEZE

THE GUARDIAN ANGEL

THE CAPTAIN

OFFICERS

SCENE I

The church of Saint Nicholas of Mala Strana at Prague some time after the battle of the White Mountain. The winter evening sun comes through the stained window above the door framed in fasces, mixed with angels and garlands of organ pipes like the prismatic spindles of Fingal's Cave. DONA MUSICA *in a great fur cloak is kneeling in the middle of the church. The chancel very dark, a lamp burns there and empty niches open on it; it is decorated with four pedestals as yet untenanted, but destined to receive the illustrious bishops who are coming on presently. There is nothing to hinder a little vague music during this scene, let us suppose the organist putting his instrument in order, not too disagreeably.*

First enter SAINT NICHOLAS *preceded by the three little children.*

SAINT NICHOLAS.   To-morrow is my feast-day.

And even now, by God's command, over the country all trampled by the war, over castles, ruined churches and monasteries, over crumbling villages,

The angels have unrolled a great carpet of snow for the passing of the purple bishop. Everything now is one under the same blanket, Catholics and sour-faced Protestants; all is reunited, all is pulled together, the very rivers have stopped sundering and carrying, nothing moves.

It is too cold outside for the men of war; the lords are warming themselves by their own fireside, fed by bundles of sacristy furniture and sawn-up saints; the theologians are disputing in the taverns;

And the poor folk, like a bird frozen up among a few holly leaves,

Are very gently beginning to hope again and live,

"'Tis not for ever" perhaps.

Wake up, good people! You must not count on me to weep into your soup! Look at this little peering sun coming through!

I get on only with little boys and my day is not lost when I have put into their heart a bit of boisterous joy, a good shout of rude laughter!

I revive the frost-bitten, rubbing their muzzle with snow.

And as the winter sun in one burst fills a hundred thousand cottages,

If with the tip of my glove I scratch the hoar-frost on your panes, in a second 'twill be Saint Nicholas all over Germany!

(He takes his place on his pedestal.)

DONA MUSICA, *with a deep sigh.* O my God, how good it feels here and how happy I am with You! One could not be better off anywhere else!

There is no need to say anything, I have but to bring You my heavy self and stay in silence at your feet.

This secret in my heart You alone know. Only You and I understand what it is to give life. Only You and I share this secret of my motherhood:

A soul making another soul, a body feeding another body within it, from its own substance.

My baby is in me and we are together with You.

And we pray together for this poor, distracted, and wounded and trampled people around me, that it may let itself be bandaged and hearken the counsel of winter and snow and night—

Things which I should not have listened to in days gone by, before this child was in me, when my joy was still without.

Let wrath and fear and sorrow and revenge

Yield to the covering hands of snow and night.

Ah, I see them still, those gory heads between which I had to pass and which were planted on each side of the Charles bridge by my husband's order!

(Enter SAINT BONIFACE *preceded by a thick-set Frisian with a huge head like an ox; two little horns are sprouting in his curly red hair.)*

SAINT BONIFACE. And what other way was there to prevent this foolish people from giving itself to my Saxons? Was the black friar to be left to plant himself in the heart of Europe, to poison the wells? Let him stay with the will-o'-the-wisps in the middle of his marches and his turbaries!

Glory to God, what Poitiers was against Mahomet, the White Mountain was against the heretic!

Honour to all those worthy captains enlisted from every corner of Christendom who at Prague rallied round the image of the Virgin Immaculate!

Their task is done and I, Saint Boniface, am left with mine, which is a heavy one. Ah, it's no small thing to be Apostle of the Saxons and bishop of the introvert, shut-up flock of a people corked, fermenting!

God has not made them to be His arms, or His oarsmen on the sea or that wing behind His shoulders,

But to be trampled down and pressed together under His feet, to be on all sides harried and hampered and hindered, mixed up with incompatible peoples and irreconcilable beliefs, to be for ever in travail, the matter for ever looking for its form, the impulse for ever dissatisfied with equilibrium, and oh! how they love what you can put in your belly!

Between those two great rivers, one going, as 'twere unawares, towards the sea, and the other going back towards Asia and the beginning,

There was a wavering and spongy mass without form, without external appeal, without vocation, without any destiny but this ferment and this slow and heavy expansion,

A people accustomed not to see about it and its warring desires those frontiers that nature made, but only its difference from other men and those languages which do not mix in with its own.

To know it you must look at its heart, for it has got no face.

I brought Christ to the Saxons and, what I had done, Luther ended by undoing.

For of no saint is it written that he was necessary, but of Luther, that he had to be.

And, besides, how should they have seen the whole Christ for any length of time in the fog? And how should the flesh, wherever goaded, lead anywhere like as the eyes do?

For some the truth and for others remorse and ill-ease, dissatisfaction and craving.

I will have a people more akin to matter and more bent thereon and more mingled therewith and more fit than any other to soak into it and be imbued therewith,

A people outside of all dry categories, outside of all the unbending nations, to be at the stage of longing, in face of everything, a mighty storehouse in the centre of Europe, semi-fluid, a conforming negation, an impulse thrusting and filling and maintaining all together, an inward and shrouded man in whom the word of God does not turn at once into action but to simmering deep-down fermentation.

That is why now that Europe is conquering the earth and that her heart be big enough for all this new body, God has set this contradiction in her midst. (*He takes his place on his pedestal.*)

DONA MUSICA. The shadow grows, the lamp burns and I hear about me the sighing of all these peoples trying to settle themselves in the night.

It needed night for that lamp to show forth, it needed all this overthrow around me, this world around Prague, where there is nothing more to look at,

To make me, closing my eyes, find my baby in me, this simple little life beginning!

By my husband's will and by his prevailing sword, the avalanche of crumbling Europe

Has been arrested half-way! It divided round this little column where Mary rises and winter spreads her cloak over the tumbled pieces of broken-down Christendom!

My king is come, he is there, forcing all this chaos to end.

Willy-nilly this folk must accept the tyranny, as they call it, but I, who knew it before them, know that it is good, and in his arms this new life in me takes rise.

Now that all their power for ill is checked, it is time for captive good to be set free.

Instead of all this evil which they strove so hard to do, my God, what surprise 'twill be for them all, that joy they may give for the asking!

See what human eyes can get or even just a singing voice!

My God, You have given me this power that all who look at me should have a mind to sing;

As if I gave them a lilt in undertone.

I give them tryst upon a lake of gold!

When you cannot take a step without finding on all sides barriers and deep cuttings, when you can no longer use speech except for disputing, why not then take note that, across the gulf, there is an unseen ocean at our disposal?

He who can no longer speak let him sing!

It is enough for a small soul to be so simple as to begin it and lo, now all souls unwittingly start and listen and reply. They are attuned.

Over the frontiers we will set up this enchanted commonwealth, where souls will call on souls in those airy cells which one tear will do to ballast. It is not we that make the music, 'tis there, nothing escapes it, we have but to attune ourselves, we have but to plunge into it even above the ears.

Rather than set ourselves against things, we have but to embark with skill upon their happy tide!

The King, my master, has brought this country stability and peace, but he has brought with him his beloved wife and here it is I wish to stay for ever out of sight, I, Musica, heavy with the fruit I bear.

(*Enter* SAINT DENIS OF ATHENS *preceded by an angel like Bernini's, carrying a great green palm upon his shoulder.*)

SAINT DENIS OF ATHENS.   Yes, how good it feels in this deserted church,

Empty of all congregation save one unseen, officially suggested by those niches right and left above us,

Listening to this small creature praying with all her heart, hands joined and the feet of her spirit unshod.

Nothing seen but the lamp, a point of fire upon a drop of oil, but for her the hollow of this place is as full of awe

As if, through a gap in the dark smoke of this world, she

Saw before her the burning bush or the propitiation amid the thunder or the Lamb upon his sealed book.

It is good to hear her coming thus to God amid this world, half-way to dissolution, which for a moment, with an ill grace, yields itself up to peace; she thinks she has but to let her heart speak to gather all these creatures into that happy circle!

But man well knows that he was not made to be happy.

There is no order in the world that can shut him in, there is no king whom all his powers accept, there is no mechanics suited to his style of moving.

While the West plans some one of its splendid geometries, a law, a system, a parliament, a king so ponderous that no stone of the builder can escape him,

Suddenly mankind goes distracted, through the seasons renewing it has caught the new piping,

It feels that the never-returning melody of this world has altered, that the lilt is no longer what it was, a different watchword is passed to it from those Angels one above the other whom I have described.

For there is no order but in heaven, no music save only there, and that of this world keeps it from being heard.

There is nothing upon the earth made for man's happiness; and all the keenness of thy Saxons, O Boniface, will not suffice to find it, that obstinate exploitation of matter which, the better to imbue it, makes itself formless like the matter.

And that is why exists, by all accounts, the sea of the Slavs, that uncharted abyss where Europe has her roots, and which will always cater her her sorrows if she runs short. There, far from the ocean which comes to her only through small inlets, only though narrow wickets closed with locks and complicated padlocks,

Churn together the waves of humanity that has no shores but Purgatory,

In cold, in night, in wind, in snow and mud which clog both soul and foot, in the lack of all guidance other than that retrograde river towards a dead Caspian, and of every other visible aim above itself.

And so to what is the greater part of mankind devoted except to realise all round its incompatibility with everything? And there is what makes its torment and its glory.

There is nothing to be seen. Mankind escapes from torture only to suffer boredom. It has but to look about it to be sure that nothing present to it is sufficient.

Eastward of all behold the true level of mankind, there is the horizon of ponderous mercury which I, pilot of the heavens, had to find as base for my observations.

That is why at the voice of Saint Paul I left Athens; oh, what distaste I had for all those academies and my lady Saint Minerva, head-goddess of professors!

I did not go towards the East. I saw that in order to save Europe, to lay in one piece the keel of that great vessel which, buffeting the waves with formless wings, endeavours to loose itself from land, to get away from that mass of mud, to find direction, it was the prow that I needed, 'tis at the point I had to take my place there beyond, with nothing before me but the stars, it was the entire world that I had to put behind me.

And, to guide men through the surges and the night, what better lantern than that of my severed head within my hand?

> (*He takes his place upon the pedestal.*)

DONA MUSICA.   My God, who art to-day!

My God, who wilt be to-morrow, I give You my child, O my God he leaps in me and I know that he is there.

What matters the present when even now my child in me is fully formed?

In him I multiply myself like a grain of wheat that will feed whole nations, 'tis in him I gather myself together and stretch my hands on all sides to those people who are yet to be,

May they sense my flesh with their flesh and their soul with a soul which makes no reproach to God, but says with a will Alleluia and thanksgiving!

What matters the disorder and the sorrow of to-day since it is the beginning of a new thing,

Since there is a morrow, since life goes on its way, using up with us the immeasurable reserves of creation,

Since the hand of God has not ceased moving and writing with us on eternity, in lines short or long,

Down to the commas, down to the least perceptible full stop,

That book which will have no meaning until 'tis finished.

Thus, by the poet's art, an image in the last lines awakens the idea which slumbered in the first, brings to life many faces half-formed which waited for the summons.

Of all those scattered movements well I know a harmony is making ready, since already they are close enough together to make discord.

My God, grant that this child in me, which I am to plant here in the centre of Europe, may be a creator of music, and may his joy be a meeting-place for all the souls that listen.

> (*Enter* SAINT ADLIBITUM *preceded by a kind of nymph with green hair twined with rushes and holding a golden oar.*)

SAINT ADLIBITUM.   Europe is asleep under the snow, ah, hardly has she won this brief moment of repose.

But lo! soon again her strength comes back to her service and, in an ever-fresh beginning, she feels on every side the inexhaustible interest of the sea.

I love this land of wells, where every drop of falling water hesitates between the watersheds which offer, but there is one that I prefer.

All the rivers go towards the sea, which is like chaos, but the Danube flows towards Paradise.

Vain for them to tell us that there is nothing on that side but the desert, mountains piled so high that 'tis truly seen they are beyond the human standard.

Doubtless the primal garden had to be blotted out like a condemned town, where you turn up the soil and encumber the approaches with stones, like a heart ravaged with repentance.

Space at least abides, free and tenantless, the Wind of God blows, and never has anything human been able to take root there.

There is our native land, ah, how great is our mischance to have left Thee, from thence every year gives back the sunshine and the spring!

There blooms the rose, thither, thither my heart is making with delight unutterable, over there it listens with untold longing, when the nightingale and the cuckoo sing!

Ah, there would I live, that is where my heart is bound!

(*He turns towards the pedestal.*)

SCENE II

DON FERNANDO, DON LEOPOLD AUGUSTUS

At sea, Latitude 10° *North, Longitude* 30° *West. The back of the stage is formed of a blue map squared in lines indicating Latitudes and Longitudes.* DON FERNANDO, DON LEOPOLD AUGUSTUS *both dressed in black with small cloaks, small ruffs, and big peaked hats. They are leaning on the bulwark and looking at the sea.*

DON FERNANDO.   The sea is sprinkled with little islands decorated each with a white tuft.

DON LEOPOLD AUGUSTUS.   We have chanced, it appears, on the middle of a school of whales. Whales, the commander told me, is the vulgar term for those animals: *Cetus magna.*

Their head, which is like a whole mountain full of liquid sperm, shows in the corner of the jaw a little eye no bigger than a waistcoat-button and the bore of the ear is so narrow that you would not push a pencil through it. You think that is as it should be ? It is simply revolting, I call it tomfoolery. And to think that nature is all full of those absurd, revolting, overwrought schemes!

No common sense, no feeling for proportion, measure and honesty anywhere—one does not know what to look at.

DON FERNANDO.   Quite—hold! Here is one standing up on end like a tower and with a flick of its tail twisting round to sweep the horizon. As simple as that!

The gardens of Thetis are all full of bell-glasses, whirlpools, spouting fountains and fancy water-works,

Like those at Aranjuez in the annual fortnight when the rain allows the architect's imagination to work!

God forgive me, I see one of those monsters turning on its side and a young whale fastened to its dug—

Like an island all given over to the sucking of a mountain!

DON LEOPOLD AUGUSTUS.   Revolting, disgusting, scandalous. My, my, a fish giving suck under my very eyes!

DON FERNANDO. It is a great merit of your Magnificence to expose yourself to all these unseemly encounters,

Giving up that sublime chair at Salamanca where you lay down the law to a whole nation of students.

DON LEOPOLD AUGUSTUS.   It is the love of grammar, sir, that took me out of myself and transported me as it were!

But can one love grammar too well? says Quintilian.

DON FERNANDO.   Quintilian says that?

DON LEOPOLD AUGUSTUS. Dear grammar, lovely grammar, delightful grammar, daughter, spouse, mother, mistress and breadwinner of professors,

Every day I find new charms in thee, there is nothing I would not do for thee!

The will of all the schoolmen of Spain carried me on! The scandal was too great! I threw myself at the feet of the King.

What is going on over there, what is happening to Castilian, all those robber soldiers let loose all stark in that detestable new world,

Are they going to make us a language to their use and wont without the sanction of those who have received patent and privilege to provide for future ages the means of expression?

A language without professors is like a court without judges, like a contract without lawyers! Shocking licence!

I have been given their essays to read, I mean their memorials, dispatches, reports, as they call them; I had no end of mistakes to mark!

The noblest words of our idiom put to uses both novel and coarse!

Those words not found in the lexicon, are they Toupi, are they Aztec, are they bankers' or soldiers' slang?

Flaunting themselves everywhere without shame, like feathered Caribbees in the midst of our fellowship jury!

And their way of linking up ideas! Syntax, in order to bring them together, has contrived many a noble circumlocution which allows them to come together gradually and make acquaintance.

But those villains push straight ahead of them and when they cannot pass they jump!

Do you think that is right!

The noble garden of our language is becoming a sheep-walk, a fairground, trampled underfoot in every sense.

They say it is more convenient. Convenient! Convenient! That is the only word they have on their lips, they will see the black mark that I am going to fling them for their convenient!

DON FERNANDO.   See what it is for a country to depart from its traditions!

DON LEOPOLD AUGUSTUS.   Tradition, you have said it.

How easy it is to see that you have conned the books of our solid Pedro, as we call him, the rampart of Salamanca, Professor Pedro de las Vegas, more compact than mortar!

Tradition, that is everything! says that wise Galician. We are living on a legacy. Something enduring with us that we must carry on.

Now what is the Spanish tradition, I ask you? It is summed up in two names, the Cid Campeador and Saint Isidore the Husbandman, war and agriculture.

Outside, the Infidel, and inside, our little field of dried peas. What had we to do with the sea, what did we go to haggle about in those countries with frightful names which the ancients never knew and where our hidalgos have only won the nickname of hide scratchers and clove chewers?

Is it a good and true-born Castilian that so took us by the hand to bring us beyond the sea towards our sunset?

It is a Genoese, a half-breed, an adventurer, a madman, a romantic, a visionary, stuffed with prophets, a liar, an intriguer, a speculator, an ignoramus, that did not know how to read a map, bastard of a Turk upon a Jewess!

And that other fellow who, not satisfied with discovering another land, took it into his head to bring us another sea, as if one alone was not already enough for our poor mariners,

What is the name I ask you, Magalian Hiche! One Magellan! A Portuguese renegade, no doubt in the pay of the king of that treacherous people to put us astray.

And all to rob the coarse vulgarian of respect for his superiors, letting no one forget that the earth is round and that I,

The King of Spain, the ladies, the professors of Salamanca, are walking about head downwards like flies on the ceiling!

DON FERNANDO.   Well if the audacity of those criminals stopped there! But have you not recently heard tell of the notions of that Slav or Tartar priestling, one Bernic or Bornic, canon of Thorn . . .

DON LEOPOLD AUGUSTUS.   Hold, should it not rather be Tours in France, or Turonibus where Saint Martin was bishop and where the house of Mame turns out prayer-books?

DON FERNANDO.   No, it's Thorn in Switzerland and where the people speak Polish.

DON LEOPOLD AUGUSTUS.   It's all the same to me, there's always this barbarian region beyond the Pyrenees which a good Spaniard would blush to know even the name of. France, Germany, Poland, they are all mists behind the mountains that from time to time come down to dim our clear Spanish genius.

What says Bornic? Speak without fear, caballero, I am ready for anything. Go on, I am giving you audience.

DON FERNANDO.   He says—I hardly dare to repeat such an absurd idea—

The earth—he says it isn't the sun goes round the earth but the earth . . . (*He titters shyly behind his glove.*)

DON LEOPOLD AUGUSTUS.   Finish it, the earth that goes round the sun. You have only to take the opposite of what all honest folk are thinking, it isn't any harder than that! That is the way to get yourself, cheap, a sorry fame for originality!

Fortunately, from time to time they push the joke too far. To see that the sun really goes round the earth it's enough all the same to open your eyes. There is no need of addition and subtraction, our square Spanish common sense is enough!

DON FERNANDO.   I hate those choppers of theories, it's what would not have been allowed long ago.

DON LEOPOLD AUGUSTUS.   You have said it, caballero, there ought to be laws to protect acquired knowledge.

Take one of our worthy students, for instance, modest, diligent, who from his grammar school up has begun to keep his little notebook of phrases,

Who for twenty years hanging on the lips of his professors has ended by getting together a sort of small intellectual stock-in-trade: doesn't it belong to him as if it were a house or money?

And the minute he makes ready to enjoy in peace the fruits of his labour or is going to mount the chair in his turn,

Lo you! some Bornic or Christopher, an amateur, an ignoramus, a weaver turned sailor, a canon smeared with mathematics, comes to blow it all to smithereens,

Telling you the earth is round, that what's moving isn't moving, and what isn't moving is, that your science is nothing but straw and that you have just got to go back to school! And then all the years I have spent learning the Ptolemaic system, what use have they been to me, if you please!

I say those people are criminals, thieves, enemies of the State, highway robbers!

DON FERNANDO.   Perhaps simply fools.

DON LEOPOLD AUGUSTUS.   If they are fools shut 'em up! If they are genuine shoot 'em! That's what I think!

I always heard my old father recommending me to dread novelties.

"And to start with," he would add immediately, "there is nothing new; what is there that can be new?"

DON FERNANDO.   I should be still more strongly of that opinion did I not smell something untidy that doesn't fit in.

DON LEOPOLD AUGUSTUS.   It is because you go too far and have not read aright the solid Pedro.

No, no, what the devil, you cannot always keep eternally stewing in the same stew!

"I like new things," says the virtuous Pedro. "I am not a pedant, I am not retrograde!

"Give me the new. I like it. I demand it. I must have the new at any cost."

DON FERNANDO.   You make me afraid!

DON LEOPOLD AUGUSTUS.   "But what new?" He goes on to say "new is but the lawful issue of our past. New and not strange. New that is the development of our natural situation. New and new again, but let it be exactly like the old!"

DON FERNANDO.   Oh, sublime Guipuzcoan! Oh, word of real gold! I will write it down upon my tablets.

"New and new again, but let it be exactly like the old."
Felicitous opposition of terms that cancel out! The spice of our Castilian wisdom! Fruit of a soul perfectly imbued with classic culture! Grape of our little temperate hills!

DON LEOPOLD AUGUSTUS.   You see what a mind is when soaked in the juicy learning of our university! I want men like him, resolutely halted on their natural frontiers, on the frontiers of our God-sent Spain!

Shall I tell you all I think? Spain is sufficient to herself, Spain has nothing to look for from outside.

What is there to add to our Spanish virtues? To our pure Spanish genius, to the beauty of our women, to the produce of our soil, to the charm of our intercourse?

Ah me, if our fellow-countrymen but understood themselves, if they did themselves justice, if they took count of the benefits they have received from Heaven! But they have a great unpardonable defect, that damnable inclination to be always demeaning themselves and speaking ill of themselves!

DON FERNANDO.   How often have I not groaned over that fatal gift of criticism which spares not even my illustrious relative the Viceroy of the Indies, whom I am just now going to join up with.

DON LEOPOLD AUGUSTUS.   I did not know that Don Rodrigo was your relative.

DON FERNANDO.   He is not, if you see what I mean, my relative, but rather an ally of mine.

An ally, if I may so say, by blood. (*He laughs shyly.*)

Everyone knows, as a matter of fact, that he once made a hole in my sister's fiancé, a knight full of promise, Don Luis—I mean to say he did him the honour of an excellent thrust, in the course of an obscure scuffle which all but gave himself a long draught of Styx.

Later, Dona Isabel married Don Ramiro, whom the Viceroy's favour forthwith promoted to the first rank,

So far as to make him, if I may say so, his *alter ego*.

DON LEOPOLD AUGUSTUS.   It is a sure way to succeed him.

DON FERNANDO.   He doesn't think to succeed him, we are not thinking yet of succeeding him.

But he can make him listen to sage counsel. 'Tis his business to assert himself.

I am bringing the Madrid atmosphere. The Viceroy is not liked at Madrid. It is so long since he left.

He has become that man overseas whose voice no one has heard, whose face no one has seen.

DON LEOPOLD AUGUSTUS.   That notion of joining the two seas by a canal, what, I ask you, are the engineers and financiers saying of it?

DON FERNANDO.   It isn't altogether so absurd, it's only a matter, if I understand right, of a sort of road along which by means of cables, and I don't know what hydraulic gadgets, they will pass over ships safe bound on a sort of cart from one hemisphere to the other.

DON LEOPOLD AUGUSTUS.   And that is where the money of Spain is going that we need so much for higher education!

Ships or carts caracoling over the mountains, oh, very good!

It is on the card! It is on the card! When a weaver turns sailor a Viceroy may well turn engineer.

DON FERNANDO.   As you say, it is so much less money for Madrid, the remittances from the Indies have declined.

And the complaints of rapine and violence that we get from every corner of America! Those frightful exactions! All those people being gathered up in Pharaoh's way to be thrown into the Culebra cutting!

DON LEOPOLD AUGUSTUS.   It gives me shivers.

DON FERNANDO.   And all instead of walking in the safe way of his predecessors. An infant would understand that you cannot do anything new without setting yourself up against what is.

DON LEOPOLD AUGUSTUS, *with emphasis.   Nemo impune contra orbem!* None scot-free against the world.

DON FERNANDO.   Still he has on his side the King, who likes him and will never recall him; an error that lasts too long can no longer be confessed.

DON LEOPOLD AUGUSTUS.   I fancy you want to say something more.

DON FERNANDO.   What would you say if our Viceroy himself took leave?

DON LEOPOLD AUGUSTUS.   Himself of himself?

DON FERNANDO.   Himself by himself of himself.   (*He brings a paper from his pocket.*)

DON LEOPOLD AUGUSTUS.   What is that paper?

DON FERNANDO.   Have you never heard tell of the famous letter to Rodrigo?

DON LEOPOLD AUGUSTUS.   Indeed I have. But I always thought it was a kind of proverb or paradigm for schoolchildren, like the sword of Damocles and the house that Jack built.

DON FERNANDO.   Here it is, you can read the address.

DON LEOPOLD AUGUSTUS.   But it is sealed.

DON FERNANDO.   If it were open 'twould lose all its potency.

DON LEOPOLD AUGUSTUS.   Who got it for you?

DON FERNANDO.   A friar that got it from a penitent hanged at morning.
Its history is strange, from the day that at Mogador, you-know-who
Posted it with a certain runaway galley-slave, who a month later at Palos,
Having lost everything down to his shirt, had the notion to stake it,
Only after skinning all the crowd to perish in two hours of a knife-wound,
And for ten years the letter is going like that from hand to hand,
From Barcelona to Macao, from Antwerp to Naples,
Bringing to him who as a last resort planks it on the table,
Success followed at once by decease.
It is high time to get it through at last to its addressee.

DON LEOPOLD AUGUSTUS.   But what do you know of the effect it will have?

DON FERNANDO.   Oh well, I take my chance.

DON LEOPOLD AUGUSTUS.   This letter which may decide his departure,
Do you think the Viceroy will receive it from your hands without suspicion?

DON FERNANDO.   Eh, that's what worries me a bit.

DON LEOPOLD AUGUSTUS.   Give it me. If the Viceroy goes, all the better.
If he stays it will be a good introduction for me to the understanding of His Highness.

DON FERNANDO.   He will make you a director of education. The old one has just croaked.

DON LEOPOLD AUGUSTUS.   I feel I am the stuff of a regular emperor of public instruction.

DON FERNANDO.   You can count on me to back you up. As for my own share,
—You know that I have put together a few small works of which I took the liberty to carry the lot to your room—
When there is an opening at the academy may I hope to occupy a desk in the shadow of your Magnificence?

DON LEOPOLD AUGUSTUS.   Let us talk about Don Ramiro.

SCENE III

THE VICEROY AND ALMAGRO

At sea off the Orinoco. The bridge of the flag-ship. In the distance a country covered with rich plantations from which arise columns of smoke, a fort with the factory it commands and a whole succession of villages burning. Lowering sky, heavy with rain, on the sea are seen several ships at anchor or already trimming sail to set off. Overloaded ships'-boats bring off the whole population of the raided villages.

THE VICEROY. Almagro, you shall be hanged.

ALMAGRO. I demand first to be judged and then, if I am found guilty,
Beheaded, as befits a nobleman.

THE VICEROY. Hanged, as befits a traitor.

ALMAGRO. I am not a traitor. I have defended against you the wealth of the King, this country which I have made and which belongs to me.

THE VICEROY. The wealth of the King is the obedience of his children.

ALMAGRO. It isn't with obedience I built this new Carthage. It wasn't your money I had in my pocket to begin with, my own and my friends'! And what I went loyally to look for sword in hand and what was mine in the pocket of my enemies.
When I was the first to land on these shores among mosquitoes and caymans it wasn't for your pleasure.
That raging appetite through heat and hunger and sickness and insect plague, it wasn't another man that gave me that. It was my own idea that I followed out.
When I dug canals, When I hammered piles, when I built bridges, wharves and mills, when I went up the rivers, when I went through the forests—yes, those days when I went all alone in front

151

like a maniac, like an idiot, without bread, without water, everyone dead behind me,

When I made treaties with the savages, when I unloaded on my plantations the cargoes of blacks that I had gone to skim from the sea, when I parcelled out the land among my sons,

It wasn't another man that gave me orders on a paper, 'tis the secret between myself and God, 'tis the sacred hunger that He put into my heart.

THE VICEROY.   Then explain to me a little, Almagro. Who was driving you? All those things that you have done, what advantage and what good did you hope to get from them?

ALMAGRO.   I do not know, I never thought of it, it's like the instinct that flings you at a woman.

No, not driven, rather there was something in front that drew me on.

I had to take possession of this land, to enter in. It was the indispensable beginning of something.

THE VICEROY, *pointing to the land*.   Look, it is destroyed.

ALMAGRO, *slowly contemplating*.   It is destroyed.

THE VICEROY.   The silt will fill up your canals, wild beasts will plunder your plantations. The undergrowth will sprout apace. 'Tis finished.

In two years, of Almagro's name and work there will not remain a trace.

ALMAGRO.   It is sad enough to see an old thing crumble.

But what joy had you in destroying this new creation at its beginning?

THE VICEROY.   'Tis true, 'tis joy to me to see that fire eating up your work. Even if it had been smaller, I should have found it out. Yes, I take pleasure in destroying that work which took the liberty of existing without me.

ALMAGRO.   You never understood me.

THE VICEROY.   And who then could have understood you better? Who has watched you for ten years and with better eyes? I tried something of the kind once in Florida.

I took lessons from you. Yes, I have even helped you at times without your knowing.

I know your courage, your judgment, your deep seriousness, your justice to the Indians and the negroes,

Your damnable pride, your hatred of me, your injustice towards me, yes, perhaps it was that in you that I like the best.

ALMAGRO.   You had all America for your own, could you not have left me this corner of Orinoco?

THE VICEROY.   Orinoco, too, is mine and it suddenly transpired that I had need of it.

I absolutely must have labourers, Almagro, I had no choice.

ALMAGRO.   For the wild-cat road between the two seas?

THE VICEROY.   Don't judge what you don't understand.

You had only an estate to create and I had to make a world.

ALMAGRO.   And I, I thought that you were jealous of poor Almagro.

THE VICEROY.   It is true, and you told me just now that I had never understood. If I had not understood your work how could I have been jealous of it?

ALMAGRO.   How understand what you don't like?

THE VICEROY.   And how should I ever have liked this doltish work which stood forbidding me the one thing that I desired?

ALMAGRO.   What is that thing?

(*Silence.*)

THE VICEROY.   Your friendship, Almagro.

ALMAGRO.   The friendship of the man that you are going to hang?

THE VICEROY.   My son, can you take this joke seriously?

What, kill my Almagro, cut off my right arm! Destroy such a rival, when I don't want to give up triumphing over you every day,

Giving him at my side a share almost like my own!

ALMAGRO.   I do not want to serve you.

THE VICEROY.   The misfortune is that I have no choice but to make you serve me.

ALMAGRO.   I have never known what it was to serve another.

THE VICEROY.   You will see how interesting it is to learn.

ALMAGRO.   I prefer to be hanged.

THE VICEROY.   Is that your appreciation of the honour which I have done you in troubling about you?

ALMAGRO.   I only asked you to leave me alone where I was.

THE VICEROY.   Why talk like that when every one of your actions had no aim but to defy me and provoke me?

ALMAGRO.   Certainly I would have done more than you if I had had the same chances.

THE VICEROY.   And you want me to leave a man like that here on the banks of the Orinoco?

ALMAGRO.   If you only want my hatred I am at your service.

THE VICEROY.   Hatred can carry you far, Almagro.
How many men have died in my service regretting the day that they began to hate me!

ALMAGRO.   You are an unjust and cruel man.

THE VICEROY.   If I were not unjust and cruel you would not like me so much.

ALMAGRO.   Ah, why have I not a blade in my hand to make you pay for this mockery!

THE VICEROY.   All I ask is to give you that blade.
Look at this bad boy that wants to bite me because I have given a kick to his tin soldiers,
When he ought to thank me for coming to look for him on the banks of his dirty Orinoco.
Almagro, you are out of it by a hundred years. In a hundred years it will be time to take the ploughshare. Now it is with cold steel that we must work.
Shall I leave my lion any longer browsing grass like a horned ox?
There where my America ends, there where turning towards the pole she wavers like a needle traversed by magnetic currents.

That is the share I have kept for you. Gird on the cuirass, Almagro, buckle the sword on your thigh! Is it ploughing and harrowing while you have before you this empire all golden awaiting and in the Antarctic night those monstrous bastions to scale? Down there where the world halts, that is where yourself will halt.

To you is reserved to close the gates of the unknown and, in storm and earthquake, set the word *Finis* to the adventure of Columbus.

Below the line which I will show you on the map take all—and try to keep it if you can.

At Panama there is a whole crowd of wild young men and desperate old ones waiting you; I have picked them for you.

When you have got half of them killed, with the other half you shall enter the unhallowed temple of the demon,

You will tread underfoot the dry bones of lost peoples, you will rend his golden plates from the statue of Vitzliputzli.

And do not fear that adversaries will ever be lacking. In the fog, in the forest, in the folds of appalling mountains I have saved up as many as shall suffice you.

I do not want you to die in a bed, but slit with some good thrust alone on the roof of the world on some man-forsaken peak under the black sky full of stars, on the great tableland whence all the rivers fall, in the centre of the dreadful tableland which the planetary wind is tearing day and night!

And none will ever know where Almagro's body lies.

ALMAGRO.   You are offering me all the Indies south of Lima?

THE VICEROY.   There it is, only waiting for you.

ALMAGRO.   I accept. The worse for you.

THE VICEROY.   Take this stump of my America, catch her by the tail, I have my eye on you.

For your part, if you do not want to love me, labour to hate me more. I shall see that you lack not the wherewithal.

SCENE IV

THREE SENTRIES

The round walk on the ramparts of Mogador. Between the battlements the sea lit by moonlight.

FIRST SOLDIER. Hark! It's beginning again!

SECOND SOLDIER. I hear nothing.

THIRD SOLDIER. No fear we'll hear any more. Oh God, I'm fed up. My! but what a cry he gave.

SECOND SOLDIER. A cry like that is when the nerve is touched.

FIRST SOLDIER. What nerve?

SECOND SOLDIER. That thing the executioners try to find. In some it's here, in others not. The nerve I mean to say.

THIRD SOLDIER. Well, now it's over with Don Sebastian, he's fizzled out.

FIRST SOLDIER. Out of the depths have I cried unto Thee. . . .

SECOND SOLDIER. Saint James, what he always had in his pocket, will get him past the customs.

THIRD SOLDIER. Poor Don Sebastian!

FIRST SOLDIER. No names.

THIRD SOLDIER. It's true he let us down dirtily.

SECOND SOLDIER. What else could he do? From the minute that blasted bitch Prouheze . . .

FIRST SOLDIER. No names.

SECOND SOLDIER. . . . From the minute when our old woman married our old man there was nothing for him but to get away. And where should he get away except to the Turks?

THIRD SOLDIER.   I'd do just as bloody much if I could.

FIRST SOLDIER.   Don't talk so loud! You know our old man often takes a walk o'nights. All right for him to dress in white with a black cloak, you see him all the same. He's got two eyes shining like a cat's.

THIRD SOLDIER.   Rather like to catch him in a nice corner! Call me small potatoes if I wouldn't plug him a good one.

SECOND SOLDIER, *leaping to his musket.*   Who goes there?

SCENE V

THE LANDLADY, DON LEOPOLD AUGUSTUS

Now it is very plain that we could no longer deny to our spectators' imagination up there just near the roof this row of windows in the pleasantly pink or blue plaster of a Genoa house brought over by the needs of local colour to Panama. Each window is decorated with a string upon which hang red peppers and garlics. The middle of a small balcony.

The bodily appearance of DON LEOPOLD AUGUSTUS *is reduced to his doublet fastened by points to the trunk hose. That doesn't prevent him, blown out with air and hanging at the end of a fishing rod, from executing in the pleasant afternoon breeze a kind of special dance both majestic and merry.*

THE LANDLADY, *beating* DON LEOPOLD AUGUSTUS *with a cane.*
Tap! tap! tap!

DON LEOPOLD AUGUSTUS *throwing off a little puff of dust at each stroke,*
Poof! poof! poof!

THE LANDLADY, *beating again and again, tap! tap! tap!* I could never have believed that a learned man could hold so much dust. (*Tap!*) Take that, my old Philip Augustus!
No luck all the same! Hardly landed two days in Panama, click! In the time you lift your hat to wipe your face, a dart of Apollo the archer, as master Clerk of the Justice of the Peace says,
Stretched him all black on the side-walk. Another to whom the letter to Rodrigo brought no luck!
Then why are you so set on keeping it? Give it me, Leopold! Drop it!
You won't? I pray you (*she beats*), I beg you (*she beats*), I must absolutely have that letter so that the play can go on and not stop foolishly hung up between heaven and earth.

See now, below there, that gentleman and lady sorrowfully waiting for us.

I humbly submit my request to the benevolent attention of your Magnificence. (*She whacks.*)

You will say that I have only to put my hand into Philip Augustus to get the letter.

But I don't dare, that would bring me bad luck.

I prefer him to get rid of it naturally and of his own accord, like a plum tree of its plum. (*She whacks. Tap! Tap! and tap! Tap! Tap! and tap! Tap! Tap! and tap!*)

DON LEOPOLD AUGUSTUS, *shaken but still important,*
Poof! Poof! Poof! Poof! Poof! Poof!

(*The letter falls.*)

THE LANDLADY.   There we are, another little whack to finish. (*Tap! Tap!*)

DON LEOPOLD AUGUSTUS.
Poof!

The back cloth with THE LANDLADY *first, and* DON LEOPOLD AUGUSTUS *next, is drawn up to the roof, showing the tops of vague tropical greenery. Then there come up, beginning with the hats followed by the faces and bodies, at last the pictures painted on the cloth, of—*

SCENE VI

DON RAMIRO, DONA ISABEL

seated on a bench, both in black and absolutely of the period, like knave and queen of playing-cards. Their faces above the painted bodies come through holes in the cloth.

DON RAMIRO, *in a deep, cavernous voice.* The Viceroy no longer loves me.

DONA ISABEL. Dear me, the minute he gives you the government of Mexico,
A kingdom ten times bigger and finer than Spain, with its mines and plantations and petroleum and that opening northwards on the infinite,
I hear you complaining: the Viceroy no longer loves me.

DON RAMIRO. If he loved me he would not banish me like this from his presence.

DONA ISABEL. Isn't it yourself that asked him for Mexico?

DON RAMIRO. I let you ask him.

DONA ISABEL. Why did you let me ask him?

DON RAMIRO. I let you ask him to see,

DONA ISABEL. To see what?

DON RAMIRO. To see how you stood in the mind of His Highness.

DONA ISABEL. Blame rather your jealous and tormented disposition,
That melancholy that gets you teased and makes you bring down on yourself the very thing you dread the most.

DON RAMIRO. You please him more than I do.

DONA ISABEL. Is it my doing? And do you think I have such a good reason to like him when it's to him I owe being your wife?

DON RAMIRO. It is true. Let me meditate on this text a minute or two.

DONA ISABEL. He doesn't care for me.

DON RAMIRO. Still we see you having access to him at any hour.

DONA ISABEL. The same as his dogs. How often have I gone in and out without his noticing; it is only when I sing that he listens.

DON RAMIRO. You had only to mention your health needing the climate of the heights and the next day he made me suggest Mexico.

DONA ISABEL. Yes, that's just like his queer indifference! To think that the very day before he had shown me so much careless confidence! Rodrigo almost caressing! And then I had to say but one word!
It's true I could not have believed that he would be so glad to get rid of me.

DON RAMIRO. It isn't you he has it in for. It's I that have offended him.

DONA ISABEL. Always that sickly anxiety!

DON RAMIRO. Ah, I cannot bear the thought of his contempt.

DONA ISABEL. How often have I heard you blame and curse him !

DON RAMIRO. One look, one smile of his made me forget all.

DONA ISABEL. Do you think he ever bothers his head about you or me?

DON RAMIRO. I only know that life without him is an impossibility!
When his deep eye turns on me, when I see that he is looking at me, there is something in me that leaps to salute him.
God has given him a sort of right and authority over me so that what he asks for is no longer mine.

DONA ISABEL. What ought you then to do?

DON RAMIRO. It's that job of director of works on the Royal

Road that I ought to have asked of him. That is what is next his heart.

DONA ISABEL.　Why didn't he propose it to you?

DON RAMIRO.　It was for me to propose, he expected me.

DONA ISABEL.　How! The place where one is sure to die in a few months, had you to ask it as a favour?

DON RAMIRO.　Ah, I blame him for having taken too seriously that moment of weakness.

DONA ISABEL.　What weakness?

DON RAMIRO.　A moment, a single moment of weakness, ah, I blame myself for having let you ask him for Mexico. Why does he show himself so stubborn and inexorable? By now he will have given that Panama job to another.

Why does he despise me so, what have I done to make him think I could not give my life for him?

DONA ISABEL.　Ought I to die as well?

DON RAMIRO.　You have only to go back with the children to Spain.

DONA ISABEL.　I see that I count for little with you, in comparison with him.

DON RAMIRO.　I have rights over you, but he has rights over me.

DONA ISABEL.　Well, I am going off this very minute to tell him that you don't want Mexico.

DON RAMIRO.　That will be no use. He doesn't forgive hesitation in the people that serve him.

Folk like me have had time to get to know him. He has turned me down, it's all over. He doesn't like people to draw back.

DONA ISABEL.　He has turned you down? We will turn him down too.

It is time to live on your own. Long enough have you been fascinated and captivated by that evil star.

Ramiro, I do not love you, but I am deeply involved with you. We will not go to Mexico.

It isn't a question of our going away, it is he that must go away. Rodrigo must disappear. Absolutely not be there.

The place he held you must take.

DON RAMIRO.   What, take America from him, it would be taking more than his wife.

DONA ISABEL.   What would you say if he gave it up himself?

DON RAMIRO.   He will not forsake us, he is with us always. I believe in him.

DONA ISABEL. . Oh God! why have I not that letter to Rodrigo?

DON RAMIRO.   That letter that your brother brought from Spain?

DONA ISABEL.   And that he handed through superstition to that fool

That a sunstroke put out this morning.

DON RAMIRO.   Better for that letter to get lost.

DONA ISABEL.   You dread the trial for your idol?

DON RAMIRO.   I dread nothing.

DONA ISABEL.   Only give me the letter to Rodrigo.
    (*The letter falls, a scene-shifter picks it up and holds it before* DON RAMIRO'S *eyes.*)

DON RAMIRO.   Take it, madam, there it is.

SCENE VII

DON CAMILLO, THE MAID-SERVANT

Mogador, a tent on the sand on the ocean brink. Within, a room feebly lit by a hanging lamp. Carpets on the ground. At the back a hanging of very light veiling.

DON CAMILLO, *in undertone.* Dona Prouheze is there?

THE MAID-SERVANT. She is resting and has forbidden me to wake her.

DON CAMILLO. Open that hanging.
I want to give her back this bead of her rosary that she lost and that I have spent the whole day hunting for. There it is.
(*The* SERVANT *opens the hanging,* DONA PROUHEZE *is seen stretched on a low couch. The lamp feebly lights her outstretched arm and open hand.*)

DON CAMILLO. She is stretching her hand as if to receive this drop of water I am bringing her. (*He puts back the crystal bead in her hand.*)
How strange it is! We are alone under this tent and still it seems to me full of countless onlookers.
So was it with that Marabout that I went to see, long ago in Atlas, who received me in an unlit room.
I thought I was alone with him and suddenly, while I spoke, I noticed that the room was full of an unseen, close-packed crowd listening to me—without a sound.

(*He goes out.*)

SCENE VIII

DONA PROUHEZE ASLEEP, THE GUARDIAN ANGEL

DONA PROUHEZE. I have found the lost bead! A single bead. But with a bead missing the bond of the prayer is undone.

I have found my missing number. This little transparent pebble. I hold it hard in my hand. This hoarded tear, this unalterable diamond. This pearl unmatched.

Water found at last.

This drop of water that the rich man coveted from Lazarus' finger tip, and which is the hundredfold of all things. This hope within me, the seed of the day to be.

(*On the screen at the back of the stage appears first dim, then better defined, a bluish image of the terrestrial globe.*)

But did I say that I held this drop of water? 'Tis I am held in it.

Someone has put it into my hand, this pearl unmatched, this essential bead without which the whole rosary of the heavens would be undone!

The earth saying *Ave Maria*.

How small she is among all the cities of Judah! So small, tiny, so little among so many lights.

So little, that no eye without a guide could find Bethlehem. And yet, the Son of God desired no other woman to be born of there, 'tis because of her that all the rest was made.

(*The globe turns slightly and now nothing is seen but the ocean.*)

I am thirsty!

I know that my beloved is beyond the sea. Rodrigo!

I know we both are drinking of the same cup, 'tis the common horizon of our banishment.

It is that I see every morning come up sparkling in the rising sun,

And when I have drained it, from me in the darkness he receives it in his turn.

(*The globe turns again and there is seen on the horizon on the edge of the curve the long sinuous line of the Isthmus of*

Panama, behind which the waters of a new ocean begin to shine.)

Between the two seas, the western horizon,

There where the barrier is thinner, between those two sundered masses of a continent,

There is where you have planted yourself, there is the gate given you to open.

(*Again the ocean only.*)

The sea! The untrammelled sea!

(*There is seen the shadow of a hand behind the luminous screen sweeping the whole expanse.*)

THE VOICE OF RODRIGO, *behind the screen.*   Prouheze!

DONA PROUHEZE.   Rodrigo! 'Tis me! I am there, I hear, I have heard.

THE VOICE OF RODRIGO, *lower, almost imperceptible.*   Prouheze!

DONA PROUHEZE.   Why hold me back on this threshold almost crossed? Why try to forbid me that gate which thou thyself hast opened?

Why hinder them coming to take me to the other side of that sunken barrier, 'tis not the sea in the mist, 'tis the army of God, in countless movement, coming to meet me.

The boundary between this sea and that other, two seas which seek to mingle their waters, through the intervening bulwark, did you then think it so strong?

Not stronger than what this woman's heart long since set up against thee!

Let me begin my penance in the lap of those eternal joys! Let me be the drop of water uniting them with thy heart. Let me have no more body that I may have no more bounds to thy desire! Let me have no more face that I may go right through to thy heart!

Do not hold up on this half-open threshold, this half-broken woman!

(*She hearkens.*)

I hear nothing now.

(*The globe on the screen turns again. On the horizon is seen the group of the Japanese islands.*)

What are those islands over there, like motionless clouds, which by their shape, their strongholds, their hollows, their gorges, seem like musical instruments for a mysterious concert, instruments at once gathered together and kept asunder?

I hear the sea endlessly breaking on those eternal shores!

Near a stake planted in the sand I see a stone staircase going up.

The clouds, slow to part, the curtain of the rain,

Hardly allow me at times to make out inky mountains, a waterfall with sombre trees, the fold of dark forests on which suddenly opens a revealing ray!

To the moon's torch answers the glare of subterranean fires, and the drum beneath a thatched roof joins with the shrilling flute.

Then, what mean at times these clouds of flowers—covering all? The inestimable gold of that annual consummation before the snow comes down?

Above the mountains, among forests, there is a great white angel looking at the sea.

> (*The great island of Japan slowly comes to life and takes the form of one of those guards in sombre armour that may be seen at Nara.*)

THE GUARDIAN ANGEL.   Do you not recognize me?

DONA PROUHEZE.   I do not know. I see only an uncertain shape, like a shadow in the fog.

THE GUARDIAN ANGEL.   It is I. I was there. I have never left you,

Your Guardian Angel. Do you really think that you were far from me until now? There was continuity between us. You were touching me.

Thus, when autumn comes how warm it is still! The air is blue, the swallow everywhere finds abundant provender,

And yet how does she know it? The autumn is come, nothing will hinder her departure, she must, she goes, braving the sea.

She is not troubled about direction.

In like manner, in a conversation, one who is all caught up and possessed by the conversation,

If he hear a violin somewhere, or simply two or three times in succession those taps one gives on a piece of wood,

Bit by bit he holds his tongue, he is interrupted, he is elsewhere, as they say, he is hearkening.

You yourself, tell me, is it really true that you have never felt in the depth of yourself, between the heart and the liver, that dull thud, that sharp pull-up, that urgent touch?

DONA PROUHEZE.   Too well I know them.

THE GUARDIAN ANGEL.   It was my hook in the very midst of you and I was paying out the line like a patient angler. Look at it twined about my wrist. There are only a few lengths left.

DONA PROUHEZE.   It is true, then, that I am going to die?

THE GUARDIAN ANGEL.   And who knows if you are not dead already, otherwise whence would come to you that indifference to place, that helpless inertia?

So near the frontier, who knows from which side I can send you, back or forward at my playful will?

DONA PROUHEZE.   Where am I and where are you?

THE GUARDIAN ANGEL.   Together and apart. Far away and with you.

But to bring you to the inwardness of this union of time with no time, of distance with no space, of movement with a different movement, I would need that music which your ears as yet cannot endure.

Where, you say, is perfume? *Where*, you will say, is sound? Between the perfume and the sound what is the common frontier! They exist together. And I exist with you.

Listen to my being. Yield to the persuasion of those waters gradually unbinding you. Give up this earth which you think solid and is but chained down.

A frail mixture, at every second thrilled with being as well as not being.

DONA PROUHEZE.   Ah, when you speak again I feel in the depths of me the fishing line, the pull of that straightforward longing against the surge, of which I have so often known the ebb and flow.

THE GUARDIAN ANGEL.   The angler brings his catch from the river to the land, but my trade is to bring to those waters where I dwell the fish that is native to them.

DONA PROUHEZE.   How shall I get there with this dense body?

THE GUARDIAN ANGEL.   You must leave it behind a little while.

DONA PROUHEZE.   Then how shall I do without it?

THE GUARDIAN ANGEL.   Is it not now a little late to ask me that?

DONA PROUHEZE.   Myself that corpse I see down there forsaken on the sand, is that it?

THE GUARDIAN ANGEL.   Try if you can again fit yourself into it.

DONA PROUHEZE.   Wax does not take a print more accurately, a vessel the water, than I fill this body in all its parts; is it filling or understanding? Bereaved henceforward
Of this fellowship that should give it life, powerless to lend it my lips.
The body, am I within it or without it? I live it simultaneously as I see it. Every movement of its life I live together in a single stroke.
Ah, poor Dona Prouheze, what pity you move in me, I see, I understand all!

THE GUARDIAN ANGEL.   Is she alone?

DONA PROUHEZE.   No, through her I make out another shadow —of a man, walking in the night.

THE GUARDIAN ANGEL.   Look closer. What do you see?

DONA PROUHEZE.   Rodrigo, I am thine.

THE GUARDIAN ANGEL.   Again the line in my hand has unrolled.

DONA PROUHEZE.   Rodrigo, I am thine.

THE GUARDIAN ANGEL.   He hears, he stops, he listens. Silence, a faint rustle in the palm-trees, a soul in Purgatory going up to Heaven,
An enormous cloud-bank hanging in the stilled air, a wavering sun, lighting up innumerable surges, a sun clearly not the sun of day, the moon on Oceania!
And again, like a captive beast worried by the gad-fly, I see him between the two walls taking up his furious race, that bitter beat of his.
Will he never stop? Ah, what a hopeless road he has already trodden between those two walls!

DONA PROUHEZE.   I know it. Day and night I hear those steps continually.

THE GUARDIAN ANGEL. Are you glad that he suffers?

DONA PROUHEZE. Hold, dour angler! Do not pull the line so! Yes, I am glad that he is suffering for me.

THE GUARDIAN ANGEL. Do you think it was for you that he was created and sent into the world?

DONA PROUHEZE. Yes! Yes! Yes, I believe from the bottom of my heart that it is for me he was created and sent into the world.

THE GUARDIAN ANGEL. Are you great enough for a man's soul?

DONA PROUHEZE. Yes, I am great enough for him.

THE GUARDIAN ANGEL. Is that the way you answer me on the threshold of death?

DONA PROUHEZE. Brother, kill this poor creature quickly and do not let her be so foolish any more.

THE GUARDIAN ANGEL. What keeps you from going to him?

DONA PROUHEZE. This line holds me back.

THE GUARDIAN ANGEL. So that if I let you go . . .

DONA PROUHEZE. Ah, then no more a fish, 'tis a bird that you would see take wing! Thought is not so prompt, the arrow does not cleave the air so fast,
As, away beyond the sea, I should be that laughing, sobbing bride in his arms!

THE GUARDIAN ANGEL. Have you never learned that 'tis the heart that must obey, and not the will materially held back by an obstacle?

DONA PROUHEZE. I obey as I am able.

THE GUARDIAN ANGEL. Then 'tis time for me to pull the line.

DONA PROUHEZE. But I can pull so hard against that it will break.

THE GUARDIAN ANGEL. What would you say if I ask you to choose between God and Rodrigo?

DONA PROUHEZE.   You are too clever an angler.

THE GUARDIAN ANGEL.   Why too clever?

DONA PROUHEZE.   To let the question be heard before the answer is ready. Where would be the angler's art?

THE GUARDIAN ANGEL. Still if I put the question?

DONA PROUHEZE.   I am deaf! I am deaf! A deaf fish, I am deaf and have not heard.

THE GUARDIAN ANGEL.   But why this Rodrigo my enemy, who holds me up, why did I not strike him? 'Tis not the line alone that my hand can manage, but the trident.

DONA PROUHEZE.   And I will hold him so close in my arms that you will never see him.

THE GUARDIAN ANGEL.   You only do him ill.

DONA PROUHEZE.   But every night he tells me something else.

THE GUARDIAN ANGEL.   What does he say?

DONA PROUHEZE.   That is a secret between us.

THE GUARDIAN ANGEL.   Your tears are enough to reveal it.

DONA PROUHEZE.   I am Hagar in the desert! Without hands, without eyes, there is someone that has foregathered with me, bitterly, in the desert!
'Tis desire that grasps despair! 'Tis Africa, above the sea, wedding the poisonous lands of Mexico.

THE GUARDIAN ANGEL.   Sister, we must learn to fare towards happier climes.

DONA PROUHEZE.   What my hand each night swears to him 'tis not in my power to belie.

THE GUARDIAN ANGEL.   So the fish thinks itself wiser than the fisherman. He labours and fights it out without more ado, not knowing that every somersault of his delights the old fellow in the reeds
Who holds him and will not let him get away.

DONA PROUHEZE.   Why do you play him cruelly and if you do not bring him to land why not give him his freedom?

THE GUARDIAN ANGEL.   But how if you were not only a catch for me but a bait?

DONA PROUHEZE.   Rodrigo, is it with me you want to catch him?

THE GUARDIAN ANGEL.   That man of pride! There was no other way to get him to understand his neighbour, to get inside his skin;
There was no other way to get him to understand the dependence, the necessity and the need of another on him,
The law upon him of that being, different for no other reason save that it exists.

DONA PROUHEZE.   Oh! And so 'twas lawful, that love of creatures for each other, 'tis true then that God is not jealous? Man in woman's arms . . .

THE GUARDIAN ANGEL.   How should He be jealous of what He has made, and how should He make anything that does not serve Him?

DONA PROUHEZE.   Man in woman's arms forgets God.

THE GUARDIAN ANGEL.   Is it forgetting Him to be with Him? Is it away from Him to be bound up in the mystery of His creation,
Crossing again for a moment into Eden by the gate of humiliation and death?

DONA PROUHEZE.   Love without the sacrament, is it not sin?

THE GUARDIAN ANGEL.   Even sin! Sin also serves.

DONA PROUHEZE.   So it was good that he loved me?

THE GUARDIAN ANGEL.   It was good that you taught him longing.

DONA PROUHEZE.   Longing for an illusion? For a shadow that evermore escapes him?

THE GUARDIAN ANGEL.   Desire is for what is, illusion is what is not. Desire through and by illusion
Is of what is, by and through what is not.

DONA PROUHEZE.   But I am not an illusion, I exist! The good that I alone can give him exists.

THE GUARDIAN ANGEL.   That is why it must give him the good and nowise the evil.

DONA PROUHEZE.   But, cruelly dragged by you, I can give him nothing at all.

THE GUARDIAN ANGEL.   Would you give him evil?

DONA PROUHEZE.   Yes, sooner than stay barren and unfruitful like this, what you call evil.

THE GUARDIAN ANGEL.   Evil is that which does not exist.

DONA PROUHEZE.   Let us then unite our double non-existence.

THE GUARDIAN ANGEL.   Prouheze my sister, the child of God exists.

DONA PROUHEZE.   But what use existing if I do not exist for Rodrigo?

THE GUARDIAN ANGEL.   How should Prouheze ever exist otherwise than for Rodrigo when 'tis by him that she exists?

DONA PROUHEZE.   Brother, I do not understand you.

THE GUARDIAN ANGEL.   'Tis in him that you were necessary.

DONA PROUHEZE.   Oh sweet word to hear! Let me say it after you. What, was I necessary to him?

THE GUARDIAN ANGEL.   No, not that ugly and ill-favoured creature at the end of my line, not that sorry fish.

DONA PROUHEZE.   Which then?

THE GUARDIAN ANGEL.   Prouheze my sister, that child of God in light whom I do hail. That Prouheze the angels see, 'tis to her he looks without knowing it, 'tis her you have to make, to give to him.

DONA PROUHEZE.   And 'twill be the same Prouheze?

THE GUARDIAN ANGEL.   A Prouheze for ever, whom death does not destroy.

DONA PROUHEZE.　Always lovely?

THE GUARDIAN ANGEL.　A Prouheze always lovely.

DONA PROUHEZE.　Will he love me for ever?

THE GUARDIAN ANGEL.　What makes you so beautiful cannot die, what makes him love you cannot die.

DONA PROUHEZE.　I shall be his for ever in soul and in body?

THE GUARDIAN ANGEL.　We must leave the body behind some little while.

DONA PROUHEZE.　What, he will never know the taste of me?

THE GUARDIAN ANGEL.　It is the soul that makes the body.

DONA PROUHEZE.　How, then, has she made it mortal?

THE GUARDIAN ANGEL.　Sin has made it mortal.

DONA PROUHEZE.　'Twas fine to be a woman for his sake.

THE GUARDIAN ANGEL.　And I will make you into a star.

DONA PROUHEZE.　A star, that is the name he calls me always in the night and my heart thrilled to its depths to hear it.

THE GUARDIAN ANGEL.　Have you not then been always like a star for him?

DONA PROUHEZE.　Far apart!

THE GUARDIAN ANGEL.　Guiding star.

DONA PROUHEZE.　Behold, 'tis quenching on the road.

THE GUARDIAN ANGEL.　I will rekindle it in the sky.

DONA PROUHEZE.　How shall I shine, blind that I am?

THE GUARDIAN ANGEL.　God will breathe upon you.

DONA PROUHEZE.　I am only a brand beneath the ashes.

THE GUARDIAN ANGEL.　But I will make of you a star flaming in the breath of the Holy Spirit.

DONA PROUHEZE.   Farewell! then, here below! Farewell, farewell, my best beloved! Rodrigo! Rodrigo! Over there, farewell for ever.

THE GUARDIAN ANGEL.   Why farewell? Why over there? When you will be nearer to him than you are now? Bound up beyond the veil with that cause which makes him live.

DONA PROUHEZE.   He is seeking and will not find me any more.

THE GUARDIAN ANGEL.   How should he find you outside when you are nowhere else but within his heart, himself?

DONA PROUHEZE.   You say true, I shall really be there?

THE GUARDIAN ANGEL.   This hook deep-bedded in his heart.

DONA PROUHEZE.   Shall he always desire me?

THE GUARDIAN ANGEL.   For some, the understanding is enough. 'Tis the spirit that speaks purely to the spirit.
But for others, the flesh also must be gradually evangelised and converted. And what flesh can speak to man more powerfully than that of woman?
Now he can no longer desire you without at the same time desiring where you are.

DONA PROUHEZE.   But will heaven ever be so desirable to him as I?

THE GUARDIAN ANGEL, *making as if to pull the line.*   For such a silly word you shall be punished here and now.

DONA PROUHEZE, *crying out.*   Ah, brother, let this moment still endure.

THE GUARDIAN ANGEL.   Hail dear-beloved sister! Welcome, Prouheze, to the flame!
Do you know them now, those waters where I willed to guide you?

DONA PROUHEZE.   Ah, I have not enough! More! More! Give it back to me at last then, that water I was baptized in!

THE GUARDIAN ANGEL.   Behold it laving and entering into thee on all sides.

DONA PROUHEZE. It bathes me and I cannot taste it! It is a ray that pierces, it is a sword that sunders, it is a red-hot iron dreadfully pressed on that very nerve of life, it is the bubbling of the spring that seizes on all my constituent parts, to dissolve and recompose them, it is the nothingness I drown in every moment, and God upon my lips reviving me. And beyond all delight, ah, is the pitiless drain of thirst, that horror of dreadful thirst that lays me open crucified!

THE GUARDIAN ANGEL. Do you ask me to bring you back to the bygone life?

DONA PROUHEZE. No, no, do not separate me any more for ever from these desired flames! I must give up to their melting and devouring this frightful shell. I must bring my bonds to the fire to be burnt! I must hug it to the destruction of all my horrid sheathing, all that God did not make, all this rigid bristling wood of illusions and sin, this idol, this abominable doll that I built up in the place of the living image of God, whose seal my flesh bore printed!

THE GUARDIAN ANGEL. And this Rodrigo, where do you think you can be useful to him, here below
Or now in this place that you know?

DONA PROUHEZE. Ah, leave me here! Ah, do not draw me out yet! And, while in that dark place he finishes his course, let me burn myself out for him like a candle at Mary's feet.
And let him feel on his forehead from time to time a drop of this glowing oil.

THE GUARDIAN ANGEL. 'Tis enough. The time is not yet wholly come for you to cross the sacred frontier.

DONA PROUHEZE. Ah, 'tis like a bier that you lay me down on, see my limbs again take on the sheath of narrowness and weight, once more upon me the yoke of the finite and the accidental!

THE GUARDIAN ANGEL. 'Tis now but for a little time.

DONA PROUHEZE. Those two beings who from far apart without ever touching keep each other in balance as the opposite plates of a scale,

Now that one has shifted his place will the position of the other not be changed thereby?

THE GUARDIAN ANGEL. 'Tis true. What you weigh in heaven we must put him on a different scale ere he can feel it.

He must complete his narrow orbit on this little globe in imitation of those huge distances in the sky which we are going to give you unmoving, to annihilate.

DONA PROUHEZE. He asked but a drop of water and do you, brother, help me to give him the ocean.

THE GUARDIAN ANGEL. Is he not waiting for it on the other side of that mystic horizon which was so long

The Horizon of bygone mankind? Those waters that you so craved, are they not making ready to cure you of earth?

The passage he has opened will not he be the first to go through?

Across that supreme barrier from one pole to the other, already half eaten away in its middle by the setting sun,

Across the New World, he is on the march to find again the eternal.

DONA PROUHEZE. At the ocean's other end there are Isles awaiting him,

Those mysterious isles at the end of the world whence I saw you rise,

How draw him thither—now that you no longer have my body for bait?

THE GUARDIAN ANGEL. No longer your body, but your reflection on the bitter waters of banishment, on exile's moving waters unceasingly fading and reforming.

DONA PROUHEZE. Now I see your face, ah, how severe and threatening it is!

THE GUARDIAN ANGEL. You shall know another face later on, this one goes with this place of justice and of penance.

DONA PROUHEZE. Is it penance he is going to, he also?

THE GUARDIAN ANGEL. The straightforward ways of God, his time is come to begin to tread them.

DONA PROUHEZE. Is it I shall have to open him the approach?

THE GUARDIAN ANGEL.   What he desires cannot be at once in heaven and on earth.

DONA PROUHEZE.   What are you waiting for, to let me die?

THE GUARDIAN ANGEL.   I am waiting for your consent.

DONA PROUHEZE.   I consent, I have consented.

THE GUARDIAN ANGEL.   But how can you consent to give me what is not yours?

DONA PROUHEZE.   Is my soul no longer mine?

THE GUARDIAN ANGEL.   Have you not given it to Rodrigo in the night?

DONA PROUHEZE.   Then you must tell him to bring it back to me.

THE GUARDIAN ANGEL.   'Tis from him that you must get leave.

DONA PROUHEZE.   Leave me, my beloved, let me go!
Let me become a star.

THE GUARDIAN ANGEL.   This death that will make a star of you; do you consent to receive it at his hand?

DONA PROUHEZE.   Ah, I thank God! Come, dear Rodrigo! I am ready! Over this thing which is thine uplift thy slaughtering hand! Sacrifice chattel of thine own! To die, to die by thee, is sweet!

THE GUARDIAN ANGEL.   Now I have no more to say to you except farewell until we meet! I have finished my task with you! Until we meet, darling sister, in the everlasting light!

DONA PROUHEZE.   Do not leave me yet, eagle of God, take me for a moment in thy claws, lift me up while I count one! The finished round of our two existences, let me see it!
The road he is to follow, let me wind it round my arms so that he may not take one step without me, and that I be at the end of it and that it guide him towards me.
—What is that stone you are showing me in your hand?

THE GUARDIAN ANGEL.   The rock on which presently his ship

will founder. He escapes alone, his head white with the foam, he lands in this unknown country.

But what matters the shipwreck, he is landed. It was not a matter of discovering a new world but of finding again the old one which was lost.

He has laid upon it the impress of his foot and of his hand, he has finished the enterprise of Columbus, he has carried out the promise of Columbus.

For what Columbus promised to the King of Spain was nôt a new district of the universe, 'twas the reunion of the earth, 'twas the embassy towards those peoples that you felt close behind you, 'twas the trampling of man's feet in the land behind the morning, it was the highway of the sun!

He has got back to the beginning of all things by the way of the rising sun.

See him linking up those darkling expectant peoples, those allotments beyond the dawn of day where imprisoned multitudes are trampling!

(The globe has turned, showing the whole continent of Asia, then India as far as China.)

Think you that God has given up his creation to chance? Think you that the shape of this earth which he has made is void of meaning?

While you are going to Purgatory he also upon earth is going to reconnoitre that image of Purgatory.

He also, the barrier once crossed,

That double purse, America, after he has taken it in his hand and thrown it away, that two-fold breast presented in your after-noon hour to your material greed,

He joins up with the other world as before, having taken it in rear.

Here they suffer and wait. And, behind that partition, as high as the sky, above, below, begins the other slope, the world from which he comes, the Church Militant.

He is going to survey those kneeling populations, those enclosed and dense-packed regions which are looking not for a way out, but for their centre.

One in the shape of a triangle and the other of a circle,

And the other is those torn islands endlessly tormented with storm and fire.

India hangs done to a turn in scorching vapour, China for ever in that inmost laboratory where water turns to mud, tramples down that slime mingled with her own scourings.

And the third is tearing herself with rage.

Such are those peoples groaning and awaiting, facing towards the rising sun.

'Tis to them he is sent as ambassador.

He bears with him enough sin to understand their darkness.

God has shown him joy enough for him to understand their despair.

That nothingness on whose brink they have sat so long, that Void made by the absence of Being, played upon by the reflex of heaven, he had to bring them God to make them understand it quite.

It is not Rodrigo that is bringing God, but he must come so that the lack of God in which those multitudes are lying may be looked into.

Oh Mary, Queen of Heaven, round whom unrolls the whole chaplet of the skies, have pity on those waiting people! (*He goes back into the earth which shrinks and becomes no bigger than a pin's head. The whole screen is filled with sparkling sky across which looms a gigantic image of the Immaculate Conception.*)

SCENE IX

THE VICEROY, THE SECRETARY, DONA ISABEL

A room in the palace of the Viceroy at Panama. It is a vast apartment with walls slightly mouldy. Part of the ceiling has fallen down and lets the laths be seen, there is still some plaster on the floor. Disordered furniture, some of it magnificent, some garish, some crippled. Through the open door in a corner is seen a chapel, furnished with blue porcelain and carved and gilt wood in the heavy overdone taste of the period. A lamp is burning. Afternoon. It is damp and hot, rainy sky through the windows, the Pacific slate-colour. The VICEROY *in an arm-chair. The* SECRETARY *near him in front of a table heaped with papers, sedulously making notes. On a footstool* DONA ISABEL, *in rather undress costume, holding a guitar and sitting on her foot. Behind the scene a little orchestra, rather bad, is playing a kind of jig or pavan.*

THE SECRETARY, *without lifting his head.*   This orchestra is very bad, I don't understand how Your Highness can put up with it.

THE VICEROY.   If it were better, I should hear what it is playing, and that would be extremely tiresome.

THE SECRETARY.   For my part in everything I prize perfection only.

DONA ISABEL, *accompanying each syllable with a note on the guitar in an ascending key ending in a transposition.* Don Rodilard . . .

THE SECRETARY.   Madam?

DONA ISABEL.   Ah, how nice it would be of you to introduce us to that poetry of your own making which sometimes, they tell me, you read to your friends.

THE SECRETARY, *shy and resolved, continuing to write.* " 620 bales of quinquina, 200 of campeachy wood."

DONA ISABEL, *half singing*.   The syllables are so justly counted, the rhymes so exactly pondered, measured, and adjusted that a single grain of snuff would capsize the fragile wonder.

THE VICEROY.   For me a perfect poem is like a stoppered jar.

THE SECRETARY, *handing him a letter to sign*.   I know that Your Highness worships comparisons.

THE VICEROY, *signs, yawning*.   Who suggests me this other one? A bit of broken jade is worth more than a whole tile.

THE SECRETARY.   That is a Chinese sentence.

DONA ISABEL.   I suppose it's those fishermen, whom our police galley roped in the other day near Tortoise Island, who brought you that.

THE VICEROY.   No, not Chinamen, these are Japanese.
Now recall to me the song they sang together, that I liked so much.

DONA ISABEL, *singing*.   On the plain of ocean
Towards the four-and-twenty isles
I row my little boat along
Ta-ra ta, ta ta ta, ta-ra, ta-ra, ta ta ta!

> (*She hits the wood of the guitar with her knuckle. The orchestra, which had started accompanying on muted strings, goes on alone for a few moments and then suddenly stops.*)

THE VICEROY.   Ah, myself, too, on the ocean plain towards the four-and-twenty isles, when shall I get under way?

DONA ISABEL.   What, my lord, are you tired of your America?

THE SECRETARY.   It is more than one day now that His Highness and myself are a bit tired of our America, as you say.

DONA ISABEL.   Have I not heard you often say, when you were building this palace now so sadly damaged,
That she was like your own body?

THE SECRETARY.   One gets tired of one's own body.

DONA ISABEL. In all that you have undertaken have you not succeeded?

THE SECRETARY. We have succeeded only too well. That Almagro, for instance, on whom we built so much hope, a regular bleating sheep!

DONA ISABEL. This America that you have made, will she be able to do without you?

THE SECRETARY. Quite well. She does without us only too much.

DONA ISABEL. Sir, why do you keep silence thus, saying nothing and letting this groom answer in your stead?

THE VICEROY. Are not his answers as good as another's? I love to listen to Rodilard.
All day while I am doing Viceroy he keeps at his task, writing, copying, transferring from one paper to another—
My destiny no doubt.
And from time to time he favours me with some reflection and marginal note or other.

DONA ISABEL. You love me not.

THE SECRETARY, *with a small screech*. Hi, my word, you are making me make mistakes. I was going to write: "You don't care for me" on the envelope. Señor Corregidor Ruiz Zeballos at You-love-me-not. That is no country for a Corregidor.
I don't know if Your Highness has noticed how far this lady here present is in love with us. A taking of the heart. A tender feeling.
Is it Don Rodrigo she is in love with? Or is it the Viceroy? No knowing.
It is easy to interest those ladies who are getting on, beginning to age.
Getting on—but still pretty.

DONA ISABEL, *singing very low*. Forgotten . . . (*Carried on by a shrill flute on a single note decrescendo ppp.*)

THE VICEROY, *with lowered eyelids, almost inaudible*. No, no, my dear love, I have not forgotten you.

DONA ISABEL. Ah, I knew well that I should get the word that thrills your heart.

THE SECRETARY. You will not get his heart except through the gate of remembrance.

DONA ISABEL. To make myself heard it's enough to put on another woman's voice.

THE VICEROY. Finish it. I want to hear the rest.

DONA ISABEL. I have forgotten it. (*Some notes on the guitar. She sings.*) I have forgotten. (*Speaking.*) I don't know any more, I have forgotten, I have forgotten myself. (*Singing.*) Since you are no longer with me I have forgotten myself!

(*Music in the wall pianissimo and entirely cacophonous. It ceases, one instrument after the other.*)

THE VICEROY. I like the way our Isabel sings, they are not notes but lines; so in the forest sings that bird they call the *rialejo!*
I like, too, that small row in the wall that goes on after she has finished.
So when you throw a stone into a thicket you hear the other stones shifting and every sort of winged thing flying off.
Sometimes even some animal far away making off in bounds.

DONA ISABEL. When I am in company I do not sing the same way.
Why compel me, my lord, to stumble in these darkling ways?
When I am alone I like rather to go over one of those songs of that old Spain of ours.
One of those airs you hear at evening, round the fountain, under the big chestnut trees.
"Oh, far brighter than the moonbeam." "Ever since that sad moment."
That Spain that neither you nor I will ever see again.

THE VICEROY. That is all the same to me. Who was talking of remembrance just now? I have a horror of the past! I have a horror of remembrance! The voice I thought I heard just now deep down in me, behind me,
'Tis not behind, 'tis in front, it calls me on; if 'twere behind me it would have no such bitterness and no such sweet,

Thrill my heart with that unknown voice, with that song that
never was!

I like that broken rhythm and that quavering note!

Thrill me with that song which says the opposite of the words,
the same thing and the opposite!

With that voice that tries to impart the unknown and does
not manage to say orderly what it wants; but what it does not want
is pleasant to me too!

THE SECRETARY.   I cannot express the scandal and reprobation
that Your Highness' words wake in me.

> (*The music in the wall quietly feeling for an air which takes
> shape gradually.*)

DONA ISABEL, *listening to the music.*   Forgotten,
I have forgotten myself,
But who will take care of thy soul—

> (*The singer and the music break off together.*)

THE SECRETARY.   It ought to be something like "Now that thou
hast let me out."
But it is second-rate prosody.

DONA ISABEL, *singing sola, the music silent.*
But who will take care of thy soul
Now I am there no more,
Now I am with thee no more,
But who will take care of thy soul, now I am with thee no more.
(*Speaking.*) No more. (*She sings.*) No more! No more! Now I
am with thee no more!

THE VICEROY, *with downcast eyes.*   There was but one word to
say and I was with thee evermore.

DONA ISABEL, *singing.*   Forever with thee, forever with thee.
(*Speaking.*) But that word, who knows if she has not said it?

THE SECRETARY.   His Highness probably has never heard tell
of the letter to Rodrigo.

THE VICEROY.   There is no letter to Rodrigo.

DONA ISABEL.   There is a letter to Rodrigo.
And over there behind us beyond the sea
There is a woman awaiting the answer these ten years. (*She sings, countered by the orchestra in the wall.*) In the night when I lie lonely
Even to the break of day
How the time is long in passing
How the hours are loth to go
Know you, know you, say, oh say.

THE SECRETARY.   His Highness will perhaps allow me to answer in his stead that he does know.

(*Night falls. A lighted candelabrum is carried to the table.*)

THE VICEROY.   Isabel, where is that letter?

DONA ISABEL.   There on that table, I gave it to your secretary.

THE SECRETARY.   Your Highness will excuse me. I thought to hand it to you in a moment once the signing was over.

THE VICEROY.   Give me the letter. (*He looks at the address.*)
It's my name all right, it's her handwriting all right. Prouheze ten years ago. (*He opens the letter and tries to read, his hands tremble.*) I cannot read.

SCENE X

DON CAMILLO, DONA PROUHEZE

At Mogador, a tent on the seashore. Carpets spread over one another. Impression of great light and heat outside. DON CAMILLO, *in a big Arab burnous, holding in his hand the little Mahometan chaplet.* DONA PROUHEZE, *half-lying on a divan, also in Arab vesture.*

DON CAMILLO, *with downcast eyes, in undertone.* All I should have to do is to take hold of that little bare foot.

DONA PROUHEZE. 'Tis yours like the rest; have I not the honour to be your wife?

DON CAMILLO. I have sworn not to touch you again, I have given in to your insulting indifference.
There is no lack of women for me up there in that poultry yard catered by Africa and the sea.

DONA PROUHEZE. I am flattered by the passing preference you grant me.

DON CAMILLO. Confess, if I were not here looking at you you would feel the want of something.

DONA PROUHEZE. It is true that I am inured to those mocking, mournful eyes glancing from my face to my hands, and to that burning question.
What pleasant afternoons we have passed that way together,
Without a single word.

DON CAMILLO. Why did you marry me?

DONA PROUHEZE. The troops had betrayed me, was I not in your power?
My husband was dead, how should we not have profited by the occasion of that brave little Franciscan whom we had just captured?

DON CAMILLO, *smiling at his chaplet.* 'Tis I that am in your power.

DONA PROUHEZE. Once more that smooth, false smile on your face.

That smile which my lady your mother loved and hated and which makes even me, yes me, a little sick.

DON CAMILLO. But 'tis true that I am in your power.

DONA PROUHEZE. 'Tis half true. Naturally, if I had not been sure of a certain power over you, why should I have married you!

The King has not relieved me of this charge he has laid upon me, Don Camillo, on the African coast.

'Tis my presence here that hinders you from doing all the evil that you would.

DON CAMILLO. Is it so? Do I often chance to ask your precious counsel, Madam?

DONA PROUHEZE. Should I have granted it? There is no need of words between us, you guess everything.

There is not one of your actions from which I am absent, not one that is not done on purpose

Either to please me, in your mischievous way, or to do me hurt; and then how sure I am of seeing you trot up at once and oh! that hungry look!

Say if you ever found me at fault; I read you through and through and you get nothing out of me.

DON CAMILLO. There is at least one thing that I can do, and that is to have you whipped.

DONA PROUHEZE. My body is in your power, but your soul is in mine.

DON CAMILLO. When you twist my soul have I not the right to torment your body a little?

DONA PROUHEZE. The main thing is that you do what I want, and that these ten years. Yes, putting aside from time to time those absurd outbreaks of your savage humour,

Generally speaking, I have no reproach to make you and I believe the King is satisfied.

DON CAMILLO. What luck! So to do him service it is enough that I give up obeying.

DONA PROUHEZE. It was not so easy to give up obeying me. One who is always before you is not so easily forgotten.

DON CAMILLO, *gently*. But who knows if, very soon, this act of a coarse bodily presence will still be feasible for you?

DONA PROUHEZE. If that is death you are announcing in those elegant terms there is no need of circumlocution. I am ready.
Thanks to you the idea has never been so far from my mind that a bird's cry, the noise of a piece of plate falling, a white word written with the finger on the ground, a grain of incense burning out,
Have not been sufficient warning.

DON CAMILLO. Take it from my mouth.

DONA PROUHEZE. I have already received it—last night, from another.

DON CAMILLO. Your constant visitor, doubtless, and the father of my child.

DONA PROUHEZE. Who would come to visit me, lonely, in the depths of my prison?

DON CAMILLO. Rodrigo, last night, every night, whom neither the walls nor the sea can contrive to hinder.

DONA PROUHEZE. You alone, Ochiali, you know it, have inflicted me your coarse bodily presence.

DON CAMILLO. But I know that he and none other is the father of that girl whom I gave you and who resembles none but him.

DONA PROUHEZE. Is it true that on thy head, darling child, comes down our triple legacy?

DON CAMILLO. Mine too? You do not doubt, Prouheze, that I go with you where you are going.

DONA PROUHEZE. What do you think yourself?

DON CAMILLO.   I think that the letter to Rodrigo is not going to stray forever without one day getting to its destination.

DONA PROUHEZE.   That appeal which, in a moment of despair, I threw into the sea, with my eyes shut?

DON CAMILLO.   For ten years it has been running from Flanders to China, and from Poland to Ethiopia.
Many a time even, I know, it has passed back to Mogador.
But, in the end, I have reason to believe that Rodrigo has at last received it and is getting ready to respond.

DONA PROUHEZE.   All over with Señor Cachadiablo and his little kingdom in Africa!

DON CAMILLO.   All over with Prouheze and her little captaincy in hell!

DONA PROUHEZE.   All over with the subtle sitting on the fence, with that dainty balance
Between the King and the Sultan, between Christendom and Africa,
And in Africa itself all those princes, caids, marabouts, rogis, bastards and renegades,
You in the middle, holding the bank and selling the gunpowder, chancy and common resort of all parties, feared and managed by all,
And suddenly, at the chosen point, coming in like thunder.
Those great plans that you unfolded to me. . . .

DON CAMILLO.   Even before you granted me the honour of this interview, they were beginning to lose their interest.
And as I received no news from that line of cocoa palms, of white sand and foam which make an invisible frontier to Spain overseas,
By now, that sensitiveness to balance, which always was my little speciality,
That sort of Cardan compensation as of the ship's compass, that is, a head well screwed on,
The eye that sees from top to bottom and the ears that listen left and right,
No longer minister to that second thought in me to pull the

imperceptible trigger of action, that position between opposing forces in which rapidity has to make up for weight.

Desire in me is slowly yielding place to curiosity,

And that curiosity itself is heavily compromised. People are on their guard against me. They have ceased to understand me.

There is even a crowd of idiots that has begun to plot clumsily against me,

Both in here and outside the gates. I get news of it from time to time.

But nothing can break the charm of this half-hour's wait. All those Turks with scimitar uplifted and me at your feet telling my beads under the palm trees,

That makes up a kind of *tableau vivant*, spellbound by the magician's wand for the pleasure of the onlookers.

DONA PROUHEZE. So all these things about us which seem present are really past, if truth were told?

DON CAMILLO. Dost not feel how far thee and me have already mysteriously detached ourselves?

DONA PROUHEZE. I don't much care for *thee* and *me*.

DON CAMILLO. A wrinkle has reached us from the sea which presently will cure me of thee, my rose, forever.

DONA PROUHEZE. If you lifted your eyes on me I should read other words there.

DON CAMILLO. Why lift my eyes when I know beforehand what I should read in yours?

DONA PROUHEZE. It is worth while to look at the one portion of the universe which still has some interest for you.

DON CAMILLO. This little bare foot is enough for me.

DONA PROUHEZE. Farewell, señor, I withdraw my foot, some-one has come for me and I am free.

DON CAMILLO. I am free too.

DONA PROUHEZE. I am glad to be free, but I don't like the idea of your being equally so. While I was alive I always felt that you had no right to be free.

DON CAMILLO. Death is come to your relief.

DONA PROUHEZE. I don't know, I am uneasy at leaving you. And who knows if my body has not shared with you such a secret as my soul itself knows not?

DON CAMILLO. It is true, you have not been able to prevent us making a kind of truce
And from going on in spite of you in sulky correspondence.

DONA PROUHEZE. Soon I shall have no body.

DON CAMILLO. But your religion says that you keep with you all that is needed to set it up again.

DONA PROUHEZE. There your power stops.

DON CAMILLO. Are you so sure? Is it all in vain that for these ten years I make you live in the habit of mind which my opposition imposed on you?

DONA PROUHEZE. Have you the impertinence to think that there was anything in me made specially for you?

DON CAMILLO. If not where is to be the power that keeps me at your feet
And for ten years has forced me to listen to that heart within you beating?

DONA PROUHEZE. Another is the occupant.

DON CAMILLO. He occupies your thought but not that heart, busy every second with making you.
The heart that makes you Rodrigo did not make.

DONA PROUHEZE. It was made for him.

DON CAMILLO. I hear all right, but that is not what I am told by that thing beating in you, much older, that beating since the creation of the world which you have inherited from another,
It utters no mortal name.

DONA PROUHEZE. I know that there starts in me a Name.
Of which Rodrigo on the other side of sea is the finish.

DON CAMILLO.   I say rather that he helps you to stifle that spirit in you.   Sighing.

DONA PROUHEZE.   Is it not through Rodrigo that I am here with you, is it not he that taught me to sacrifice the whole world?

DON CAMILLO.   He is enough to take its place.

DONA PROUHEZE.   Himself have I not renounced in this world?

DON CAMILLO.   So as the better to possess him in the other.

DONA PROUHEZE.   Shall I be left without reward?

DON CAMILLO.   Ah, I was expecting that word! Christians have no other in their mouth.

DONA PROUHEZE.   All the better if it serves me to batter that of a renegade.

DON CAMILLO, *confidentially*.   Tell me, you who stayed at home, I have always been curious to know the effect here of my brilliant sortie.
And if I really succeeded in hurting the old landlord.

DONA PROUHEZE.   He Who is the cause of all joy cannot be hurt anyhow.

DON CAMILLO.   Ta, ta, ta, you talk like a little starling repeating the air one whistles to him!
I believe otherwise, try to follow my reasoning. To the rescue, my schoolday memories! The Agent—yes, that is the word I was looking for. (*pedantically*.)
All that is against the will of the Agent inflicts upon that Agent a suffering in accord with His nature.
If I knock against the wall I hurt myself, and if I knock with great force I hurt myself greatly.

DONA PROUHEZE.   It is true.

DON CAMILLO, *knocking his two fists against each other*.   And if I knock with infinite force I do myself infinite harm.
So when I am done with, if I hold good, I hold up omnipotence; the Infinite suffers limit and resistance in me; I force that upon Him

against His nature, I can be the cause to Him of infinite harm and suffering! Such a passion as has rent the Son from the Father! According to what you Christians tell us.

DONA PROUHEZE.   We say grace freely given and not extorted; goodness and not just suffering.

DON CAMILLO.   Say what you will, what will He do if I don't want any of that goodness?

DONA PROUHEZE.   God does not trouble about the apostate, he is lost, he is as though he were not.

DON CAMILLO.   And I say that the Creator cannot let go His creature; if it suffers He suffers as well, and He it is that causes in it what suffers.

It is in my power to hinder that shape that He wanted to mould me to, in which I know that I cannot have a substitute. If you think that every creature is forever irreplaceable by another,

You will understand that it is in us to deprive the sympathetic Artist of an irreplaceable work, part and parcel of Himself. Ah, I know He will have always this thorn in His flesh, I have found the way to the very depth of His Being. I am the jolly lost sheep whom the hundred others will never suffice to make up for,

I suffer from Him in the finite, but He suffers from me in the infinite and to everlasting. This thought consoles me here in Africa where I am condemned.

DONA PROUHEZE.   What frightful wickedness!

DON CAMILLO.   Wickedness or no, I have to do with someone difficult and not so simple as you think, I have no advantage to give away.

I hold a strong position, I keep back something essential. There is need of me, I am here.

I am in a position to deprive Him of something essential.

(*Sneering.*) Many ignorant admirers, who can only say Amen to everything, are not worth one enlightened critic.

DONA PROUHEZE.   If God has need of you don't you think that you also on your side have need of Him?

DON CAMILLO.   I have now for some time nursed this prudent and wholesome thought. The dangerous Old Man that the priests tell us about, why not put ourselves right with Him?

It doesn't cost much, He is so easy to get on with and He takes up so little room!

A touch of the hat and lo! He is satisfied. A few external attentions, some cajolery, that never finds old men insensible. At bottom we know that He is blind and slightly doting.

It is easier to get Him on our side and use Him to maintain our little contrivances for comfort,

Country, family, property, riches for the rich, scabs for the scabby, little for the little folk, and nothing at all for the men of nothing. To us the profits, to Him the honour in which we share.

DONA PROUHEZE.   I shudder to hear you blaspheme so.

DON CAMILLO.   I was forgetting. A nice lover for the amorous women in this world or in the other,

The happy eternity which our parish priests talk of

Only being there to give virtuous women in the next world the pleasures which the other sort take to themselves in this; now is it I blaspheming?

DONA PROUHEZE.   All those homely things that you jeer at are none the less capable of burning away in the heart of man and turning into prayer.

With what do you want me to pray?

All that is wanting to us serves to make us ask.

The saint prays with his hope and the sinner with his sin.

DON CAMILLO.   I have absolutely nothing to ask. I believe, with Africa and Mahomet, that God exists.

The prophet Mahomet came to tell us that it is enough for all eternity that God exists. I desire that He remain God. I do not wish Him to take any disguise.

Why has He such a bad opinion of us? Why does He think that He can only win us over by presents? And why does He need to change His face to make Himself known to us?

It hurts me to see Him demean Himself so and make advances.

You remember that story of the Cabinet Minister who took it into his head to go to the wedding of his office-boy and did nothing but cause a general upset?

Let Him remain God and let Him leave us to our nothingness,

for if we cease to be entirely nothing, what will take our place to bear entire witness that God exists?

Him in His place and us in ours for evermore, Amen.

DONA PROUHEZE.   Love will have it that there be not two places but only one.

DON CAMILLO.   The thing by which He is what He is, as He cannot give us it, then let Him leave us where we are. I have no need of the rest.

I cannot become God and He cannot become a man. I have no pleasure in seeing Him under our corporeal appearance.

Our body is what it is. Who would not be vexed to see our honest working clothes turned into a disguise on the back of another?

DONA PROUHEZE.   What was nailed to the Cross was not a disguise.

The union that He contracted with the woman was true, that nothingness He went to find even in a woman's lap.

DON CAMILLO.   So 'twas nothingness that God desired in the woman's lap?

DONA PROUHEZE.   What else did He lack?

DON CAMILLO.   And this same nothingness ever since, you say that it is not ours and does not belong to us?

DONA PROUHEZE.   It belongs to us only that we may enhance by our admission of it the being of Him Who is.

DON CAMILLO.   Is prayer, then, nothing else than a confession of our nothingness?

DONA PROUHEZE.   Not only a confession, but a state of nothingness.

DON CAMILLO.   When I said just now I am nothing, was I then saying a prayer?

DONA PROUHEZE.   You were doing the contrary, since the only thing that God lacks you wish to keep to yourself, preferring it to that which is; resting content with your essential difference.

DON CAMILLO.   So, little by little, like a clever angler, I have brought you where I wanted you.

DONA PROUHEZE, *troubled, as if she remembered*.   Why do you speak of angler, why do you speak of fishing;
A fisher . . . a fisher . . . of men; it seems to me that I have seen one already.

DON CAMILLO.   Prouheze, when you pray do you belong entirely to God, and when you offer Him that heart all full of Rodrigo what room is left for Him?

DONA PROUHEZE, *sombrely*.   It is enough to do no evil; does God demand that for His sake we give up all our affections?

DON CAMILLO.   A feeble answer, there are affections that God permits and are a part of His will.
But Rodrigo in your heart is nohow the effect of His will, but of yours. That passion of yours.

DONA PROUHEZE.   Passion is bound up with the Cross.

DON CAMILLO.   What cross?

DONA PROUHEZE.   Rodrigo is forever the cross to which I am fastened.

DON CAMILLO.   Why then didn't you let him finish the work?

DONA PROUHEZE.   Is he not coming back from the world's end to finish it?

DON CAMILLO.   But you only accept death at his hand so as to bring your soul nearer to him.

DONA PROUHEZE.   All that in me is able to suffer the cross have I not given it up to him?

DON CAMILLO.   But the cross will not be satisfied save when it has destroyed in you everything that is not the will of God.

DONA PROUHEZE.   Oh, dreadful word!
No, I will not give up Rodrigo!

DON CAMILLO.   Why then I am damned, because my soul cannot

be ransomed except by yours, and it is on that condition only that I will give it you.

DONA PROUHEZE. No, I will not give up Rodrigo.

DON CAMILLO. Die, then, by that Christ stifled in you
Who calls me with a fearful cry and Whom you refuse to give me.

DONA PROUHEZE. No, I will not give up Rodrigo.

DON CAMILLO. Prouheze, I believe in you; Prouheze I am dying of thirst! Ah, cease to be a woman and let me see upon your face at last that God that you are powerless to hold in,
And let me reach at the bottom of your heart that water of which God has made you the vessel!

DONA PROUHEZE. No, I will not give up Rodrigo.

DON CAMILLO. But how else should come that light upon your face?

SCENE XI

THE VICEROY, DON RAMIRO, DONA ISABEL, DON RODILARD

The Spanish Fleet off Darien, in the gulf of Mexico, making ready to fit out for Europe. The poop of the flag-ship.

THE VICEROY.   Señor lieutenant, I am truly sorry to deprive you of the fleet at this critical moment.

I know in fact that the buccaneers are preparing an expedition against Cartagena.

And if you ask me how you are to put up any resistance to those gentlemen without ships, without munitions, with which I have had to provide myself at your expense,

Without your best troops, which I have taken the liberty of borrowing; without money,

I answer that you will have to do what you can.

DON RAMIRO.   I will try all I can.

DON RODILARD.   And besides, once His Highness has gone it would be immoral and shocking if all were to go right.

THE VICEROY, *vague and off-hand*.   The King is calling me.

DON RODILARD.   One of those silent appeals in the secrecy of your inmost shrine which it is the duty of a subject not only to guess, but even to forestall.

THE VICEROY.   I have a great mass of silver and gold to carry to Spain and I will leave to no one else the care of its convoy.

I must show myself at Madrid,

And I will take advantage of my crossing to settle up with those African looters who attack my convoys every year. Between the two Spains the thread must be secure.

DON RODILARD.   Just as the municipal orator said the other day,

199

That thread which over the Andes and that monstrous limb
between the two Americas by which the world is bolted

Has just drawn your ship like the very car of Jupiter

From the Pacific expanse even to the domain of these impatient
and ever-chafing waters.

THE VICEROY, *stamping his foot on the bridge.* 'Tis done, Master
Wit, I have succeeded! That great machine that my mind imagined
over the mountains has worked! That thing which all reasonable
minds refused with fury, is alive; is working. All that great assem-
blage of ropes, pulleys, and counter-weights is grinding from shore
to shore in its triumphal absurdity; the Greeks and the Romans
never saw the like! Why do they talk in class about Hannibal and
his elephants? Myself at the head of twelve vessels have crossed
the mountains, and flights of parrots have settled in my rigging,
I have opened up under my keel a wake of mountains and forests!

And a hundred thousand men, lying below-ground on both
sides of that road which I set up, bear witness that, thanks to me,
they have not lived in vain.

I have not worked as engineer, but as statesman.

I created the central passage, the common organ which makes
these two sundered Americas a single body. I hold the middle
position across the continents, astride upon the great watershed,

This bar which allows no enemy of mine to join hands with
another, the shortest crossing between all points. This key which
every moment justifies the whole against all its parts.

It is the key which I am going to place in the hands of the King
of Spain.

It was time that we brought him news from the other ocean
which I found beyond that bar of gold, silver, and spices; time that
I turned my horse's head, and set him to jump like a riding-school
hurdle this limit where time stands still,

I see once more his foaming chest below me plunging in the
waters of that sequestered sea.

(DON RODILARD *is holding his hand stretched out in front of
him as if he were reading in it.*)

THE VICEROY.   What are you reading in your hand, master
secretary?

DON RODILARD.   The history of Charlemagne.

THE VICEROY.   And what is there interesting in the life of Charlemagne?

DON RODILARD.   Charlemagne, every spring when his huntsmen had got everything ready, was accustomed to mount his horse and go a-hunting.
They were baptising the Saxons in heaps, they were bringing to Marseilles, threaded in long strings, the worshippers of Mahomet to furnish the galleys of His Majesty. Speeches, flourish of trumpets, fireworks, triumphal arches, insertions in the papers. In autumn the emperor went back to Arcueil-Cachan
Roland remained behind:
You see him in the children's books blowing his little trumpet with all his might.
Hence the well-known expression: To do the Charlemagne.

THE VICEROY.   If I do the Charlemagne the faithful Ramiro will do the Roland, and woe to the Saracens that come to pull his beard!
Take America, my Roland, knight without fear and without smile, and try to keep it right.
For when you are in difficulties—I have left you a little book entirely copied out in Rodilard's hand, all you will have to do is to resort to it. There is an alphabetical index at the end.

DON RAMIRO.   I beg Your Highness not to go away.
In the name of all those who, from one pole to the other of this new world, believe in you and have taken you for chief, I seriously and solemnly beg Your Highness not to go away.

THE VICEROY.   And why should I not go away, master of the meanwhile?

DON RAMIRO.   You have pledged your faith to America even unto death.

THE VICEROY.   Great God! If that were true it should be enough to make me want to betray her.

DON RAMIRO.   Do not destroy in the minds of them that love you that image they have made of you.

THE VICEROY.   It doesn't interest me.

DON RAMIRO.   Do not leave for a woman's sake the post entrusted to you.

THE VICEROY.　A woman, what woman? It isn't a woman that makes me go.

DON RAMIRO.　Do you mean to say, my lord, that it is not for a certain woman's sake that you are going?

THE VICEROY, *off-hand and jeering.*　Not at all, master questioner, duty alone (*almost yawning*), duty alone, duty alone calls me.

DON RAMIRO, *bowing profoundly.*　It remains for me but to take leave of Your Highness. I wish Your Highness a good passage.

THE VICEROY.　Farewell, sir.

(Exit DON RAMIRO.*)*

DON RODILARD, *bowing in his turn and handing a small volume.*　I take the liberty to hand to Your Highness my complete works; it is a token of the esteem that I have for Your Highness.

THE VICEROY.　Good-bye, dear Rodilard, you alone have understood me.

(Exit DON RODILARD.*)*

DONA ISABEL.　Only Rodilard has understood you, my lord?

THE VICEROY.　Only Rodilard has understood me.

DONA ISABEL.　Why did you lie so to Don Ramiro?

THE VICEROY.　It amuses me to lie sometimes and to go about my business under cover of that sham Rodrigo that I have set up on a pole.

DONA ISABEL.　He loves you.

THE VICEROY.　I detest intimacy.

DONA ISABEL.　And will you not say a nice word to me before setting off?

THE VICEROY.　Farewell, I will think of you sometimes.

DONA ISABEL.　I loathe you.

THE VICEROY.　All the better. My character is so constituted that the scorn and the hatred of people are easier to bear than their admiration.

And forthwith—

SCENE XII

Two months later. The Spanish Fleet off Mogador. A lowering afternoon, without a breath of wind. Enter a CAPTAIN *holding a telescope which he hands to the* VICEROY.

THE VICEROY, *looking at the land.* It is all over, the Moors are running for their lives. 'Sdeath, they have had their quietus. They will not begin to attack again to-day.

THE CAPTAIN. Faith, Ochiali is a stiff chap. It would be a pity for him to finish his course anywhere else but at the end of a Christian rope.

THE VICEROY. Perhaps you would have liked us to lend him a hand against the infidel.

THE CAPTAIN. Yes, my word, the whole army would have gone with pleasure to the rescue of Devil-catcher.

THE VICEROY. 'Tis much more amusing to see him go down like this under my eyes, without firing one cannon shot,
I fancy him every morning looking at the sea and this lowering presence of our ships night and day closing up the horizon.
I had no need to take all these troops from Don Ramiro.
It was to be foreseen that, as soon as our intentions became known, the Moors would not want to leave us so rich a booty and Mogador once more to Spain.

THE CAPTAIN. But the Moors at Mogador, are they worth much more to us than Camillo?

THE VICEROY. It is a temptation that I suppress, that ancient pox that is in our blood,
I give short shrift to all those ill-smelling tricks, working us up again to some expedition à la Don Sebastian.
It doesn't enter into my calculation that Spain should again have interests in Africa. The New World is enough.

THE CAPTAIN.   But what will the King of Spain say?

THE VICEROY, *laughing drily*.   I have done nothing, sir, I have
not fired one gun.
Is it my fault if this untimely calm keeps us a fortnight before
Mogador?
Am I responsible for the interpretation which those idiotic
savages have put upon our presence?
And could I have guessed that our renegade's forces were ready
to mutiny?

THE CAPTAIN.   But will you not do anything at least for Don
Pelagio's widow whom this robber holds captive?

THE VICEROY.   Not captive, sir, so far as I can tell, but his
honoured wife.

THE CAPTAIN.   Perhaps he would release her if we made him
some promise.

THE VICEROY.   I have no promises to make, I await his
suggestions.

THE CAPTAIN, *seizing the telescope and sweeping it towards the
land*.   A signal! I see a white flag going up and down on the mast
of the citadel. They are asking to send us a parley.

                                                    (*Silence.*)
What shall I reply?

THE VICEROY.   I do not care to reply.

THE CAPTAIN.   My lord, I beg you to hear what those unhappy
Spaniards have to say.

THE VICEROY.   Very good, let them send their parley.

            (*An officer goes to carry out the order. Silence.*)

THE CAPTAIN.   I see a boat leaving the port.
There is a woman on board. It is a woman, yes, there is a
woman and a child in the boat.

THE VICEROY.   Give me the telescope. No, you can see better
than I. You are absolutely sure there is a woman?

SCENE XIII

THE VICEROY, DONA PROUHEZE AND OFFICERS

The bridge of the flag-ship, enclosed with awnings so as to form a kind of great tent. A big lantern lit before the painting of Saint James on the bulkhead of the stern-castle. THE VICEROY *seated in a great gilt arm-chair. About him and behind stand ship captains and chief officers.*

Enter an OFFICER. The envoy of the commandant of Mogador is here.

THE VICEROY. Show him in.

(*Enter* DONA PROUHEZE *holding a little girl by the hand. A silence.*)

THE VICEROY. You are the envoy of the lord Ochiali?

DONA PROUHEZE. His wife and his envoy, here are my credentials.

(*She hands him a paper which he passes unread to an officer behind him.*)

THE VICEROY. You have our attention.

DONA PROUHEZE. Must I speak like this before this gathering?

THE VICEROY. I want the whole fleet to hear.

DONA PROUHEZE. Go you away and Don Camillo keeps Mogador.
You may have seen just now how we are still capable of defending ourselves. And we have spies among the attackers.

THE VICEROY. It matters very little whether Don Camillo, as you call him, Ochiali, or whatever be his renegade name,
Keeps Mogador.

DONA PROUHEZE.   Gentlemen, I beg you to listen to what your general is going to reply. I ask you: is it by the will of the King of Spain that you are here?

THE VICEROY, *with a sardonic smile*.   A letter brought me here, an appeal, a will against which I had no counterpoise.

DONA PROUHEZE.   You heard it late.

THE VICEROY.   As soon as it reached me I left all and I am here.

DONA PROUHEZE.   So you preferred a woman's appeal to the service of your sovereign?

THE VICEROY.   Why should I not make a little war under my own flag?
Like that other Rodrigo, my patron, who was called the Cid.

DONA PROUHEZE.   So it was to make this private war on us that you have let go the Indies?

THE VICEROY.   Why should I not have brought in Morocco to this new configuration of events? Your appeal,
Completing the general aspect and momentum of the universe like an horoscopic plan,
Called on me to crown them by my departure.

DONA PROUHEZE.   There is no one calling you now: go away.

THE VICEROY.   There is no appeal now, say you? Not so says the listening heart in me.
A stiffening sea in front of Mogador holds down my keel.

DONA PROUHEZE.   Gentlemen, if the King of Spain had wished to destroy Ochiali do you think he had no means of his own?
And that, having so long put up with us, he had some reason why?
This Africa at the gates of the kingdom, this immense storehouse of locusts which since the time of Tarif and Yousouf and the Almohades has thrice engulfed us,
Do you think it could be left without watch and ward? And that it was not good to keep in reserve some interior way of knowing and intervening?

Ochiali the renegade has served the King of Spain better than Don Camillo the steward.

THE VICEROY.   I will never let it be said that the King of Spain has need of the service of a renegade.

DONA PROUHEZE.   And I, who know that against evil there is always in a lowly way something that may be done,
I say that if the royal shepherd had not put trust in that dog that I have been here for ten years,
The wolf would have eaten up many more of his sheep.

THE VICEROY.   No dog, but a faithful wife whom we admire.

DONA PROUHEZE.   His wife it is true, I consented to be his wife! Since I had no more troops and there was no other way for me to carry on at Mogador
That captaincy which the King had entrusted to me, the constraint and the ordering for ten years of that ferocious beast.

AN OFFICER.   It is true and I am bound to bear witness. Many a captive set free, many a ship by her orders aided against the pirates, many shipwrecked men sent home without ransom
Are witness to what Dona Prouheze has done here through ten years for the kingdom.

THE VICEROY.   The list of Ochiali's misdeeds would be longer still; all that came from my quarter was his favourite booty.

DONA PROUHEZE.   I could not hinder everything, still I was the stronger.
Several times he has whipped and tortured me. But he had obeyed.

THE VICEROY.   You say that he has whipped and tortured you?

DONA PROUHEZE.   The first time was when I wrote you that letter, the letter to Rodrigo.

THE VICEROY.   Ah, I ought never to have left you with him.

DONA PROUHEZE.   Why so? The blows of a beaten man do not hurt.
Besides, you also tortured him.

THE VICEROY.   Am I to think that your body alone was with this man?

DONA PROUHEZE.   Rodrigo, what I have sworn to you every night is true. Beyond the sea I was with you and nothing kept us apart.

THE VICEROY.   Bitter union!

DONA PROUHEZE.   Bitter, say you? Ah, if you had listened better and if your soul on leaving my arms had not drunk of the waters of oblivion
What things it might have told you!

THE VICEROY.   The body is powerful over the soul.

DONA PROUHEZE.   But the soul is more so over the body.
As witness this child whom my heart, filled with only you, has borne you.

THE VICEROY.   Is it to bring me this child that you are come?

DONA PROUHEZE.   Rodrigo, I give you my daughter, keep her when her mother is no more with you.

THE VICEROY.   So as I had guessed, you wish to return to Ochiali?

DONA PROUHEZE.   I have still to hear you refuse this last proposal that I am charged to make to you.

THE VICEROY.   Speak.

DONA PROUHEZE.   If you withdraw your fleet, he proposes to let me go with you.

(Silence.)

THE VICEROY.   What do you think, gentlemen?

AN OFFICER.   I do not see what should hinder us from saying yes and saving this woman who, after all, was the wife of the noble Pelagio.

ANOTHER OFFICER.   And I am of opinion that we ought to finish what we have begun and make no covenant with this sworn renegade.

DONA PROUHEZE.   Before all things he wants to get rid of me, he wants to try to live over again, 'tis I that hinder him from going on. Shall I say what he added, my lord?

THE VICEROY. Well?

DONA PROUHEZE. That he was very glad to create this small obligation from you to him.
He gives me to you, he says. He puts me in your hands.
He entrusts me to your honour. His idea is to humble us through each other.

THE VICEROY. I came here in answer to your appeal, which was to free you from this man.
And I will free you. I will have no further bond between this wretch and you.

DONA PROUHEZE. Dear Rodrigo, there is no other means of setting me free but by death.

THE VICEROY. What, who will hinder me from keeping you on board here while the Moors over there are ridding me of Camillo?

DONA PROUHEZE. Honour hinders. I have sworn to the man to come back if his conditions are not accepted.

THE VICEROY. I am no party to that promise.

DONA PROUHEZE. You will not make me fail my word. You will not give him this advantage over you and me.

THE VICEROY. Must I give you into the hands of the Moors?

DONA PROUHEZE. All is ready to blow up the citadel to-night. At midnight there will be a great flame and when that goes out an explosion.
Then go, something will be over and done.

THE VICEROY. What will be over, Prouheze?

DONA PROUHEZE. All is over for Prouheze, all that kept me from beginning!

THE VICEROY. Officers, comrades in arms, men gathered together here, drawing chance breath around me in the darkness,
And who all have heard tell of the letter to Rodrigo and of that

long desire between this woman and me, for ten years now a byword between the two worlds,

Look upon her, like them who with eyes long shut may have looked upon Cleopatra or Helen or Dido or Mary of Scotland,

And on all those women who have been sent on earth for the ruin of empires and of captains and for the loss of many towns and ships.

Love has done its work in thee, my best-beloved, and the laughter on thy face has given way to sorrow, and the gold of thy crown to the mysterious hue of snow.

But that in thee which once made me that promise, under that form which now is well-nigh waning,

Has never for a moment ceased to be itself.

That promise between thy soul and mine in which for a moment time stood still,

That promise you made me, that undertaking you gave, that duty towards me which you took upon you,

Is such that death in no wise

Can free you from it in my sight,

And such that, if you keep it not, my soul, from the depths of hell for all eternity, will accuse you before the throne of God.

Die since you will, I give you leave! Go in peace, withdraw forever from me the feet of thine adored presence!

Consummate the severance!

Since the day is come when you fade from this life and since no one but me by the design of Providence

Keeps you evermore from being a danger to morality and society,

And heap upon this promise which you have made me that very death which makes it irrevocable.

A promise, I have said, the old eternal promise!

All the same, whence could have come to Cæsar and Mark Antony and those great men whose names I have just now given you to recall

Whose shoulder I feel on a level with my own,

Whence could have come to them the sudden power of those eyes, that smile, those lips, as if never before they had kissed a woman's face,

If into their life, all busy steering the onrush of time, had not burst the unlooked-for intervention of beatitude?

There flashed on them a lightning that struck their world dead for evermore, cut it away from them,

A promise that nothing in the world can satisfy, not even that woman who for a moment makes herself its vessel to us,

And whom possession merely turns to a void and mocking image.

Let me make it clear, let me untrammel myself of these tangled threads of thought! Let me unroll, before the eyes of all, that web which for many a night,

I have woven, flung from one wall to the other of that bitter verandah like a shuttle in the hands of the dark weavers.

Is not a being's joy in its perfection? And if our perfection is to be ourselves, just that very person whom fate has given us to fulfil,

Whence this profound exultation like that of the prisoner who hears in his wall the sap at work to set him free, when the dart of death is buried quivering in our side?

So to me was the sight of this angel like the dart of death! Ah, it takes time to die, and the longest life is not too much to learn to answer that long-suffering call!

A wound in my side, like the flame that little by little sucks all the oil from the lamp!

And if the perfection of the eye is not in its own geometry but in the light it sees and in every object it discerns,

And the perfection of the hand not in its fingers but in the work which it engenders,

Why nevertheless should the perfection of our being and the kernel of our substance be evermore bound up with opacity and resistance,

And not with worship and desire and the preference of something other than self and with giving one's dross for gold and one's time for eternity and with giving oneself up to translucency and splitting at last and opening up into a state of ecstatic dissolution?

Of this self-undoing, of this mystic deliverance we know that of ourselves we are incapable, hence this power over us of woman like to that of Grace.

And now is it true that thou art leaving me so without any bond?

The paradise that woman has shut, is it true that thou couldst not reopen?

Those keys of my soul which I gave up to thee alone, is it true that thou carriest away with thee only to shut forever the outlets

Of that hell in me which thou hast made, unveiling Paradise?

DONA PROUHEZE.   But Rodrigo, 'tis for that I came, if it is true that I have given any undertaking to thee,
'Tis for that I came, dear Rodrigo, to ask you to give it back.

THE VICEROY.   Such, then, was that unflagging appeal, night and day, which for ten years sought me across land and sea and never let me rest!

DONA PROUHEZE.   Dear Rodrigo, that promise which my body made you I am powerless to fulfil.

THE VICEROY.   What, would you have me believe that promise lied?

DONA PROUHEZE.   What do you think yourself?

THE VICEROY.   You may lie but I know deep down that your body did not lie nor the joy it promised me.

DONA PROUHEZE.   Behold it breaking up.

THE VICEROY.   It breaks, but the promise which you made me does not break.

DONA PROUHEZE.   And so can I give thee joy?

THE VICEROY.   I know that thou canst if thou wilt—and eternity, were it but a moment.

DONA PROUHEZE.   But how can I will it, dear Rodrigo, how will it when I have given my will over to another? How move a single finger when I am taken and held? How speak when love is mistress of my soul and my tongue?

THE VICEROY.   Is it love that, having forbidden you to me in this world,
Refuses me any promise for the next?

DONA PROUHEZE.   'Tis love that refuses ever to leave this eternal freedom in which I am bound.

THE VICEROY.   But what good is this greedy, barren love which holds naught for me?

DONA PROUHEZE.   Ask me not what good it is, I know not, blissful creature, sufficient for me that I am good to it.

THE VICEROY. Prouheze standing there, hear this despairing cry that for ten years I have unceasingly sent up to thee!

DONA PROUHEZE. I hear it, but how answer else than by that soundless growing of the everlasting light in the heart of this woman brought low?

How speak when I am captive? How promise as if there were still in me something left of my own?

The will of Him who possesses me is my will alone and the will of Him in whom I am annihilated, in that Will it is for you to find me again!

Blame only yourself, Rodrigo, what no woman could have provided, why ask it of me?

Why have fixed upon my soul those two devouring eyes? What was asked of me I tried to have, to give thee!

And why resent it now that I can no longer promise but only give and that the vision and the gift now make in me but this single flash?

You would very soon have done with me if I were not now made one with what has no limits!

You would very soon cease to love me if I ceased to be a free gift! He who has faith has no need of promise.

Why not believe this word of joy and ask nothing else but this word of joy here and now ; which 'tis my very being to make known to you, and no promise, but myself!

Myself, Rodrigo!

Myself, myself, Rodrigo, I am thy joy! Myself, myself, Rodrigo, I am thy joy!!

THE VICEROY. No word of joy but of deceit.

DONA PROUHEZE. Why pretend not to believe me when you believe me despairingly, poor unhappy man!

Where there is most joy there is the most truth.

THE VICEROY. What good is that joy to me if you cannot give it?

DONA PROUHEZE. Open and it will enter in, how give you joy if you do not open the only gate by which I can come in?

Joy is not possessed, 'tis joy possesses you. One does not lay down conditions.

When thou hast set up order and light in thee, when thou hast made thyself fit to be embraced 'tis then she will embrace thee.

THE VICEROY. When will that be, Prouheze?

DONA PROUHEZE. When thou hast made room for her, when thou hast withdrawn thyself to make room for her thyself, for that joy most dear!

When thou askest her for her own sake and not for the increase in thee of what is set against her.

THE VICEROY. Oh, companion of my banishment I shall then never hear from thy lips aught but that *no*, and *no* again?

DONA PROUHEZE. Why, noble Rodrigo, wouldst thou then have wished me to put into thine arms an adulteress?

Even later on, when Don Pelagio died and I flung that appeal to thee,

Yes, perhaps 'twas better that it never reached thee.

I should have been but a woman soon dying on thy breast and not this eternal star thou thirstest for.

THE VICEROY. What good is that star that is never reached?

DONA PROUHEZE. Oh, Rodrigo, it is true that the distance which sunders me is impossible to clear by our strength alone.

THE VICEROY. But then where is that road between us two?

DONA PROUHEZE. Oh, Rodrigo, why go looking for it when it has come looking for us? That force that calls us out of ourselves, why not

Trust to it and follow it?

Why not believe in it and yield up to it? Why strive to know, and to make all those motions which trammel it and why lay any condition on it?

Be generous in thy turn, as I have done canst not thou do likewise? Strip thyself! Cast off everything, give all to get all!

If we are going towards joy what matters that here below 'tis inverse to our bodily nearness?

If I am going away towards joy why think that that is for thy grief? Dost thou really believe that I came into this world for thy grief?

THE VICEROY. No, never for my grief, Prouheze, my joy! No, never for my grief, Prouheze my love, Prouheze my delight!

DONA PROUHEZE.   What have I willed but to give thee joy! To keep nothing back, to be entirely that sweet balm! To cease to be myself that thou mightest have all!

There where joy is most, how believe that I am far away? There where joy is most, that is where Prouheze is most!

I will to be with thee in the beginning, I will to espouse thy cause! I will to learn with God to keep nothing back, to be that thing of goodness and of giving that holds nothing back and from whom all is taken!

Take, Rodrigo, take, my heart, take, my love, take this God Who fills me!

The strength by which I love thee is none other than that by which thou art in being.

I am made one forever with that thing which gives thee life eternal!

The blood is not closer to the flesh than God lets me feel each throb of that heart in thy bosom which for every moment of blissful eternity

Unites and sunders.

THE VICEROY.   Words from the other side of death, and I hardly understand! I look upon thee and that is enough for me! Oh, Prouheze, do not go away from me, stay and live!

DONA PROUHEZE.   I must go.

THE VICEROY.   If thou goest there is no other star to guide me more, I am alone!

DONA PROUHEZE.   No, not alone.

THE VICEROY.   By dint of never seeing it in the sky I shall forget it. Who gives thee this assurance that I cannot cease to love thee?

DONA PROUHEZE.   While I am in being I know that thou art in being with me.

THE VICEROY.   Only make me that promise and I will keep mine.

DONA PROUHEZE.   I am unable to promise.

THE VICEROY.   I am still the master! If I wish I can keep thee from going.

DONA PROUHEZE. Dost thou really believe that thou canst keep me from going?

THE VICEROY. Yes, I can keep thee from going.

DONA PROUHEZE. Thou thinkest so, well say only one word and I stay. I swear it, say only one word, I stay. There is no need of violence.

One word and I stay with thee, one only word, is it so hard to say? One only word and I stay with thee.

(*Silence. The* VICEROY *bows his head and weeps.* DONA PROUHEZE *veils herself from head to foot.*)

THE CHILD, *suddenly crying out*. Mother, do not leave me.

(*A long vessel with two banks of masked oarsmen comes along- side the vessel of the stage. Two black slaves come out and take her by the arms and carry her into the funeral barge.*)

THE CHILD, *with a shriek*. Mother, do not leave me! Mother do not leave me!

THE FOURTH DAY

To windward of the Balearic Isles. The whole of this day passes at sea in sight of the Balearics. In twelve bars the orchestra defines the horizon once and for all.

ALCOCHETE

BOGOTILLOS

MALTROPILLO

MANGIACAVALLO

CHARLES FELIX

DON RODRIGO

THE JAPANESE DAIBUTSU

DON MENDEZ LEAL

DONA SEVENSWORDS

THE BUTCHER'S DAUGHTER

THE KING OF SPAIN

THE CHAMBERLAIN

ACTRESS I

ACTRESS II

THE CHANCELLOR

COURTIERS

PROFESSOR BIDENS

PROFESSOR HINNULUS

THE MAID

DIEGO RODRIGUEZ

THE LIEUTENANT

DON ALCINDAS

MINISTERS I, II, III, IV, V and VI

SOLDIERS

BROTHER LEO

THE USHER

THE NUN

SCENE I

FISHERMEN : ALCOCHETE, BOGOTILLOS, MALTROPILLO, MANGIACAVALLO

The last is black and hairy and looks especially stupid.   Behind, the boy CHARLES FELIX *holding in his hand a line.*

ALCOCHETE, *dipping his finger in the sea and sucking it thoughtfully.* 'Tis sweet.

BOGOTILLOS *takes the water in one hand, passes to the other, rubs both together hard, and inhales the bouquet.*   If that don't give you a bit of vintage flavour, may I be scuppered into the Inland Revenue.

MALTROPILLO *dips a cup in the sea, and rolling his eyes, rinses his mouth from the cup, then spits it back like a wine-taster.*   I tell you—if that's like anything, it's like the Malvoisie the father porter at the convent treated me to one evening.

ALCOCHETE.   Taste it, so, Mangiacavallo.

MANGIACAVALLO, *wavering and already bending down.*   You want to pull my leg.

BOGOTILLOS, *pushing his head into the sea.*   Taste, I tell you, conosser.

MANGIACAVALLO, *dripping and sneezing.*   Pooah! Frrt! Atishoo!

MALTROPILLO.   Is it dry or oloroso?

MANGIACAVALLO.   Blasted fools! I never tasted anything so salty! It's warehouse bilge.

ALCOCHETE.   Look out, our Charles Felix thinks he has a bite!

MANGIACAVALLO.   The idea, making a lad of ten feel the bottom of the sea like that.

ALCOCHETE.   Well, what could you feel with your hoofs thicker than shark-skin? You could hold red-hot coke in them without hurting.

BOGOTILLOS.   This is a fine thing! This line, chaps, is made of Manila hemp, finer than a nerve. It's as live as a snake. A watch, a shoe, a saucer—that there line would find them for you at the bottom in a second. But to make it work you want a little delicate body, you want a hand as dainty as a roseleaf. Look out, *cuchinillo!*

MALTROPILLO.   That's all my eye, but whose idea was it to put that hand at the end, I ask you?

MANGIACAVALLO.   What hand?

MALTROPILLO.   — knows nothing — sees nothing — looks at nothing. You don't see a hand at the end of the line, son of a sea-cook?

MANGIACAVALLO.   I did see a sort of a yellow stump.

MALTROPILLO.   A sort of a yellow stump, that's Levi the jeweller's hand, what was hung last month for coining real money.
The hangman sold it me, honest, for a pound and a half of fresh fish; I was after it a long while.
A moneylender's hand, why it goes hunting all of itself. Where there is gold and silver it goes stiff on the spot. It would feel in your pocket for your purse.
If there is anything at the bottom of the sea, the Levi hand'll get it you for sure.

ALCOCHETE.   If it's wine you want you'd better put a boozer's nose on the line 'stead of a jeweller's hand.

MALTROPILLO.   Eh, for that my own'll do. Everyone knows that round here the sea is always a rum colour.
Gone bad, as you might say.
The other day when Bogotillos brought me a tub from the fleet what he took just by this here spot,
Bet your boots it tasted all alike same as that Canary wine they have in Greece.

MANGIACAVALLO.   Tastes all alike as salt water what is salty.

BOGOTILLOS. Say, you're not here for talking. You gets paid for rowing. Row! When we want your opinion we will ask you.

Everyone knows that somewhere about here is a wine well, sort of unplugged hogshead.

MALTROPILLO. A wine well; no more surprising than the oil wells they are finding down Brazil way. There is a blaze over them.

ALCOCHETE. Is it round here Shirty found the Chilly Woman?

MANGIACAVALLO. Who is the Shirty?

MALTROPILLO. Easily seen you don't belong to these parts, son of a Sardinian sardine!

Everyone knew Shirty, the big, black ragged-arse that had a wife what leathered him.

And he always looked as though he were splitting laughing as if he wanted to get his breeches in his teeth. One day he went down to free his anchor what had got stuck, and look you! he 'appened to get his foot on the bridge of an old ancient ship what went to the bottom long ago.

And while he was kicking about in her, he all of a sudden feels as if he had his arms round the Chilly Woman.

A big woman's corpse, all bare, as hard as stone.

Ever after that he did nothing but go looking for her: it turned his head.

BOGOTILLOS. It were right on this here spot.

ALCOCHETE. And what he told me, he did; it wasn't a woman but a sort of a big jug or jar, so big he couldn't hardly get his arms round it.

All alive and boiling like a witch's belly.

BOGOTILLOS, *pointing to a ship coming*. Look out! Pretend to be doing something else, there is someone coming on! Everyone try to look as if you weren't looking.

(*Back stage, behind a light veil*, DON RODRIGO'S *ship goes by under a single jib-sail. Between the two masts stretch lines on which swing rows of large pictures, daring both in drawing and colour.*)

MALTROPILLO.   It's Don Rodrigo's ship.

ALCOCHETE.   What ho! He has hung his whole picture shop out to air! All the saints in Paradise have been over his counter! Look at the bunting he's 'oisted! A boat coming back from three days' fishing isn't more cluttered up with sails and nets a-drying.

BOGOTILLOS.   It's a right time for doing trade. The fleet arriving from America with gold and silver from Peru is here. The fleet that's going off to batter the Turks under Don John of Austria

Is here going to set off. And the convoy catering our Armada against England is there just the same as well. The king is there with all his Court.

Finance, diplomacy, law-courts, the whole bag of tricks.

All Spain is there dancing on the bonny sea. Folk are coming to see at last that you cannot live anywhere but on the water.

And the fishermen in the middle of all that, my lads! The barges for the victualling, the servants, the play-actors, the mountebanks, the priests with the Mass-ship ringing the bell, the police!

You see nothing but black dots all over the place like flies on gummy paper.

MALTROPILLO.   Oh, and at night it's a fair knock-out with all the lights,

The sky-rockets, the kitchen fires flaring and crackling, the singing out from ship to ship, dances and concerts, choirs of men and women singing like one voice, 'tisn't every day you see that.

Or a lovely great funeral convoy at sea like my lord Admiral's the other day,

The whole Spanish grand Ramadan on sea!

The sea, I mean to say, like a sort of wopping great band you can't shut up, away down below always humming the tune to itself, and beating time to itself and dancing under you!

No one dreams of getting back to land; the boats go to Majorca to get the needful.

(*The shadow of an orchestra illustrates what they are saying.*)

ALCOCHETE.   If I were the King of Spain, it would make me tired to see Don Rodrigo going about in the middle of all that with his one leg.

BOGOTILLOS.   It isn't the King of Spain that's to blame for his one leg.

ALCOCHETE.   All the same he was ten years Viceroy of the Indies; then they sent him to the Philippines in disgrace, and it was there making war on the Japanese he got took prisoner.

And now he's forced to sell sheets of holy pictures to poor fishermen to earn his living.

BOGOTILLOS.   The sea is just the place for wrecks. The King of Spain isn't bound to bother with all that end up here sailing near the wind.

ALCOCHETE.   Yes, but this one sails under his nose as haughty as a three-decker.

BOGOTILLOS.   Well, if I were him I'd jolly well show all those goldy curly courtiers what happens to a fellow I have lost interest in.

MALTROPILLO.   But it's him rather that looks as belike he'd lost interest in the King of Spain. You should see how he looks, perking himself up on his wooden stump, how he bangs it on the bridge of his boat.

Halt! 'shun! it's me!

As if he were saying same as to say there was no more to be said but naught. How he turns at bay to talk to you!

BOGOTILLOS.   I've a notion that it'll end up bad for him.

ALCOCHETE.   Meanwhile everyone buys his sheets of saints. There's never enough. You see nothing but them on the wall in the islands and right away to the Bagnios in Algiers. The Fathers of Ransom send 'em by parcels to the poor prisoners.

MALTROPILLO.   The funniest thing is that he has never tried to paint or draw, but he explains his idea, an' there at the side of him is a Japanee he brought back from Japan, and he works out everything for him on a wooden board. With ink and colour and press you pull as many sheets as you like.

BOGOTILLOS.   The other day he gave me a grand Saint James. You see him landing in Spain.

He has a kind of black whiskers, no eyes, a big nose like a

bill-hook; he is tucked up like a sailor to the waist and it's all legs and muscles.

He has his right foot planted on the prow of his ship, the knee up to his chest.

And he's throwing over Spain a sort of warp in spirals that goes on uncoiling and twisting in the sky,

Towards a kind of a pillar you see there.

The pillar of Hercules, that stake that pins Europe by the middle. The last rivet screwed tight to keep Europe from shaling.

MALTROPILLO.   I've got a different Saint James. He's as big as the whole distance between sky and land.

He's coming out of the sea. He still has a foot in it up to the ankle, and he's so big he has to stoop under the ceiling of the clouds.

He has a huge arm hanging from the right shoulder, and a hand at the end of it swaying like a grappler,

And underneath on the shore, with its shops and its steeples, you see a little town all white like a smudge of flour.

ALCOCHETE.   There is a Saint Joseph, too, on Mount Ararat, getting a lease of Noah's ark. But the one I bought is Saint Jude, the patron of desperate cases.

You see a kind of cross-roads down a mine where three or four galleries meet, miles underground.

There is a man all by himself sitting down with his head on his arms, on a table. And out of one of the galleries comes a shaft of light like a lantern coming towards him.

BOGOTILLOS.   There's lots more! You haven't done looking at them all, by you get home. You might say someone finds him the pictures, and he chucks it over to the Japanee there, always by him like a cook with his frying-pan all full of fry on the fire.

MANGIACAVALLO.   All that doesn't say what we will do with that big tun of wine under the wet once we have fished it up.

ALCOCHETE.   There will be nothing more to do but turn innkeepers and give all Spain a drink.

BOGOTILLOS.   And what would the Holy Inquisition say, not counting the Ministry of Customs and Excise? I think we ought to offer it to the King of Spain, and His Majesty will make us all gentlemen.

> (*Just here the line pulls hard and pays out in the hands of* CHARLES FELIX.)

CHARLES FELIX.   Help! Help! I've got something! I've got a bite!

SCENE II

A cabin in Don Rodrigo's ship. He is standing, aged and growing grey; he has a wooden leg. Near him at a table loaded with papers, brushes and colours, THE JAPANESE, DAIBUTSU, *is drawing. In a corner, a graving-press. In another corner,* DON MENDEZ LEAL *hanging upside down. He is a mere silhouette cut out in black cloth.*

There may be, if desired, at the back of the stage a screen on which can be projected scenes and paintings so arranged that the public can pass the time while the actors tell their little tale.

DON RODRIGO, *describing.* Right above two big pillars, broadly marbled, with very massive yolk-yellow capitals carved in the romanesque manner.

The Virgin sits leaning against the right one in dark blue garments. On her breast no colour, nothing seen but a little infant's hand, well drawn.

Beneath her feet a stairway going down right to the foot of the picture. At the top the two Magi; make me some gentleman or other of your country in state dress with a huge *kammori* on his head, his body and limbs swathed in twelve thicknesses of silk, and near him at his back, making one mass with him,

Put me in a kind of big sausage-hanger of a European, all black, stiff as the law, with a big hat, and enormous nose and wooden calves, and the Golden Fleece around his neck.

Lower down to the left the negro king, back view, with a topknot of lion's mane like an Abyssinian, and a necklace of claws.

Leaning forward on something, and the other arm stretched out full length holding an assegai.

The base is composed of a camel cut off half-way, making a humpy line. Saddle, trappings, a red plume on his head, a bell under his chin.

Behind the pillars, high up, mountains like those you see beyond

Pekin, with their towers and battlemented walls chance-flung on the hills like a necklace. You sense Mongolia behind them.

Wakarimaska?

THE JAPANESE. *Wakarimass.*

DON RODRIGO. All that takes up only the left side of a long roll of paper. To the right, underneath, there is room for a screed of little Spanish verses with their y's and their inverted question marks. It is to be pious, full of queer turns and mistakes in spelling.

I once had a secretary who loathed that kind of goody-goody poetry. It makes me want to write poetry when I think of poor Rodilard.

THE JAPANESE, *pointing to* DON MENDEZ LEAL. Isn't this good gentleman here going to weary of waiting for us in that uncomfortable posture?

DON RODRIGO. Finish your work while we are both red-hot; I feel it's going to go! I feel inspiration going from me right to the ends of your ten fingers.

THE JAPANESE. How could Your Excellency ever have done anything else but draw?

DON RODRIGO. That's what I often ask myself. All the time I wasted! And besides, how could I so long have been easy on those paws of legs when even now it's a great deal too much to hold on to the earth by one?

Yet now it's amusing to flop about like this between heaven and earth with one leg and one wing!

THE JAPANESE. The other leg, thanks to me, is perpetually honoured by a little monument on the battlefield of Sendegahara.

DON RODRIGO. I am not sorry! Oh, men of Japan, I was too fond of you! It was worth losing a leg to get into your country!

THE JAPANESE. Was it with cannon-balls that you reckoned to show your sympathy?

DON RODRIGO. One uses what one has, and I have never been free with flowers or fondling.

You were too well off in your little dry hole in the middle of the ocean, in your little tight-shut garden taking your tea in little sips out of little cups.

It worries me to see people well off; it's immoral; I itched to butt into the middle of your ceremonial.

THE JAPANESE.   Whether you liked it or not you had to spend some time with us learning repose and stability.

DON RODRIGO.   I can see myself yet on that top floor of the castle of Nagoya which was given me for prison! What a prison! It was I rather who held all Japan across the joint of her main articulation, all Japan I kept through my seventy windows!

Good God, how cold it was!

On one side the country, it was winter time, the country all crackled, the earth pink, the little woods black, and the least detail delicately drawn as with a boar's bristle on finest porcelain,

On the other side the town filled up a full half of the view from my windows towards the west. And I remember well that single dark blue blot made by a dyer's establishment on the scaly grey of the roofs.

There I made your acquaintance, friend Daibutsu! How many holy pictures we unfolded together! What long bands passed slowly through my fingers like a flood of images and lettering.

THE JAPANESE.   If you had wished, I could have taught you to draw in our manner.

DON RODRIGO.   I never could have done it. I should not have had the patience! I have a hand like a wooden glove; I could not have yielded my mind up to Nature like a perfectly blank sheet of paper, a fasting thing,

On which one by one the shadows appear and outline themselves and tinge themselves with various hues.

What can be said out and not what is meant to abide for ever in the delight and concealment of a light ineffable,

Like those waters out of which the lotus springs, like your own very islands that are just four or five rocks in the ocean.

I did not come on earth to get spellbound.

THE JAPANESE, *speaking as if he were setting down each idea in hieroglyphics on the paper*.   It is written that great truths are not imparted save by silence. If you want to tame Nature, you must not make a noise. Like a land with the water sinking in. If you don't want to listen you cannot hear.

DON RODRIGO. And do you think that I heard nothing, all those long, legless winter days when I was deciphering the archives of your priests and hermits?

When I was rattling one after another the panels of that room where you had me shut up? Prisoner not of walls and iron bars, but of the mountain and the sea and the fields and the floods and the forests,

Everlastingly around me drawn out on the shifting paper.

I was hearing! I have heard.

Two words for ever kept me company on that wonderful pilgrimage, step by step along a road of paper.

One of those words was *Why?*

Why? What is the secret within secret bound up and folded in the knot of the hieroglyphics, like bubbles mounting from a single plunge of thought?

There is something saying Why? In the wind, in the sea, in the morning, in the evening, in every tiny feature of the inhabited earth.

"Why the wind, for ever teasing me?" says the pine-tree. "To what must I needs be thus fastened?" "What is it that dies like this in ecstasy?" says the chrysanthemum.

"What is there so black that makes me be?"—the cypress. "What is called azure, making me so blue?" "What exists so lovely that I be such a rose?" "What the unseen taint that forces my petals one by one to fade?" "How strong the water is to warrant me this flicking tail and scaly sheath!" "Of what ruin," says the rock, "am I the rubble? For what far-off inscription is my side made ready?" All rises and upsprings smiling to itself within the great gap enwrapped in golden mist.

THE JAPANESE. What is the second word?

DON RODRIGO. There is nobody in all those paintings! It is all very well to dot a few ships on the sea, to dust down a big town there at the head of that darkling gulf.

No more does that fulfil the expectancy of those mountains tiptoeing over one another to see better—

It no more lessens the loneliness than the chorus of frogs and tree-crickets.

THE JAPANESE. Yes, 'tis a great lesson in silence that the painters hang up around us. Even that crowd of children at play becomes in an instant as soon as the paper catches it from the brush,
Silence and stillness, a sight for ever and ever.

DON RODRIGO. Friend Daibutsu, 'twas not to become in my turn silence and stillness that I broke a continent in half and crossed two oceans.
It is because I am a Catholic man, it is in order that all the sections of mankind may be joined together and not one think itself entitled to go on living in its heresy,
Severed from all the others, as if it had no need of them.
Your own barrier of flowers and witchery—yes, that too had to be broken like the rest, and therefore did I come, forcer of gates and trudger of roads!
You will stand no more alone! I bring you the world, the total word of God, all those brethren, whether you please to take up with them or not, all those brethren in a single parent.
And since you cut off my foot, since you shut up in a prison what body was left to me,
I had only the soul left to go through with, the mind, and, by means of those hands of yours, brother Daibutsu, which I took possession of,
Those pictures to which you egged me on, those great possibilities in myself which I drew, on bits of paper.

THE JAPANESE. Do you say that all those saints are images of yourself?

DON RODRIGO. They are much more like me than I am to myself with this withered body and this still-born soul!
They are something in me that has succeeded and won its attainment!
They are entirely alive! No more resistance and inertia in them! They answer wholly to the mind which gives them life, they are excellent brushes in the hand of a perfect artist like that which Sesshiu took when he drew that circle, a standing perfection on the wall of Kyoto.
You have nothing else to do but decorate your prison. But I with my designs build something that goes right through every prison!

I have laid down the plan of something which fits the movement of your heart as the mill-wheel fits the water dropping! The man who through his eyes receives to the soul within, the plan of that sort of tireless engine which is nothing but movement and longing,

Takes to himself a power for ever incompatible with any wall!

As was shown by your martyrs of the southern isle when I was there, who were crucified and sprayed with melting brimstone!

THE JAPANESE. Señor Rodrigo, your words are hindering me from drawing. I have understood what you wanted. I have made good your remarks. The business is yours no longer, and by your leave I will finish it alone.

DON RODRIGO. At least try not to let it misfire, as you did that Saint George. You had no understanding of it, my poor old fellow.

I must use you for want of a better. Don't put on your suffering look!

And finish your work quickly, because there is another idea coming to me. It is much more amusing to plan out a saint than to make oneself into one.

THE JAPANESE, *pointing to* DON MENDEZ LEAL. What shall we do meanwhile with this good gentleman there in that corner, all thoughtful and mumchance?

DON RODRIGO. It won't do him any harm to ponder and ripen yet awhile the message that the King has given him for me. It shakes down his ideas.

I have noticed that most people have a certain void in the head where the green mould gets in.

They must be looked after like bottles that you are careful to slope a bit all the time they are waiting at the bottom of the cellar

So that the wine constantly presses a little on the cork.

THE JAPANESE. Are you not curious to know what the King, through the channel and orifice of Don Mendez Leal, here present, has to impart to you?

DON RODRIGO. Yes, indeed, I am dying to know, and you make me think of it. Especially as the good gentleman is impatient and I see his ribs moving and wrought up with longing to exist. Up, sir! (*He puts him upright.*) Good morrow, sir, I am all attention.

THE JAPANESE.   But how do you expect him to speak when he is all flat?

DON RODRIGO.   I am going to stop up his nose, and you will see him fill up at once with that air on which he lives.

THE JAPANESE.   But prithee whence will come that air, that small substantial wind?

DON RODRIGO.   Poor Daibutsu, I see that you are not up in modern science

Which tells us that everything comes from nothing, and that it was the hole that by degrees made the cannon.

Thus did the primitive amœba,

Blowing out its own bubble by the might of the goddess called Evolution, end up as an elephant, to which is promised in its turn, rest assured, a no less flattering future.

See, our man is even now fulfilled with anxious rumblings!

Look at His Excellency giving way to his inmost idiosyncrasy and, as it were, gathering together the arcane emanations of a telluric spring, beginning to rear and kick; and wanting to escape the enlivening pinch that I am applying. One moment, sir, if you please.

I am going to tie up his nose; that will be safer. Pass me your shoelace. (*He ties up his nose with a shoelace.*)

THE JAPANESE.   Why are you tying up his nose?

DON RODRIGO.   I am tying up his nose to make him tell the truth. It is down the nose that all the lies come. That is why they say to children "the end of your nose is moving."

THE JAPANESE.   You are right, the nose is like the finger-post in the middle of the face showing the locality. With us when anyone wants to say "it's me," he points to his nose.

DON RODRIGO.   Well, I have made a knot in his ego, he cannot now get away like a gas. Look at him gradually filling and taking shape and rotundity.

The nothing brought forth the void, the void brought forth the hollow, the hollow produced the puff, the puff produced the bellows, and the bellows produced the blown.

As witness the ambassador here all stretched and blown out and made real all over like a little india-rubber pig.

Don Mendez Leal, I offer you my humble respects and I beg you to pardon the extreme lowliness of this place whither you have not shrunk from bringing with you

This faithful comrade who always goes before you,

Madam, or, shall I say, Miss Excellency.

DON MENDEZ LEAL, *speaking lightly through his nose.* Don Rodrigo, despite your goings on and your poverty and the disgust you awake in everyone, I am still interested in you, and am ready to stretch out to you the right hand of magnanimity.

DON RODRIGO.   I thank you, sir.

DON MENDEZ LEAL.   You shall thank me presently, but first be so good as to listen when I speak to you.

DON RODRIGO.   I beg your pardon.

DON MENDEZ LEAL.   Yesterday, was not His Majesty still disposed to make you the warden of one of his principal tobacco warehouses in the fairest town of Andalusia?

DON RODRIGO.   Tobacco makes me weep.

DON MENDEZ LEAL.   Weep, weep, sir, weep your insolence and your ingratitude! After your signal disobedience in Morocco, after your adventures in Japan, a prison should long since have hidden you away.

DON RODRIGO, *pointing to his leg.* Impossible to put me in prison altogether. There will be always something left outside.

DON MENDEZ LEAL.   The King, at my petition, has consented to bear in mind the services that you rendered him long ago in the Western Indies.

There are those who maintain that it was you in reality who had the first idea, who pencilled, so to speak, the rudimentary plan

Of that enterprise realised by Don Ramiro, the royal road of Panama which will always bear the name of that great man.

DON RODRIGO.   It is a very great honour to me that my name should be humbly linked with his.

DON MENDEZ LEAL.   And how, I ask you, have you thanked
His Majesty for the favours which he but sought occasion to
shower upon you?

DON RODRIGO.   I shudder to hear it.

DON MENDEZ LEAL.   What is this unheard of insolence, parading
thus under the King's eyes at the very moment that he is holding
his solemn session at sea,
This kind of rag and tatter of a man whom once he had charged
to represent
In the other world
His own Majesty in person?

DON RODRIGO.   I will answer you presently, but is not John
Hay your Christian name?

DON MENDEZ LEAL.   My name is not John Hay; my name is
Inigo, and my family is the best in the Asturias.

DON RODRIGO.   I say this because I have Saint John Hay over
there just finished. Saint John Hay, patron of provender-men and
graziers. Green on green, it's a relief to the eye, a pure delight
just to look at. Go on, I pray you.

DON MENDEZ LEAL.   I don't know now where I was.

DON RODRIGO.   You were at "unheard of insolence," and I
was asking you your Christian name.

DON MENDEZ LEAL.   Yes, and while we are at it, is it not
shameful for a gentleman to make himself a hawker of daubs
like these?

DON RODRIGO.   Daubs of saints, my lord.

DON MENDEZ LEAL.   What familiarity is this, to represent the
saints like ordinary men on some foul paper that the fisherman or
the carpenter pins up on the wall of his cabin, amid the most
repulsive sights?
Is it not lacking in respect for holy things? Let us leave those
venerable and respectable figures in their place on the altars and in
the oratories, and let them be glimpsed only through the smoke
of incense.

If they must be represented let it be by the hallowed and consecrated brush of some church-warden of art, duly commissioned,

A Velasquez, a Leonardo da Vinci, a Luke Oliver Merson.

DON RODRIGO. I must confess to you, sir, that my principal reason for taking up the career of fine art

Has been the desire not to resemble Leonardo da Vinci.

DON MENDEZ LEAL. A saint must have a face . . . *common*, if you see what I mean, since he is the patron of many folk;

He must have a decent demeanour, and gestures meaning nothing in particular.

DON RODRIGO. Trust the painters for that. It isn't imagination that chokes them! (*He spits.*)

Myself, I have a horror of those salted-shark mugs, those faces that are not human faces, but a little virtue-show!

The saints were nothing but flame, and nothing is like them unless it warms and enkindles!

Respect, ever and always respect! Respect is due only to the dead and not at all to those things we need and use!

Amor nescit reverentiam, love knows not reverence, says Saint Bernard.

DON MENDEZ LEAL. And is it Saint Bernard, for instance, that advised you to make that horseman I see there on the other side, his head under his cloak, and most indecently uncovered,

Bestriding that upright horse?

Never did a horse behave like that.

DON RODRIGO. It is Saint Paul that I want to represent. And it is on a horse like that that you go up to Heaven.

But if you are a fancier I would rather advise you to buy this fine picture of the Fourteen Helping Saints on which Daibutsu has bestowed all his pains.

And here again are Saints Cosmas and Damian, patrons of doctors and of all the learned men in whose hands we slowly recover from health.

DON MENDEZ LEAL. Everything I see is an offence against tradition and taste, and comes from the same perverse desire to surprise and vex honest people.

DON RODRIGO. That's possible; but what would you do now, for instance, if they ordered the earthly paradise?

DON MENDEZ LEAL. The earthly paradise?

DON RODRIGO. Exactly, the earthly paradise. If you had been told just like that to make the earthly paradise on a scrap of paper?

DON MENDEZ LEAL. I don't know; I suppose I should try to make a kind of jungle or hopelessly entangled thicket.

DON RODRIGO. You are out of it, you have not thought upon it.
The earthly paradise was the beginning of everything, consequently there was no thicket, but a well-groomed sample of each species, each in its square of ground with the proper instructions. The Gardens of Intelligence!
It must have been like the plantations of the School of Pharmacy at Barcelona with nice labels in porcelain. A place of delight for classic poets.

DON MENDEZ LEAL. There is no talking seriously with you.

DON RODRIGO. All I ask is to listen.

DON MENDEZ LEAL, *friendly and confidential.* Don Rodrigo, I have no use for you, but who can know the mind of the King? Who can penetrate the designs of this sovereign who keeps his Court on the ever-changing sea?
Is it to be admitted that you are coming back to favour and that I have not been the first to seek out this surprising spot on which His Grace's ray has rested?
One could not find a more unpleasant one.
When you are in power I trust that you will give me a great deal of money.
Oh! how I long for all that you can give me!
The King has spoken of you twice the same day. It is a sign that he either wants to hang you or name you chancellor,
To good understanding, good luck. (*He makes as if to go away.*)

DON RODRIGO. Before leaving you will surely take a glass of wine?

DON MENDEZ LEAL.   Excuse me. Your boat is pitching; I am a little seasick.

DON RODRIGO.   Then let me at least offer you a little picture; here is Gabriel, the patron of ambassadors; see how gilt he is and shiny!

It is in remembrance of him that those gentlemen have the right to wear a white feather in their hat.

SCENE III

DONA SEVENSWORDS, THE BUTCHER'S DAUGHTER

A little boat at sea. The BUTCHER'S DAUGHTER *at the fore.* DONA SEVENSWORDS *at the stern holds the tiller and steers. Both are quite young girls, dressed as men. Early morning.*

DONA SEVENSWORDS, *to the* BUTCHER'S DAUGHTER, *throwing water in her face.* Stop crying, at once, Butchie, or I will chuck in your face all the salt water you have spilt into the sea since we left Majorca.

THE BUTCHER'S DAUGHTER, *sniffling.* What will my father say? What will my mother say? What will my brother say? What will the registrar say? What will the Reverend Mother at the convent say, where I have been so well brought up?

DONA SEVENSWORDS. What will my young man, the splendid owner of the Progressive Butchery, say?

THE BUTCHER'S DAUGHTER. Ah, the mere thought of my young man lends me wings! And I feel that just to get away from him I would gladly go with you right to the end of the world!

DONA SEVENSWORDS. You shall go with me if I want you to, for as soon as I get tired of you I will shove you down into the sea with a good whack of an oar on the head.

THE BUTCHER'S DAUGHTER. All right, you can do what you like with me, miss; I am satisfied! Since I saw your pretty face, since you looked at me and smiled, I have felt that there was nothing for it but fly after you, wherever you go!

DONA SEVENSWORDS. We must look alive, quick, Butchie; it feels so good! There is no time to lose if we want the world to stay as lovely as it is just now! It isn't possible! Perhaps it is only going to last a second! That is the way the gnat loses no time, going straight to the lovely clear flame that has just been lit!

But we are not a gnat; we are two little comrade larks pricking and singing towards the sun!

At least I am a lark and you are only a big blow-fly. That doesn't matter, I love you all the same.

THE BUTCHER'S DAUGHTER.   Where do you want to take me?

DONA SEVENSWORDS.   Oh my Butchie, how happy I feel; how nice it is going to be with me; what fun! The other girls always have that long boring life in front of them; husband, children, soup to make every day, the everlasting plates to wash and wash, that is all they think of!

People walk in pain and they don't notice that it is so much easier to fly; you have nothing to do but give up thinking of yourself!

That beautiful sun—it was not for nothing that God put it there! We have only to go to it, let us go up! But no, no, 'tis not the sun! It is that lovely scent that pulls me! Oh, if I could breathe it all the time! The hour of death, and once again it's there! It isn't the visible sun that I want, it's that sort of wild sweetness, that lovely scent which makes my heart stop beating.

THE BUTCHER'S DAUGHTER.   Where is it, that lovely scent?

DONA SEVENSWORDS.   There, where my dear mamma is; it smells good! Many a time at night she has come looking for me, and she puts her arms round me tenderly and I am her darling girl. And I must go set her free in Africa.

THE BUTCHER'S DAUGHTER.   But didn't you tell me that she died there more than ten years ago?

DONA SEVENSWORDS.   She is dead, but she has not finished what she had to do in Africa! Is she free while there are so many Christians groaning in the Bagnios of Barbary?

I cannot go to her, but I can go as far as them.

Are we free when on every side we are bound to so many souls in trouble?

Shall I stay slack, boring myself to tears in Spain, when it only depends on me to set free the whole captive people, and mamma with them, like them? Oh, I wish I were gone now!

THE BUTCHER'S DAUGHTER. Is it you that are going to set the captives free?

DONA SEVENSWORDS. Yes, miss, and if you start any tricks I have only to twist the tiller and bring you back to the Progressive Butchery.

THE BUTCHER'S DAUGHTER. Tell me all about what we are going to do.

DONA SEVENSWORDS. As soon as we muster three hundred men (and there is nothing easier than to gather three hundred men, and lots more, for there is no good Christian in Spain would but like to be in such a noble enterprise),
We will all set off together under the standard of Saint James and of Jesus Christ, and we will take Bougia.
Bougia for a start. We must be reasonable; Algiers is too big a business.
I saw a sailor a week ago that knows Bougia. His foster-brother was prisoner at Bougia. He says there is nothing easier than to take Bougia.

THE BUTCHER'S DAUGHTER. And when we have taken Bougia?

DONA SEVENSWORDS. If you want to know what I think, I don't believe we shall take Bougia, but we shall all be killed and go to Heaven. But then all those poor captives at least will know that we have done something for them.
And all the Christians when they have seen us perish bravely will rise to set them free and drive out the Turks.
Instead of nastily fighting among themselves.
And I shall be in Heaven in my dear mummy's arms; that's what comes of being me.

THE BUTCHER'S DAUGHTER. And I will always march behind you quite close, and I will have a big bottle full of water to give you a drink every time you are thirsty!

DONA SEVENSWORDS. If my father wishes, we shall take not only Bougia, but Algiers and all the rest. You must see my father! He knows everything. There is nothing he can't do if he wants. What compared to him is Dragout or Barbarossa?

THE BUTCHER'S DAUGHTER. Is it your father that has only one leg and makes those lovely sheets of saints that all the fishermen want to have?

DONA SEVENSWORDS. My father is the Viceroy of the Indies, and 'tis he that got the ships over the Isthmus of Panama. And afterwards 'twas he that discovered China and Japan and took all by himself with twelve men the castle and town of Oshima, defended by three thousand warriors armed with bows and arrows. That is where he lost his leg; and after that, on the top floor of the castle of Nagoya, he learned the language of the bonzes and studied philosophy.

And now here he is back again with all the saints, making a great army of paper. With his brush he brings down all the saints from Heaven, and when they are all ready he will put himself at their head and me at his side and you behind me with a big bottle and we will take Bougia and Algiers for the glory of Jesus Christ!

THE BUTCHER'S DAUGHTER. John of Austria, the son of Dona Musica to whom the King of Spain has given command of his fleet and who sets off to-morrow to fight against the Turk, is a much greater general than your father.

DONA SEVENSWORDS. It isn't true, Butchie, you're a liar! I shall never let anyone say that there is a greater general than my father.

THE BUTCHER'S DAUGHTER. An old feller with his foot cut off! Who would enlist under the orders of an old chap with a cut leg when you have only to look at that lovely young man to be sure that he will lead us to victory?

DONA SEVENSWORDS. What has he done, then, your little Don John? Africa and the two worlds are full of my father's name.

THE BUTCHER'S DAUGHTER. You cannot deny it,
If you were a man and if you were not the son, I mean the daughter, of Don Rodrigo,
With what a will you'd go immediately to join the standard of Don John.

DONA SEVENSWORDS, *with a big sigh.* It's quite true, Butchie. Ah, little you know how right you are!

THE BUTCHER'S DAUGHTER. Go on, I feel you have something to tell me.

DONA SEVENSWORDS. Can you keep a secret?

THE BUTCHER'S DAUGHTER. I swear it; all that you give me I can keep!

DONA SEVENSWORDS. Don John is in love with me. He has seen in my eyes all right that I am ready to die for him. It's all over, I don't want to see him ever again. Ah, he might woo me! My heart is his.

THE BUTCHER'S DAUGHTER. But then where did you see Don John?

DONA SEVENSWORDS. This very night as I was going to your house to put the ladder to your garden-wall to help you get away.

What did I see under a street lamp at the corner of Oil Street? A beautiful young man in black, with a gold chain round his neck, bravely defending himself against three roughs.

You know I had a huge pistol that I had stolen from my father and used to play at loading up with all the powder I could find. I shut my eyes and . . . *bang!*

It made so much noise and so much smoke that you'd have said it was a cannon shot and you couldn't see anything any more,

I had my wrist all shaken to pieces with it.

When I saw clear again, the three robbers had flown and there was no one but that lovely, elegant young man in black, thanking me.

Ah, I was frightfully ashamed and I didn't know where to stuff myself; what must he have thought of me!

THE BUTCHER'S DAUGHTER. What did he say, what did he say?

DONA SEVENSWORDS. He told me to come with him on his ship and that I should be his page and his orderly and that he was setting off the day after to-morrow to fight the Turk and that his name was John of Austria and that he would die before thirty.

THE BUTCHER'S DAUGHTER. Perhaps he meant to make game of you.

DONA SEVENSWORDS. He is making game of me and I am

making game of him. His name is John of Austria and my name is Mary of the Seven Swords the daughter of the Viceroy of the Indies. You'd think it was him the Gospel speaks of at the end of Mass where it says: "There was a man whose name was John." I belong to my father and not to that nasty boy that looks so sure of himself and me.

He told me I had to come at once and that he had been told that he would die before thirty. Am I afraid of death?

Because I am a girl does he think that I am not able to serve him and to die for him?

Oh, I would be a brother to him and we should sleep together —side by side, and I should always be there beside him to defend him, oh, I should recognise his enemies at once! And if he dies I too am ready to die with him!

THE KING OF SPAIN, THE CHAMBERLAIN, THE CHANCELLOR,
THE ACTRESS

*A hall in the floating palace of the King of Spain. It is a great
gilded apartment upheld by twisted columns and lit by a broad stained
window in small sections, half open. A deep golden light comes from
below, by reflection from the sea. The* KING OF SPAIN *is a man of pale
complexion with deep-set eyes under bushy eyebrows, large bony features
never lit by a smile, thick-set, and his head sunken in his shoulders.
He looks like the King of Spades, whereas his predecessor of the first
two days resembled rather the King of Hearts.*

*His eyes are fixed intently on a death's head made from a single
piece of rock crystal, which is set upon a cushion of black velvet, in the
middle of the table, lit by a ray of the setting sun.*

THE KING. What power hinders me from flinging straight
through the window this accursed pebble, this knowledge box
which Rodrigo went and dug up for me from the bottom of a
Mexican tomb, this translucid skull that he presented to me in jest?

A spiritual sponge, between my thought and those things which
the curve of the earth hinders me from seeing, it is an unholy
go-between.

One second . . . and there's nothing. One second . . . and
all is blotted and the frightful pattern, not known if it be this
crystal or my thought colouring it, is blotted out.

A moment ago in ten leagues of tempest, in a churn of raging
waves, lighted by a raving sun, did I not see the *Rosario* go down
on fire, poop in air and the royal standard disappearing in the
foam?

Now 'tis a deathly night with slabs of snow floating and little
ghastly lights flitting on every side. I see before me a shore
covered with wreckage, little crews being put to the sword.

And of that obstinate corpse which in the waters of this prophetic
nothingness keeps floating up and drowning again, I need see only

its shoulder and its neck, encircled with a golden thread and a
screed of lace,

To recognise the admiral himself, the handsome Duke Medina
Sidonia. Philip, is it thee?

Who keeps me from throwing this pebble through the window,
this skull carven out of mind? What but the eagerness of a heart
that no disaster can glut and that opens its gates

Only to the challenge of catastrophe?

Is it unexpected, all that happened to me? Have I ever cherished
any illusion?

Was I ever fool enough to believe that I was going to conquer
England with twenty thousand men and that Armada encumbered
with convoy and service ships?

All those complications, revolts, at a hundred different points,
to be backed to the very day; Scotland, Ireland, all those ambitions,
rivalries and jarring interests to be got into step, Parma's troops
in Flanders to be embarked under the cannon of the Low Countries.

Were they not so many gates opened to ill-fortune? He who
trusts to chance, what has he the right to expect?

By what name call the king who builds on the changing sea and
entrusts to the winds his treasure and his soldiers?

And still I had no choice. I absolutely had to do something.
Hope is not indispensable to enterprise.

Heresy is such a stain on Christendom, in the universal heart a
thing so hideous and abominable,

That had I had but one throw, it was the duty of the most
Catholic King to try to crush Cranmer and Knox and nail to her
rock that cruel Scylla, that harpy in human guise, bloody Elizabeth.

I have done my task, I have stopped that hole through which
my Accuser might have passed, I now worship God on every side
a perfect rampart around my faith. (*He covers the death's head with
a corner of the black velvet cloth on which it is set.*)

> (*Enter in fearful haste the* CHAMBERLAIN. *He has a handsome
> ruff, a handsome little blond beard, handsome black breeches,
> well padded, and all his limbs and joints are awry at
> different angles like the sections of a carpenter's measure.*)

THE CHAMBERLAIN, *coming in awkwardly and rapidly.*　　Sire, good
news! Sire, excellent news! Glorious news!

Praise be to God who watches over Spain! Who could have

doubted that an expedition so well planned and with such honourable aim, under a chief so distinguished, could have any end other
than excellently, perfectly, satisfactory?

THE KING, *looking at him with a leaden eye.*   Quiet yourself, sir,
and recover your wits, and be good enough to tell me in order and
measure what it is you would have me know.

THE CHAMBERLAIN.   I humbly beg Your Majesty's pardon; on
a day so fair for Spain who could contain his joy? The very sea is
trembling deep beneath my feet and this palace, with its mirrors
and its paintings, is heaving and cracking—
As if the resistless wave, which has just been flung against the
cliffs of Dover and of Southampton,
Were making itself felt at the roots of that deep eddy which
from beneath the keel of your most royal ship
Blossoms into a triple crown upon the brows of Spain thrice-
blessed of God.

THE KING.   Drop this poetic talk and enlighten me.

THE CHAMBERLAIN.   Without any kind of difficulty the glorious
Armada, favoured by the breath of angels,
Is come to the shores of Calais and of Gravelines,
And there upon the ready ships it has embarked the troops of
Parma.

THE KING.   Where were the fleets of Frobisher and Drake
meanwhile?

THE CHAMBERLAIN.   Their *débris* strews the coasts of the Straits,
of Ireland, of the Hebrides, and the Bristol Channel.

THE KING.   That is not the same thing on the map.

THE CHAMBERLAIN.   There is no possible doubt whatever.

THE KING.   Are these the news that come straight from the
Admiral?

THE CHAMBERLAIN.   Oh no, but nothing else is spoken of at
Bayonne.

THE KING.   And who gave you news from Bayonne?

THE CHAMBERLAIN.   A Jewish merchant just come this morning, whom the police have examined.

THE KING.   It only remains to thank God for so great a success.

THE CHAMBERLAIN.   And by now our fleet going full sail up the Thames is thundering at the Tower of London!

THE KING.   We must have a solemn *Te Deum* and hold counsel upon what we are going to do with Great Britain.

THE CHAMBERLAIN.   There is but one shadow on your victory, if I must say all.

THE KING.   Speak out.

THE CHAMBERLAIN.   The poor Duke of Medina Sidonia is drowned, how is not explained.

THE KING.   God rest his soul, Amen!

>   (*Noise of a discussion is heard without.*)
What is that noise?

>   (*Enter an usher.*)

THE USHER.   Sire, there is a woman who says that Your Majesty appointed her audience and absolutely insists on being introduced to Your Majesty's presence.

THE KING.   One moment. (*To the* CHAMBERLAIN.) Did you go to find Don Rodrigo, as I had sufficiently given you to understand was our desire?

THE CHAMBERLAIN.   It was Don Mendez Leal who undertook that mission.

THE KING.   Well, what answer did he give?

THE CHAMBERLAIN.   He gave no answer, but he pinned on his back the portrait of the Angel Gabriel, and he tied up his nose with a shoelace to keep him from telling lies.
The poor gentleman is still quivering with that insult.

THE KING.   Very well.   I shall ask you, sir, to do me the favour for a moment to cease to exist!   The Chamberlain ceases to exist!

(To the usher). Show the lady in.

(Usher goes out, enter the ACTRESS.*)*

THE ACTRESS. Sire, sire, I cast myself at the feet of Your Majesty! *(She suits the action to the word in excellent style.)*

THE KING. Rise, Madam.

THE ACTRESS. Sire, my king, what shall I say, where begin? Ah, I feel the greatness of my daring! But is not the King's mercy, like that great cup in the gardens of Escurial, nourished from distant peaks and never known the hour of overflowing, where the nightingales always have leave to slake their thirst? *(She rises.)*

THE KING. Speak without fear, Madam, you have our ear. Are we not of the same trade, you and I, each in his own theatre?

THE ACTRESS *in a ringing voice.* Ah, if ever, oh my King, my voice has carried right to your heart the accents of Lope and Calderon,
If ever your heart was thrilled to see Spain in my person throw herself in billowing folds at the feet of Sertorius,
Lend favourable ear to my poor woman's supplication!
For if it is true that I have fostered with my simple affections those great words that 'twas my duty to make felt,
It is right and just that in their turn all those creatures that I have been on the stage, and that depend on me for animation, should now surround and support me like great pillars!

THE KING. I listen.

THE ACTRESS. Don Philip de Medina Sidonia . . .

THE KING. I was expecting that name.

THE ACTRESS. Sire, Don Philip, my wee Philip,
Ah, no one knows so well as I do that he is not cut out to govern England!

THE KING. And who has told you, Madam, that I had an England at my disposal to make him a present of?

THE ACTRESS. Everyone knows that Your Majesty has just conquered England and that God has scattered His enemies.

The rumour has spread around in a moment like fire in dry grass. Hearken to those songs and acclamations on every side.

THE KING. True, it is a great day for Spain. This day is granted to Spain a great and memorable day.

THE ACTRESS. Sire, give me back Philip. No one knows so well as I do that he is not cut out to govern England!

Ah, I have too well vanquished him that he should ever more be able to embrace anything but me. I am worth more than England!

When he was in my arms it was not the noise of the restless waves beyond, foaming against that lair of heretics, that kept him from sleeping!

'Twas not the smell of seaweed or turf-smoke or oak-leaves in the rain that would ever make him forget the burning perfume of rose and jasmine that brought him unto me!

THE KING. What are you afraid of, then, if you are sure of him?

THE ACTRESS. I am afraid of that Queen Mary whom the Usurper has cast into a dungeon.

My beautiful Philip sets her free and very soon she yields him her hand. Behold him King of England, in the fog and ice.

That is how things come to pass in all the histories I have ever played. Poor Philip! it's all over, I am nothing to him any more.

THE KING. Queen Mary is not in England just now.

THE ACTRESS. Where is she, then?

THE KING. Why, here at my feet; I never believed her so beautiful.

THE ACTRESS. Sire, I don't understand you.

THE KING. No Mary was ever so beautiful or so touching, 'tis thus I love to picture her to myself.

THE ACTRESS. Sire, I am afraid of you! May it please you to unfold me your thought!

THE KING. Don Philip is thine, my daughter! Take him, I give him to thee, what joy to be together again!

THE ACTRESS.   Oh sire, you are good and I kiss your hands; what, you are going to tell him to come back to Spain?

THE KING.   How strive against the impulse of my heart?
I will give you Philip if you can give me someone in his stead to govern England.

THE ACTRESS.   Sire, don't mock me, those great men and captains about you—you have but to choose among them.

THE KING.   He whom I have chosen defies me and refuses to go where I want him.

THE ACTRESS.   What, there is someone under you who dares to disobey?

THE KING.   I have given no command, he who obeys me needs no command, it is my will that surrounds him on all sides and carries him away like a torrent. But he has put himself in such a position that I have no purchase on him.

THE ACTRESS.   Ah, why am not I your Chancellor? I would in a moment find arguments that would make him give ground!

THE KING.   You are stronger than my Chancellor.

THE ACTRESS.   Is the man still young?

THE KING.   He is old and has but one leg.

THE ACTRESS.   That's Don Rodrigo you mean.

THE KING.   The same.

THE ACTRESS.   Is it Rodrigo the picture-merchant, that refuses to be King of England?

THE KING.   He will not refuse when he sees Mary in tears at his feet.

THE ACTRESS.   Am I to be Mary?

THE KING.   I know not by what perversity you insist on wanting to be anyone else.

THE ACTRESS.   Escaped from Elizabeth's prison?

THE KING.   And received in great secrecy by the King of Spain.

THE ACTRESS. What will he do when he finds out the deception?

THE KING. What does the rat do when he's caught in the trap? Duty will then be a cage around him that he cannot get out of.

THE ACTRESS. And 'tis truly Rodrigo out of all your servants that you need?

THE KING. Of all that I hold in England, none but he is fit to take possession.

THE ACTRESS. And have I to beg him to accept England?

THE KING. I await but his request to grant it him.

THE ACTRESS. And you will give me back Philip?

THE KING. All that from the midst of the sea and of my army this moment answers to the name of Philip I present to you.

THE ACTRESS. And I will bring you Rodrigo!

(*She goes out after a final curtsey. Meanwhile the hall fills up with various functionaries, officers, dignitaries, and pleni-potentiaries so as to build up a kind of tableau vivant which you could call the Court of the King of Spain something in the style of the "Governor's Round." Once this difficult composition is achieved they all stay perfectly motionless.*)

THE KING, *clapping his hands.* Gentlemen, I have need of you, kindly lend me your attention.

ALL, *answering in unison.* We are Your Majesty's to command.

(*They start to set up an imitation of attention in the most fictitious and conventional way that can possibly be imagined.*)

THE KING. I suppose you have all already heard these great news that have come to us,
Our enemies scattered by the tempest, our forces rallied and reassembled, the heretic armies divided against themselves, and our mighty army in concert with our fleet marching upon London?

THE CHANCELLOR. We must thank God Who has marvellously accomplished His work through us, contrary to all human wisdom.

THE KING.   To Him alone be the honour as to the great invisible Star Who guides the ebb and flow of temporal affairs,
And for the nations that He loves makes defeat of no less advantage than victory, and to receive no less than to give.

THE CHANCELLOR.   The rumour has reached me that Don Philip de Medina Sidonia is dead.

THE KING.   It is true ; that is news that it behoves us to keep secret as yet.

THE CHANCELLOR.   Who is to govern England instead of our handsome Duke?

THE KING.   Yourself, my lord Chancellor, if it suits you.

THE CHANCELLOR.   My place is to oversee and not to govern.

THE KING *to the courtiers*.   If any of you asks England of me I will give it him.

(*They all stay motionless and dumb.*)

What, not one of you wants England?

THE CHANCELLOR.   They are afraid of Your Majesty and of those designs which It hides at the bottom of Its unsearchable heart.

THE KING.   Oh well, I know, I have already settled to whom I will give those islands in the mist, those dark and sodden lands,
Which at last have been touched through the tempest by a ray of our Catholic sun.

THE CHANCELLOR.   We await his name.

THE KING.   I await the man himself to come and suggest himself to us.
Too long has he fled Our presence to the very ends of the earth, boasting to do Our work where We were not and of winning for Us the length of his shadow through means by himself invented and put together.
Thus you have seen him by turns flinging himself at the gates of West and East.
And now the swell that carried him to the very ends of the earth brings him back resistlessly to Us,

Now that of his sunken fleets there is left beneath his feet only that broken ship,

On which he has the insolence to go on flouting Our royal vessel.

Well, I swear that if, instead of playing with the inverted reflection of my standard, he comes straight to me, I will give him all he asks and will show him countenance.

THE CHANCELLOR.　Why, having dropped him when he was young and powerful, take him up again now that he is weak and old?

THE KING.　It isn't I, it's the nature of things that dropped him, he was no longer in harmony with them;

You could say that he and they no longer lived by the same life, that they did not chime together, did not understand each other.

Was it not my duty to remove at once the machinery that stuck and creaked?

'Tis not the same thing to impose his will, to mould the plastic material, as he did erstwhile with America,

As to fall in with things already existing, and to intervene, pat to the point with faultless ear,

For 'tis existing things that provide the movement and we the intelligence.

All those things which seem disparate do still by nature make for harmony.

And now that he is old I suppose that he has realised the time for him is come not so much to act as to listen,

And to guide human interests and passions to that politic marriage to which they are predestined.

THE CHANCELLOR.　And so 'tis to this wooden-legged hawker —'tis to him that you are going to sign over the inheritance of the leopards and the harp?

THE KING.　I await but a sign.

THE CHANCELLOR.　What sign?

THE KING.　I will not go looking for him, I will give him no command. But let him ask England of me and I will give it him. You never venture to ask me for anything, or rather only titles, a few bits of ribbon, a few bags of crowns, a few slices of land,

But this beggar who has no refuge but three planks on the sea,

Let him ask me for England and I will give it him.

SCENE V

The scene-shifters set up carelessly in the middle of the sea a sort of pierced rockery as light as puff-pastry. The characters of the Scene come on divided into two gangs, and accompanied by as many supers as may be needed to give them body. On one side of the puff, MANGIACAVALLO, ALCOCHETE, *and* PROFESSOR BIDENS. *On the other side* BOGOTILLOS, MALTROPILLO *and* PROFESSOR HINNULUS. *The legs of these gentlemen can be seen below the gunwales of the boats they are handling, as everyone knows quite well that without legs boats cannot get on.*

FIRST GANGER, BIDENS.   That's our buoy, here it is, I recognise it by this little red flag we planted on top.

SECOND GANGER, HINNULUS.   That's our buoy, here it is, I recognise it by this little red flag we planted on top.

BIDENS.   Oh, I am dreadfully excited.

HINNULUS.   Oh, I am dreadfully excited. (*He giggles.*)

   (*Each gang fastens to the prow of the boat the rope's end affixed to the buoy.*)

SECOND GANGER.   Look out! We have only to pull all together with a will. Now or never.

BIDENS.   Why is it now or never?

   (HINNULUS *gives to understand in pantomime that he is going to say the same thing.*)

FIRST GANGER.   Haven't you heard that all the English fleet is gone to the bottom?

   (*The second ganger says the same thing in gesture.*)

BIDENS.   Well, what then?

HINNULUS.   Well, what then?

FIRST GANGER.   Then there is something going to come to the top again! When anything goes to the bottom there is always something coming to the top.

SECOND GANGER *says the same thing and adds:* That's equilibrium, what?

FIRST GANGER.   That's equilibrium, what?

BIDENS, *as if calling* HINNULUS *to witness across the puff-pastry.* What strange superstition!

HINNULUS, *in like manner calling the puff-pastry to witness.* What strange superstition!

BIDENS.   And now haul away!

HINNULUS.   And now haul away!

FIRST GANGER.   Haul away.

SECOND GANGER.   Haul away.

(*They don't haul.*)

FIRST GANGER.   If you stood a half-Douro all round there'd be better hauling.

SECOND GANGER.   Just a little Douro all round and we'd pull with better will.

BIDENS, *raising his arms to heaven.*   It's frightful extortion.

HINNULUS, *lifting his arms to heaven.*   It's frightful extortion. (*He whinnies.*)

BIDENS.   I have already stood ten Douros, and if we hoist the catch there is ten more.

HINNULUS.   That makes ten Douros I have stood already, and ten others if we haul up the bottle.

BIDENS.   And let us get on with it because I am always in dread of seeing Hinnulus turn up. The long-eared donkey, he pretends that it's a bottle you have made fast to.

HINNULUS. I am not too sure that I shan't see that cursed Bidens turn up. What a sheep-head, he reckons that what you have harpooned is a big she-fish. (*He whinnies.*)

FIRST GANGER, *cautiously*. Bottles like that—it's seldom there is any going about in the sea. Still we have managed to get hold of her. But she was too heavy for us, she's went to ground in a hole in the puff-pastry.

SECOND GANGER, *at the same time*. Those big fish like that—can't say as I ever seen 'em. Only a second I wor able to spot her in. That was enough to tie her to the hawser; she won't get away. But she was too strong for us in that hiding-hole of hers.

BIDENS, *stamping his foot*. It isn't a bottle, it's a she-fish.

HINNULUS, *stamping his foot*. It isn't a fish, it's a bottle.

BIDENS, *coaxingly*. What was she like, that fish?

FIRST GANGER. We didn't see her but a minute.

BIDENS. Round and shiny like a big bottle?

FIRST GANGER. Just what I was going to say, that's it, all pink and shiny like a big bottle.

BIDENS. And you didn't see now and again something like a light going off and on again?

FIRST GANGER. That's just it, eh? Mangiacavallo, a sort of a light, as you might say, going out and lighting up again.

HINNULUS. And what was it like, that bottle?

FIRST GANGER. It was a big bottle.

HINNULUS. Well, what was there in this bottle?

SECOND GANGER. Beg pardon, sir, we only saw it a minute. Or more like the shadow she made on the white sand at the bottom of the water with the red sun up above, that was just going to set.

HINNULUS. And you didn't see a whole lot of things moving about inside?

SECOND GANGER.　There's always a whole lot of things in a bottle.

BIDENS.　Enough said, now go ahead.

HINNULUS.　And now go ahead.

BIDENS.　Haul away.

HINNULUS.　Haul away.

FIRST GANGER.　Haul away.

SECOND GANGER.　Haul away.

(*The two gangs tied up to each other carry out on each side of the puff-pastry a sort of tug-of-war.*)

FIRST GANGER.　It's giving.

SECOND GANGER.　It's giving.

FIRST GANGER.　Eh, but it's stiff.

SECOND GANGER.　Eh, but it's stiff.

(*They stop.*)

ALCOCHETE, *obsequious*.　But before we start again, kindly explain to us, Professor, what's the make of this kind of animal that you are so anxious to collect?

BIDENS, *oracular and solemn*.　In the beginning in the limestone and cretaceous periods there ranged the steaming seas—whales of lacquered tin.

ALCOCHETE.　That's interesting.

BIDENS, *gesticulating as if he were drawing on a blackboard with chalk*.　The animal that we are hunting is a survival of those naive epochs. I saw its portrait in a German book, and I myself have gathered pieces of it here and there.

ALCOCHETE.　That's interesting, and how was it built?

BIDENS, *simple and familiar*.　There was but one eye which formed the objective and above it a kind of lighthouse or electric lantern, which it quenches and lights again at will.

The mouth, what kind of mouth? It has no mouth. It is
completely stoppered.

But in the middle of the stomach may be seen a double wheel
on which is twined in a figure of 8 an endless thong or belt,

On which become imprinted the images captured by the objective.

ALCOCHETE.   That's interesting.

BIDENS, *cantabile con molto espressione*.   On being taken up by
the second wheel they pass into a species of jawbone or brush
duly irrigated, which takes off the images and hands them on to
the digestive organs.

Nothing more beautiful has been found since the *Prapsopteron!*

ALCOCHETE.   And what name are we to give that there fish?

BIDENS, *with enthusiasm*.   We shall call it the *Georgeophagus*
from *George*, that is my name, George Bidens, and *ophagus* meaning
fish. All the he and she-fishes have names like that.

ALCOCHETE.   That's interesting. And you say that a beast like
that exists?

That's interesting.

BIDENS.   Of course it exists! It's got to exist! It is a convenient
hypothesis.

It's better than effectual, it's indispensable.

HINNULUS, *as if he were continuing the conversation*.   But if you
were able to get the bottle as near the boat as you say, certainly
you must have seen something.

BOGOTILLOS.   Sure, we did see something.

HINNULUS.   What did you see?

BOGOTILLOS.   Well, try to see it yourself a bit.

HINNULUS, *with suppressed excitement*.   If you want to know
what I think, that bottle is none other than the one that Apollonius
of Tyana threw into the sea and that Pantagruel went looking for.

BOGOTILLOS.   Who was Apollonius?

HINNULUS.   Apollonius was a great man of science, long ago, who found out how to bottle up time. You cork it up and it's over, it doesn't get away.

BOGOTILLOS.   That's a good idea.

HINNULUS.   Only tell me what you saw.

MALTROPILLO.   It isn't *seeing*, as you could say; it was so mixed up; it's more like hearing.

HINNULUS.   What did you hear?

MALTROPILLO.   It was the braying of an ass.

HINNULUS.   It was the ass of Silenus when by moonlight in the midst of the bacchanale he climbed to Parnassus. (*He whinnies.*)

MALTROPILLO.   A splash, splash, like big fishes jumping out of the water.

HINNULUS.   It was Proteus feeding his singing seals with four trombones.

MALTROPILLO.   A galloping like horses unharnessed among rolling stones.

HINNULUS.   It was the centaurs stumbling among the oleanders on the rocky slopes of Cithœron! Well done. (*He whinnies.*)

SECOND GANG, *as if it had been waiting for this signal, with one voice, spitting in its twelve hands and triumphally uplifted by the music which sustains it to the end of the scene.* Well done, and now go ahead.

FIRST GANG.   Go ahead, go ahead.

(*They all go backwards.*)

BIDENS and HINNULUS.   Haul away, haul away.

FIRST and SECOND GANGS.   Haul away, haul away.

(*They haul, tug-of-war.*)

It's giving! It's giving! Pull hard, oh but it's stiff, it's stiff! Go ahead! Go ahead!—back away! Back away!

(*The rope breaks, they all fall upside down.*)

SCENE VI

The ACTRESS *on the proscenium in front of the lowered curtain, uncorseted, throat and arms bare. She is supposed to be in her dressing-room making up for the scene that she is going to play. A great mirror in front of her, on her table among the toilet implements a few rumpled sheets of paper. All the furniture and fittings are fastened to the curtain by strings easily seen.*

THE MAID, *handing the* ACTRESS *a little pot of black.* Madam has forgotten her Rimmel.

THE ACTRESS. You are right, a little Rimmel will just make my eyes flash better. The arrow of personality flies with greater force from the bow of a darkened eyelid. (*She touches her eyelids with a little brush, then she slowly rolls her eyes from right to left and then from left to right, opens, shuts, opens, shuts.*)

THE MAID. And all that to get an old muck-merchant, half croaked, to accept a kingdom at our hands.

THE ACTRESS. Don't say that, Mariette; you don't understand at all, Mariette, it is a superb situation and the most beautiful part I ever had in my life, a golden part. What a pity there is no one to see us, but I will use it for the season in Madrid, it will make a little sketch at the Alcazar, you will see!

And not a scrap of rouge on the face. Only a little carmine on the lobe of each ear. What do you say?

THE MAID, *clapping her hands.* Just right, lights up everything.

THE ACTRESS. Must be simple to begin with so as to work up the development and all the shades. Quite tranquil and gentle, quite tuneful with a sorrowful undertone, simplicity, simplicity! A kind of submission and resignation full of dignity. (*Trying her voice.*) La, la, la la, little pot of butter, little pot of butter; the notes of the middle register a trifle dull,

Simplicity, but greatness too! I begin in high-born simplicity: "I have summoned you hither, sir." (*She refers to her paper.*)

THE MAID.   Would Madam like me to go for the book of words?

THE ACTRESS.   There is no book of words, Mariette, it's much finer as it is. I have to create everything, words and music. I read my answer beforehand in the eyes of my partner.

It's only a matter of managing the gesture, the words come to the top by themselves.

I begin by a kind of recitation, my story, a long tissue of pathetic taradiddles recited in the most musical of voices. And then bit by bit all the great movements of eloquence and passion, the accents of that mournful queen at the feet of that runaway, I hope he is quite hideous and brutal, and from time to time an interrogation, a word, a touching little question.

That's it, here and there a nothing, a trifle, clear, clear, tender, touching, a pretty little flirt.

And in the background always, naturally, the secret of woman, something kept back, half understood.

THE MAID.   Oh, I'll hide myself somewhere to see you; oh! if Madam is as beautiful as the other evening it will be lovely! I didn't know where to put myself, I cried all night over it.

(*Just here the curtain rises, dragging with it the looking-glass, the toilet-table, and the whole outfit.*)

THE MAID.   Oh my God! What's the matter?

THE ACTRESS.   We are on the other side of the curtain, without heeding we have got to the other side of the curtain and the action is going on without us! Oh my God, someone has stolen my part, I feel stark naked! Look quick, let us get back there within, and we will end up all right coming out at one end or another.

(*Exeunt.*)

(*The curtain rising discovers the* ACTRESS, *another in the same part, neck and arms bare, busy painting at a table, a glass of dirty water in front of her and* RODRIGO *standing over her giving directions.*)

DON RODRIGO.   Your Majesty does me great honour consenting like this to work under my direction.

THE ACTRESS, *without lifting her eyes*.   You would do better to tell me if it's green or blue you want the umbrella. I see it dark blue.

DON RODRIGO.   And I see it red, a faded red, almost yellow. And underneath an evangelist in full sail, Saint Luke, busy with his writing. A little street in Avignon under the Palace of the Popes, and above in the full azure, very high, there is a flying buttress all white (make it pink, to look whiter), a soaring buttress of unspeakable joyfulness!

Between Saint Luke and the said buttress there is a pigeon flying to perch on it.

THE ACTRESS.   I like the Saint Matthew better.

DON RODRIGO.   Yes, it's a big idea I had to put behind him that great triumphal arch in red stone with two gates and the inscription in Roman capitals, and the bull's head.

THE ACTRESS.   An angel is Matthew's symbol.

DON RODRIGO.   I am sorry, but the bull looks better. You have quite caught the shade for the sky in the background and the long, slanting clouds.

Saint Matthew the publican between two streams of traffic going up and coming down.

Yes, but he is too small, he is not seen.

Quick, another sheet, we will make another, drawn in a sort of elliptical window.

He has a kind of great Roman face with shaven jowl and double chin,

A yellow toga like a Buddhist monk's pinned on the shoulder with a great copper brooch,

And under the table a huge foot wearing a leaden sandal,

Crushing down Calvin who vomits the devil!

THE ACTRESS.   It's lucky that you met me after your Japanese left you standing.

DON RODRIGO.   Yes, he went off without notice. He must have seen a chance to get back to his country. I must have offended him, I don't know how. They are like that!

But I do not grieve for him, you work still better than he; it blends well together, you and me. When all is said and done there are things which nothing suits so well as the blend of man and woman.

What a good inspiration it was of me all of a sudden to ask you if you could draw. While you would go on talking to me of a heap of uninteresting things.

THE ACTRESS. You didn't ask my opinion, you annexed me on the spot.

DON RODRIGO. The tiresome thing is that you cannot engrave, but I am sure you will learn quickly. The Japanese left all his boards and his tools.

THE ACTRESS. That is all right, but I am going to have to get back to England.

DON RODRIGO. Not a bit of it, I have told you already that I have no desire to make the acquaintance of England.

I know a little old convent near Majorca with a courtyard full of lemons so yellow that it hurts the eye.

You will be very well off there for work. You will be able to work from morning till night without anyone coming to bother you.

THE ACTRESS. Yes, but the handsome Duke of Medina Sidonia has just conquered England for me.

DON RODRIGO. I should never have thought that the handsome Duke Medina Sidonia was able to conquer anything difficult.

THE ACTRESS. Who knows, perhaps my heart will not be so for him.

DON RODRIGO. All right, marry him! And I will go and make war on you in Ireland!

THE ACTRESS. Don Rodrigo, why are you so rough and contrary with me?

DON RODRIGO. Marry the handsome Duke of Medina Sidonia, I am old, a poor chap with only one leg.

THE ACTRESS. If I marry anyone it will be the son of the King of Spain.

DON RODRIGO.   All I ask is to keep friends with you.

THE ACTRESS.   'Tis you that I prefer.

DON RODRIGO.   It's nice of you to say that, even if it isn't true.
Yes, it pleases me to hear it.

THE ACTRESS.   I won't marry anyone! In the London prison I
found out that I had a soul, a living soul not made to moulder in
a prison.

I swore that never again would I let myself be cast into prison.

I swore that never would I endure a man's big carcase between
me and the sun!

I did not want to go on living half-baked!

I want someone to help me and not swallow me alive!

With you one is alive, I am alive with you these two days!
You do not ask me for anything; you are like music that makes
no demands but immediately carries you away and puts you in
tune with itself.

Ever since you have been here it's been music. I give myself
up with eagerness, trust and poise, as to the arms of a strong
dancer,

I feel that I provide your spirit with what it wanted! You are
there, and behold me strong and merry, I feel quite brilliant and
resounding!

It's like a cleansing trumpet call—like a fighting flourish that
revives the drooping spirit and fills it with courage and fire!

And meanwhile we are both free! I have no claim on you and
you have none on me. It is delightful! We are together while the
music lasts.

DON RODRIGO.   Well, we are going to make and make and
make pictures without end.

THE ACTRESS.   But supposing I want to make something else
with you than pictures and sand-pies?

DON RODRIGO.   Is it by the desire of the King of Spain that
you came looking for me?

THE ACTRESS.   Why should I not confess? Medina Sidonia is
no use for anything but the happiness and unhappiness of a weak
woman.

'Tis you that the King has need of in England with me. He awaits but one gesture of yours towards him.

DON RODRIGO.   I will not make that gesture.

THE ACTRESS.   What, will you not help me?

DON RODRIGO.   I don't understand why His Majesty bethought himself of me all at once!

He had no need of me whole and sound, why does he gather me up all broken?

THE ACTRESS.   His confidence does you honour.

DON RODRIGO.   It offends me. He is not afraid of me,

There is nothing to fear from a cripple. I shall be more than happy to carry out his orders.

The ascendancy that the handsome Medina Sidonia may have established over you has nothing to fear from me.

THE ACTRESS.   Is that true, dear Rodrigo?

DON RODRIGO, *with a wry smile*.   It isn't altogether true.

THE ACTRESS.   Your sovereign is mighty politic. I suppose that really he wanted to use us against each other.

Well, why not strike up alliance as he asks us, it will be his doing?

DON RODRIGO.   Is any alliance possible with you?

THE ACTRESS.   Dear Rodrigo, I am with you these two days and it seems to me that never before has anyone known me,

So much so that it irks me.

You have aroused in me unknown forces; when I listen to you everything shifts about and makes for a different order. I seem to have something deep and novel in me that cannot help responding to your wooing.

Ah, and for your part don't you think that I have found you out a little?

DON RODRIGO.   It is too true!

Would you call it not delightful, this young intent face a-listening?

That beam of intelligence in those fine eyes looking at me,
that's as good to me as a white body!

THE ACTRESS, *covering her shoulders with the mantilla.* I don't
like this country.
If I stay much longer under this burning sun, I feel that I will
wither up like seaweed on the shingle.

DON RODRIGO. And meanwhile from the head to your little
feet your Aragonese mother made you Spanish.
Your face is pale, and still I don't know what gives it such
brilliance.

THE ACTRESS. The eyes, maybe? No,
It's this touch of carmine that I put just on the very end of
the ears.

DON RODRIGO. Why, that's it! See the importance of a just
touch! Hum! Where were we?

THE ACTRESS. We were at England, where you are coming
to-morrow with me.

DON RODRIGO. So I have the pleasant mission of managing
that conquered people?
To work under the lash, every Sunday good as gold, go listen
to the parish priest, and every month put in a bag for you the
money that you will send to the King of Madrid every year, as
little as possible,
That is the job you are giving me to explain in Spanish to my
sympathetic subjects.
It reminds me of my friend of long ago, Almagro on his
plantations.

THE ACTRESS. What would you have us do?

DON RODRIGO. Madam, who gets the most out of a horse,
He that mounts him and digs both spurs into him, or he that
holds him by the bridle and whips him for all he is worth?

THE ACTRESS, *clapping her hands.* I understand! Ah, you are
the man I want!
A horse that needs his master never dreams of throwing him off
and he will not philosophise or theologise!

You must keep him busy!

Ah, you are lame, but I am going to put a superb animal under you. My people, how I love them!

You shall love them as I do.

You and I are going to show this people its vocation.

DON RODRIGO. Do you think the King of Spain will be pleased with this little programme?

THE ACTRESS. He will have time to get used to it bit by bit.

DON RODRIGO. So it's to deceive my sovereign that you propose?

THE ACTRESS. That's it, we will hoodwink him a little bit, of course!

DON RODRIGO. And once more you are going to send me back to walls and furniture and papers? The immense spaces and the sun to be mine no more?

The sea that I have felt so long alive beneath my heart and which has been so long my bed-fellow, the imperial couch beneath me, must I tear myself away from that?

THE ACTRESS (*the orchestra plays an arrangement of "Fingal's Cave"*). But in England we are never far from the sea, 'tis throbbing right to the heart of our counties.

The island is like an immense harp tuned to catch its notes and its music.

Twice a day it comes to feed and nourish us through every sort of channel and opening, right to the centre of the country.

How lucky to have it all round one and be cut off from everything in that great garden full of grazing beasts, that meadow in whose heart the rainbow always plants one foot!

That's what an artist like you wants! Away from everything, the ready means of intervening in the affairs of Europe without ever anyone bothering with ours, always half-enveloped in mystery and mist.

The absurd conquest by the Armada will never happen again. Ah, well will I punish the traitors and the boobies who could not defend themselves!

You Continentals,

You cannot get into your heads that there is something else

besides land on this planet. But the sea comes first and the land is in it.

This ocean you did not see—you Spaniards have hurried across it with your eyes shut so as to get quickly to batten on that land which you found on the other side.

But we English have the whole sea for our own, not merely this sort of puddle, your Mediterranean,

But all the sea wholesale,

The land that happens to be in it over and above, enough to fasten a few barges to it here and there.

We soak in it! We stick at nothing! We are free! We are open at all ends! The infinite water on every side comes kissing the steps of our castle!

Come with me to the top of Europe, to that dove-cote, as it were, surrounded with flickering wings, with my gulls, my carrier pigeons, forever setting off to quest all the seas of the world! Here where we are there isn't even a tide! But in London one's finger is night and day on the throbbing pulse of the world!

While you are busy at your desk, suddenly the light is intercepted, a great four-master going up the Thames!

DON RODRIGO.   When the sun gets to shine through the mist, you see the muddy water livening into a million golden scales, that is the ægis of Britannia.

THE ACTRESS.   Will you come with me to England?

DON RODRIGO.   I will come if I want to, but first I would like to try to realise with you this great projection of the frieze,

To be called the Kiss of Peace ; I got the idea of it looking at the monks in choir passing on to one another the kiss which the first of them received at the altar from the celebrant.

They cast their shadows on one another.

But instead of monks we will put women wrapped in long veils.

They are passing the Peace to each other.

I have a kind of great cloth: we will tell the little cabin boy to wrap up in it, or perhaps I shall do it myself; I will pose for you.

SCENE VII

DIEGO RODRIGUEZ, THE LIEUTENANT

*An old, patched and battered boat painfully beating about for port.
(If this is too complicated to show, a simple bottle in the hand of
DIEGO RODRIGUEZ containing a ship in sail will do the trick.) On the
bridge the commander, DIEGO RODRIGUEZ, and his LIEUTENANT, a
young man.*

DIEGO RODRIGUEZ. Since the middle of the night I have
recognised the smell of Majorca as if a woman were sending it me
whiff by whiff with her black fan. Only Corsica smells as good.

THE LIEUTENANT. There is also the town of Marseilles.
Wouldn't I give Corsica and the three Balearics to get the
smell of the damp wood burning on the Timor shore!

DIEGO RODRIGUEZ. If I hear you say those villainous words
again, I will send you to the bottom, head first.

THE LIEUTENANT. I only put my lips to it and you snatched it
from me at once! Why did I not drink deeper of that poisoned cup!

DIEGO RODRIGUEZ, *sweeping with his telescope.* Nothing is
altered! There is the notary's house, there is the bailie's, there is
the Poor Clares' convent among the cypresses! It's absurd.

THE LIEUTENANT. Show me the house of Dona Austregesila.

DIEGO RODRIGUEZ. It isn't visible. It's on the other side of
the point.

THE LIEUTENANT. We will be there in a few minutes with this
good wind. You can go ashore this evening.

DIEGO RODRIGUEZ. No, we make no headway with this old
tub all barnacled to the keel. It's too late, I will tell them drop
the anchor.

THE LIEUTENANT. Are you afraid, Captain?

DIEGO RODRIGUEZ. I am afraid! I am afraid! That's true.

THE LIEUTENANT. Afraid of the joy in store for you?

DIEGO RODRIGUEZ. What joy? Dona Austregesila has had time to get married and widowed twice or three times. At least I have no illusions! I am not green enough to believe that she kept faithful to her oath these ten years gone by.

THE LIEUTENANT. No, I don't believe it either.

DIEGO RODRIGUEZ. If she loved me she would have managed to write to me.

THE LIEUTENANT. Certain sure.

DIEGO RODRIGUEZ. True, she didn't quite know where I was. But after all, everything hangs together at sea, and a letter always ends by getting there.

THE LIEUTENANT. That's what I say.

DIEGO RODRIGUEZ. Who would trust a woman's oath? There is not a book that doesn't tell you what to think of that. It is made quite clear.

THE LIEUTENANT. Of course.

DIEGO RODRIGUEZ. Besides, what can I offer her now to tempt her? I am old and this old patched boat ready for the knacker is my whole fortune. Neither war nor commerce, nothing that I have tried on land or sea has turned out well.

THE LIEUTENANT. There's no denying that.

DIEGO RODRIGUEZ. I have not even managed to discover anything. Other navigators have countries full of men, vast rich countries to show and to share their name with.
But Diego Rodriguez has a cake of red slag in the middle of the Atlantic Ocean, a home for seals and penguins.

THE LIEUTENANT. Just as you say. An accursed place, you can't even water there.

DIEGO RODRIGUEZ. She is beautiful. She has land and money.

One of the good families of Majorca. She cannot have lacked for suitors.

THE LIEUTENANT.   Very likely, very likely.

DIEGO RODRIGUEZ.   It isn't likely, it's sure.

THE LIEUTENANT.   Quite sure, quite sure.

DIEGO RODRIGUEZ.   No, it isn't quite sure, don't be impertinent! It's a great shame, I say.

Why did I set out if not for her? To become worthy of her! There wasn't enough gold in the whole world for me to cast at her feet!

Ah, I should never have believed that she would betray me thus! I should never have believed that she was like other women.

THE LIEUTENANT.   Just the same.

DIEGO RODRIGUEZ.   If you go on talking like that you will get my fist on your snout!

THE LIEUTENANT.   What would you have, captain? You have been so long talking to me about Dona Austregesila! First I tried to defend her, but you have an answer for everything, and I admit that you have convinced me.

DIEGO RODRIGUEZ.   Get wise. I know more than the length of my arm about it. You will see what women are, and life.

(*Enter* DON ALCINDAS.)

DON ALCINDAS.   I salute Diego Rodriguez, captain of the *Santa Fé*. I am Don Alcindas.

DIEGO RODRIGUEZ.   A very good day, Señor Alcindas, are you the Customs?

DON ALCINDAS.   No, I am not the Customs.

DIEGO RODRIGUEZ.   I thought nothing but the Customs would warp us up so quick.

DON ALCINDAS.   There are good eyes at Majorca watching the seas. There are good memories that have not forgotten the *Santa Fé*.

DIEGO RODRIGUEZ.   I understand, you represent my creditors. Well, I won't pay you, you can have me put in jail.

The money that you lent me ten years ago—you can write it off.

I have nothing left but this old boat. Pay yourself out of that if you can.

The cargo isn't mine.

DON ALCINDAS.   You are offensive, Don Diego. You have no other creditor here than one from whose debt 'tis not in your power to escape.

DIEGO RODRIGUEZ.   What rigmarole is this? I don't understand you.

DON ALCINDAS.   Why, have you forgotten Dona Austregesila?

DIEGO RODRIGUEZ.   Is Dona Austregesila alive?

DON ALCINDAS.   She is alive.

DIEGO RODRIGUEZ.   Go on. Tell me what name she bears at present. What is her husband's name?

DON ALCINDAS.   Did you think she would wait for you these ten years? So beautiful and so desirable? Who were you to deserve such faithfulness?

DIEGO RODRIGUEZ.   I am Diego Rodriguez who discovered in the middle of the Atlantic Ocean a brand-new pebble that no one had ever seen before.

DON ALCINDAS, *looking him up and down.*   The more I look at you the harder I find it to believe that once upon a time you could pretend to the hand of the most beautiful and virtuous lady of Majorca.

DIEGO RODRIGUEZ.   Is it you she married?

DON ALCINDAS.   Alas! she rejected the respectful request which I cast at her feet.

DIEGO RODRIGUEZ.   Then who is the happy man that she found worthy of her choice?

DON ALCINDAS.   No one. She isn't married.

DIEGO RODRIGUEZ. And may I know why, though rich, virtuous, and the noblest woman of Majorca, she still has found no husband?

DON ALCINDAS. Come, come, Don Diego, can't you guess?

DIEGO RODRIGUEZ. No, I don't know! No, I don't know!

DON ALCINDAS. In a few minutes more now she shall tell you herself. 'Tis she that recognised your ship; every day she climbed that tower to look at the sea. 'Tis she that sends me.

DIEGO RODRIGUEZ. Why did she never write to me?

DON ALCINDAS. She never doubted that your faithfulness was as great as her own.

DIEGO RODRIGUEZ. Don Alcindas, what am I to do?

DON ALCINDAS. I don't know.

DIEGO RODRIGUEZ. I will sink this ship and send us all to the bottom! It cannot go on like this! I am not worthy to lick the sole of her shoe.

DON ALCINDAS. That is true.

DIEGO RODRIGUEZ. But does she know what state I am coming back in, an old man, a defeated conqueror, a cracked sailor, a broken merchant and the most ridiculous poor fellow in all the Spanish seas?

DON ALCINDAS. You are not poor. Dona Austregesila has taken care of your property in your absence, and you are the richest man in Majorca.

DIEGO RODRIGUEZ, *to the* LIEUTENANT. And that is the woman, sir, that you are always throwing up to me as faithless!

THE LIEUTENANT. I beg your pardon.

DON ALCINDAS. Don Diego, down on your knees and take off your hat and salute the native land where such a bride after so many voyages is in store for you.

SCENE VIII

DON RODRIGO'S *ship*. DONA SEVENSWORDS *is seated at the table, her head in her arms.*

DON RODRIGO *approaching softly from behind and laying his cheek on the head of* SEVENSWORDS. What is my little lamb thinking of?

(DONA SEVENSWORDS *makes no answer and does not change position, but passes her arm round her father's waist.*)

DON RODRIGO. Well, is there some vexation? Doesn't want to say anything to her poor daddy?

DONA SEVENSWORDS. If I tell you what I think, I am sure that you won't answer me as I would like.

DON RODRIGO. And what would you like?

DONA SEVENSWORDS. I don't want you to keep company with that woman that you call the Queen of England.

DON RODRIGO. Her Majesty the Queen of England. Isn't she Mary the Queen of England? Have you not seen our own sire the King of Spain treat her as such?
She came and threw herself at my feet. Could I repulse her? Am I free to refuse that task in which no one could take my place—
My conscience bound me to listen to her;
To me alone she will be a docile pupil. All that our armies have conquered she puts at my disposal.
There is something about her indescribably attentive and submissive that has touched my heart.
It is interesting to write her name royally across all that white page.

DONA SEVENSWORDS. I count for nothing any more, and she does whatever she likes with you.

DON RODRIGO. Are you jealous, little girl?

DONA SEVENSWORDS. Another is jealous.

DON RODRIGO. Yes, I know whom you mean, I am looking at her in your eyes.

DONA SEVENSWORDS. My mother, who gave me to you so that you might always be hers.

DON RODRIGO. Yes, I know that you have always been hers and a part of herself.

DONA SEVENSWORDS. If she were not with me, I should not sense you so much.

DON RODRIGO. So there is no chance of getting away without any noise, on tiptoe?

DONA SEVENSWORDS. I am not her only, I am you also; there is something in my soul which is you and spies out your movements. You shall not get away from your little Sevenswords.

DON RODRIGO. When your mother was not there, then was the time I used to speak with her.
When she was not there, then was the time that I spoke to her best.

DONA SEVENSWORDS. Speak, daddy darling. She is dead, she is not here.

DON RODRIGO. But maybe her Guardian Angel is here listening.

DONA SEVENSWORDS. He is tired with following you; he is asleep; he doesn't hear you.
He is here asleep, a bitter sleep like a desperate tramp at the inn who sleeps because he cannot stir another step.

DON RODRIGO. I am alone with my darling child?

DONA SEVENSWORDS. Yes, father.

(*He moves his lips without any audible word. She looks at him tenderly and close, then turns away his face, putting her hand on his eyes.*)

DON RODRIGO, *very softly, laying his hand on her other hand.* The tears that are in my heart the sea would not be wide enough—

DONA SEVENSWORDS. What, you are not comforted?

DON RODRIGO. My soul is empty. Because of her who is not here, heavy tears, my tears, could feed the sea.

DONA SEVENSWORDS. But she is going to be here presently. Very soon. She whom you loved, very soon, she whom you loved —you will see her again, very soon.

DON RODRIGO. And I think it will never be! That essential absence, yes, my darling, and even when you were alive and
I held you in my arms in that
Embrace that quenched hope,
Who knows if it were other than
The commencement and apprenticeship of that
Fathomless and hopeless craving to which I am
Predestined, bare and with no counterpart?

DONA SEVENSWORDS. But that is hell you are saying! Those are guilty thoughts sprung from doing nothing.
While there is love there is something to be done.
Instead of thinking of yourself, why not think of her?
Who knows whether herself has not need of you, who knows if she is not saying: Rodrigo! Who knows if she is not in a place unknown to us fastened with bonds that you are able to undo?

DON RODRIGO. More daring than Columbus to get right to where she is,
Can I avail to cross the threshold between this world and the next?

DONA SEVENSWORDS. There is what one ought to do, and not bother if one avails or unavails; nothing is simpler.
Why do you talk of threshold as if there were separation? There is no separation when things are as close as the blood is to the veins.
The soul of the dead like breath penetrates our heart, our brain.
I hear my mother at night speaking to me so sweet, so tender! So substantially. There is no need of words between us to understand each other.

DON RODRIGO.   Tell me what she says, Sevenswords.

DONA SEVENSWORDS.   Not one word that could sound in this outer air which we are breathing.

DON RODRIGO.   How understand her in that case?

DONA SEVENSWORDS.   What can a prisoner ask for? 'Tis heart-rending!

DON RODRIGO.   What hands can send deliverance to her?

DONA SEVENSWORDS.   Where the body cannot go, charity can, for it is mightier than all.

DON RODRIGO.   What bread and what water can reach her lips in the grave?

DONA SEVENSWORDS.   She has no hands nor mouth, but there is no lack of people in her place in Africa who have the wherewithal night and day to howl despair against the Spain which has forgotten them! Do not all things hang together? Is theirs not the same privation and the same grieving?
While knights and ladies dance to the sound of lute and flageolet, while the lords in the tourneys prod one another with great sticks—

DON RODRIGO.   While a certain old fool amuses himself drawing images with the remaining stump of his mind—

DONA SEVENSWORDS.   While our merchants are going to the very end of the earth to bring back a fistful of pearls, a few barrels of oil, a few bags of spice,
A fatter oil is forgotten,
A more generous wine, that water, the true, regenerating us,
Tears upon our hands of the captives we have set free and are bringing back to their wives and their mothers.

DON RODRIGO.   God alive, Sevenswords, you are right, forward! What are we doing here? Why are we not already *en route* for Barbary?
Why look for any other Africa than that very one from which I am so long accustomed to demand the impossible?

DONA SEVENSWORDS.   Is it true? You want us to set off? I

have one little soldier with me already, a butcher's daughter that I have brought from Majorca.

DON RODRIGO. That makes three; let me find another forty stout fellows of the same kidney.

DONA SEVENSWORDS. 'Tisn't forty we shall find, ten thousand if you like! You can ask anything from Christians; if you get nothing from them it's because you aren't daring, because you don't ask enough!

If you made a little shift to ask them for something?

Do you think they would enjoy themselves so much as all that, in Spain, in the middle of their little businesses?

Tell them that's all over. Tell them you are going to Africa and to come with you, and that they will all die, that not one will come back!

It isn't ten thousand we shall get, it's a hundred thousand; we shall never have enough ships! But we will not accept every one!

The King of Spain himself. Oh! but for that matter how funny it must be to be the King of Spain!

When he sees us going off, hurray! I am sure he will want to come as well and fight with us in such a noble cause like a good little man.

DON RODRIGO. It's Don Rodrigo will stump along first at the head of all that army.

DONA SEVENSWORDS. You are making game of me.

DON RODRIGO. May my stump take root if I make game of you. And may the graft of an old swashbuckler on this briar-stock make it grow red hips every winter, enough to keep two chaffinches.

DONA SEVENSWORDS. Then when do we begin?

DON RODRIGO. It's those "tears on my hands" that hold me up. I don't like to be wept over.

How much pleasanter it would be if one could do good without anyone taking notice,

In silence, like God, and without any sort of chance of being thanked or recognised and smothered from head to foot in gratitude!

Instead of smashing up doors with axes,

How much jollier it would be to get in stealthily from behind like poison and to humbug the prisoners and their keepers by opening up everything without their noticing!

And to give rise somewhere to a liberty resistless like the sun, slowly overcoming all the cloud-veils without anyone dreaming of saying thank you!

DONA SEVENSWORDS. Why refuse anything that a poor man can give, or the tears of a simple heart?

Besides, it isn't what you think queer and amusing, dear father, that's the principal point, but to set the captives free for the glory of God.

DON RODRIGO. When I have delivered the captives (come on, I am quite willing, they shall weep on my feet),

There will still be others left.

DONA SEVENSWORDS. But we shall be left as well or else we shall be dead, and that will quit us of our duty.

DON RODRIGO. Sevenswords, my child, will you think little of me if I speak my mind?

DONA SEVENSWORDS. Say on, father.

DON RODRIGO. It is curious how the idea of good Mister Alonso Lopez in chains, and of turning over Alonso Lopez to the bereaved Mrs. Lopez and to the little Lopezes,

And taking from this time forward Alonso Lopez in this African episode of his temporal existence for my pole star,

Has very little effect on me at all.

DONA SEVENSWORDS. Father, I shall never believe you so cruel and so light-minded.

DON RODRIGO. Neither am I, devil take me! But I get my thought out by the first end I can, I would like to try to explain myself!

Tell me now, child, who has done most service to poor fever patients,

The devoted physician who never leaves their pillow and bleeds them and takes their life to cure them at peril of his own,

Or that sort of ne'er-do-weel who one day taking it into his head

To go to the other side of the world,
Discovered quinine?

DONA SEVENSWORDS.   Alas! the discoverer of quinine.

DON RODRIGO.   And who has freed most slaves, the man who
selling his patrimony ransomed them one by one, or the capitalist
who found out how to make a mill go by water?

DONA SEVENSWORDS.   Everyone his own way, it isn't so much
patient well-doing to our brothers and sisters that is commanded us
As doing what we can to love the captive and the suffering, the
image of Jesus Christ, and to lay down our life for them.

DON RODRIGO.   Come, once again I am repulsed with loss, and
yet I am convinced that there must be some way of explaining
to you
Why it is when I am called to the north I at once have the
feeling that it's to the west I ought to look.

DONA SEVENSWORDS.   But here is neither north nor south, but
you are drifting at random on a backwater,
Giving up to the winds everything that springs from your
imagination.

DON RODRIGO.   And why should I not have the right to bring
forth my fly-leaves like the cherry-tree its fruit, or, if it is too
much honour to liken me to that tree of sweetness,
The juniper its berries?

DONA SEVENSWORDS.   Because I have need of you. My mother
has need of you and all those captives in Algiers have need.
We need you very deeply, and not your fruit, but your wood.

DON RODRIGO.   But does it mean needing me to ask me what
any other in my place could provide much better?
For instance, if you need a table, certainly you can apply to a
locksmith and perhaps he will make you something rather like.
But if I were you I would think of a cabinet-maker.

DONA SEVENSWORDS.   And so it is not in your line to trouble
about your suffering brethren?

DON RODRIGO.   My special line is not to do them good one by
one. I am not a man of detail.

My line is not to save Alonzo Lopez from the Turkish Bagnios and Maria Garcia from the small-pox.

DONA SEVENSWORDS.   But don't say, dear father, that you are no use at all!

Don't hurt me so! Don't say that in this miserable world you don't want to be useful to anything or anyone!

DON RODRIGO.   Yes, rather, Sevenswords, yes, I believe that I did not come into the world for nothing, and there is in me something necessary that could not be done without.

DONA SEVENSWORDS.   What did you come to do among us?

DON RODRIGO.   I came to enlarge the earth.

DONA SEVENSWORDS.   What is enlarging the earth?

DON RODRIGO.   The Frenchman living in France, for instance, it is too little, he chokes! He has Spain underfoot, and England overhead, and at his sides Germany and Switzerland and Italy; fancy moving free with that!

And behind those countries, other countries and other countries again, and finally the unknown, no one fifty years ago knew what there was. A wall.

DONA SEVENSWORDS.   Do you think to abolish the unknown?

DON RODRIGO.   When you talk of delivering the captives, is it setting them free to pass them from one prison to another, to change compartments? Spain long since to me was not less insufferable a hole than Algiers.

DONA SEVENSWORDS.   There is always on one side or another a wall that keeps us back.

DON RODRIGO.   Heaven is not a wall!

There is no other wall or barrier for man except Heaven! All that is earthy upon earth is his to walk upon, and 'tis unthinkable that he should be shut out from any portion—

Wherever his feet will take him he has the right to go.

I say the Whole is indispensable to him. He cannot do without it. He is not built to walk with one leg and breathe with half a lung. He needs the whole lot, all his body.

It is another thing to be limited by God or by things which are of the same nature as ourselves and are not meant to hold us in.
I want the fine perfect apple.

DONA SEVENSWORDS.   What apple?

DON RODRIGO.   The globe, an apple that you can hold in your hand.

DONA SEVENSWORDS.   That which grew long ago in Paradise?

DON RODRIGO.   'Tis always there! Where is order there is Paradise. Look at the sky and the astronomers will tell you if order is lacking there.
Now, thanks to Columbus, thanks to me,
We are makeweights in this astronomic affair,
Blissfully cut off from everything else but God.
We hold by nothing now but Law and Number, which unite us to the rest of the universe. What stars! How rich is God! And we, too, may add our ha'porth of gold to the inexhaustible wealth of God!

DONA SEVENSWORDS.   And while you are looking at the sky, you don't see the pit at your feet, you don't hear the cry of those unfortunates who are fallen into the cistern beneath you!

DON RODRIGO.   It's to do away with the hole that I have tried to enlarge the earth. Evil always brews in a hole.
You do evil in a hole, you don't do it in a cathedral.
For every wall that is removed is like the broadening of consciousness. There are more eyes looking on at us. There are more things perturbed by the disorder which we cause.
We ourselves, when the bulkheads are down, notice that there are occupations more interesting than gnawing each other like insects in a pot.

DONA SEVENSWORDS.   I wonder however you became aware long ago of that woman who was my mother.

DON RODRIGO.   I didn't become aware of her, I was delivered into her hands.

DONA SEVENSWORDS.   And now her death has set you free again, what luck!

DON RODRIGO.   My child, don't speak of things which she and I alone can know.

DONA SEVENSWORDS.   The bond with her, a touch of death was enough to break it. When I ask you to come to her rescue you will not.

DON RODRIGO.   Another task is calling me.

(DONA SEVENSWORDS *does not reply, and draws lines on the table with her finger.*)

My little teacher has something to say.

DONA SEVENSWORDS.   Father, I love you so! But need you talk to me of enlarging the earth and all those big things?
I can no longer follow you, it's too big; I no longer know where you are, and I feel all lonely and I want to cry!
It isn't worth while having a father if one isn't sure of him and if he isn't quite simple and small like us.

DON RODRIGO.   Then I have no right to live for anything but you?

DONA SEVENSWORDS.   You have just said that you have been delivered into her hands; why then are you trying to escape her? that is not honest;
You ought not to have allowed a woman once to get the better of you. Now what you promised her you have no right to withhold, and I am here to claim it in her stead.

DON RODRIGO.   But how if what you ask me I am absolutely unable to give?

DONA SEVENSWORDS.   It's your business to put yourself straight —so much the worse for you! It's a command, mark you! Nothing but obedience!
I am not pleased with you for putting this kind of custom-house at the gate of your heart to let in what pleases you and the rest not.
When I command you something and you say to me "I cannot," what do you know about it? You know nothing at all. Try to see!
It's so good, so mighty to obey!
Naturally one can fancy a heap of things to oneself. Imagination offers you a heap of good things all equally alluring.

But a command received, there is no choice. It is like natural hunger that seizes you by the guts—you leave everything standing to go and sit at table.

DON RODRIGO. Then what must I do?

DONA SEVENSWORDS. You must promise.

DON RODRIGO. Well, I promise.

DONA SEVENSWORDS. You mustn't say it like that, but simply: I promise—spitting on the ground.

DON RODRIGO. I promise. (*He spits on the ground.*)

DONA SEVENSWORDS. I promise too.

DON RODRIGO. I promise but I won't keep.

DONA SEVENSWORDS. Then I won't keep, either.

SCENE IX

THE KING OF SPAIN AND HIS COURT, DON RODRIGO

The Court of the King of Spain on his floating palace, as already described. It is made of several pontoons paired together and ill-joined, always cracking, rising, falling and changing level, so that not one of the actors has sure footing, and the architecture of this fine place varies in the strangest ways.

Pantomime of courtiers doing their best; it is evident that they are doing their utmost to be all there, and by means of diverse head-shakings, hand-joinings, arm-crossings, eyes raised to heaven or fixed on floor, and corroborating gestures, are expressing (in rhythm with a little tune both smart and funereal) their profound consternation. The moving floor forces them besides to knee-bending and body-bowing so as to keep their place, and sometimes throws them into amazing zigzags, most unexpectedly.

ONE. My cousin is among the lost.

TWO. So is my uncle. He leaves me all his fortune; I shall be very rich. Hurrah! Alas! Alas!

THREE. Alas! Alas! Alas!

FOUR. And to think that I had just got the monopoly of smoked haddock in Scotland for seventy years! What will my creditors say?

FIVE. The Duke of Medina Sidonia had his head caught between the two shells of a huge oyster.
You can see him when the sun shines gently waving in a sort of draught at the bottom of the sea,
Ending in elegant little shoes with diamond buckles.

THE CHANCELLOR, *in a cavernous voice.* What a strange turn in human affairs! (*Before he is quite done, a roll of the ship sends him express across the hall into the arms of an insignificant hidalgo much embarrassed by the honour.*)

ONE. Even yesterday on the faith of that absurd sub-prefect of Bayonne—

TWO. Yesterday and to-day!

THREE. All is lost! This time there is no doubt. Nothing will come back to Spain.

FOUR. Alas! Alas! our army!

FIVE. Alas! Alas! our ships!

SIX. Alas! our ships, the *Lion of Castile*, the *Sun Royal*, the *Elephant of Asturias*, the *Rampart of the Pyrenees*, and the *Grand Blank of Spain!*

ONE. The guard-ship of the Bidassoa.

TWO. The *San Fernando*, the *Saint Ferdinando*.

THREE. The *Saint Pontius*, the *Saint Alphonsus*, the *Saint Ildephonsus*.

FOUR. The *Saint Mark Girardin*, the *Saint Mary Perrin*, the *Saint René Taillandier*, and the *Bartholomew Saint Hilaire*.

FIVE. All gone to the bottom, *de profundis*, never mind, don't let us think of it!

ONE. The most wonderful thing of all is His Majesty's bearing. His face has not altered.

TWO. He has not countermanded any celebration.

THREE. Nor any audience.

FOUR. What, the audience with Don Rodrigo, does that hold still?

THE CHANCELLOR. Express command of His Majesty. Nothing is altered. Don Rodrigo is to be solemnly invested with his English command.

FIVE. What, does he know nothing about it?

THE CHANCELLOR. He has been isolated these two days on a ship. Strict orders to keep everything from him. Orders for you all, gentlemen, to behave respectfully to him as befits the Viceroy of England, the chosen of His Majesty.

ONE.   It's going to be funny!

TWO.   That, then, explains this strange choosing of Don Rodrigo?

THE CHANCELLOR.   We have a great sovereign. As soon as he heard of the disaster to the Armada, at the very moment when our own false news came to us of our victory, he thought of Don Rodrigo.

THREE.   Here he is.

> (*Enter* DON RODRIGO *in splendid black garments, a gold chain round his neck, leaning on a page and between two tall lackeys. All bow respectfully, with variations introduced by the motion of the sea. The curtain parts at the back of the stage and the King appears upon his throne. The whole Court does reverence. As he is on a different pontoon from that of* RODRIGO *and the courtiers, sometimes he rises above them to an amazing height, sometimes he disappears below, and nothing of him is seen but his head encircled by the gold crown with its cusps on a level with the floor. The orchestra fails to be interested in all that is coming, and to kill time busily imitates the dip and surge of the sea and the feelings of seasick folk.*)

THE KING.   Approach, Don Rodrigo, and let me at last gaze upon that forehead whence have sprouted so many noble thoughts, that arm which has laid its law on fortune.

I have been shown on the map that cutting which you had the idea of making between the two Americas;

An ingenious little thing from which the talents of Don Ramiro have been able to draw marvellous results.

For it is through that, could you believe it, sir, that from now onward peace reigns over this vast empire, and secure from sedition, we extend to both continents the benefits of religion and taxation.

And later on 'twas you that in the midst of ocean on the very flank of China and Japan,

Welded as it were those rings, the scattered Philippines where this ancient vessel of Spain has cast her furthest anchor,

Not without expenditure, of which our minds, more slow and heavy than your own, may still come some day, I am sure, to acknowledge the usefulness.

So many services deserved a recompense. But what position find for you where you should not be cramped?

Great minds have no needs. They mock at titles and money. What better recompense than to give free field to your genius and let you cruise at large in the sunshine of our benignity?

Then did we admire your Christian spirit when, void of any mercenary afterthought,

You consecrated yourself wholly to the moral welfare, so closely bound up with their material development, of our labouring populations on the seaboard.

What more meritorious than to bring home to the disinherited class by means well suited to their rude and simple mind

Some ray of the ideal, some reflex of higher beauty; in a word, the feeling for fine art?

Again what nobler subject of inspiration than those great men who all their lives did but teach the scorn of riches and respect for the State,

And who now in Heaven perpetual functionaries, share with the sun and moon the honours of the calendar?

Forgive me, Don Rodrigo, if the consideration of your artistic efforts has sometimes brought to my lips a good-natured smile.

In turning over those humble pictures I met with happy inspirations, the treasure-trove of a generous imagination, unhappily ill-served by insufficient means and ignorance of all the rules.

You have made me marvel once again how nature by herself cannot make up for the lack of good teaching.

Believe me, sir, our academies are full of abounding imagination, of quivering sensitiveness, of volcanic passion;

But all those fine minds could not have attained to clear and harmonious expression, to their own true social usefulness, they could not have exploited with economy their small domain, they would not enjoy without tiring our eyes and our brain that temperate brilliance which we admire,

Unless in dread of their own transports they had not eagerly seized on all the curbs which the wisdom of our ancestors has given to our hand, and had they not strictly laid down for themselves this rule of practice:

He who does what another has done before him is in no danger of going wrong.

Forgive me for enlarging at such length on this frivolous subject:

Perhaps you will deem me not altogether void of light upon these questions, having once taken lessons from Raphael,

I mean from Raphael Colin, and from Cormon.

But I desist. I know that in amusing yourself with these simple compositions your aim was not to augment the artistic patrimony of the Spanish nation,

But that the spirit guiding you on was that of vulgarisation, edification and philanthropy.

DON RODRIGO.   Nothing could escape Your Majesty's piercing gaze. What honour, and at the same time what confusion, to have held for a moment the attention of that eagle eye,

As well accustomed to take the measure of an empire as to follow the poor rabbit trying to hide between two clumps of heather.

So did the great Napoleon once with a glance bring to light Lucius de Lancival!

Those drawings that Your Majesty has just sentenced have cost me, who am but a poor workman, much trouble, many years of study, experiment and reflection,

But one look, a few moments of attention was enough for Your Majesty to discover their defects.

Ah me, I know them only too well! *Defuit mihi symmetria prisca.* I lacked the olden symmetry.

And to orientate me into my true direction (*laying his hand on his heart*), Your Majesty's words shall be my most precious treasure; yes, I will take them henceforward for my rule of art and of life,

Which shall be consecrated entirely not only to the uplifting of the moral tone of our tunny-fishers,

But to the glory and illustration of Its reign. (*He bows.*)

THE KING.   I approve of your intentions as much as of your modesty.

(*Flattering murmurs from the bystanders delicately underlined by the orchestra. Little thumps on the big drum.*)

But I spoke to try you. The serenity and deference with which you have replied prove to me that the artist in you has not won over and corrupted everything.

'Tis not an artist that I need in England.

'Tis not those hands spreading colour on paper that I need, but those that long ago fashioned America.

You have leave to speak, Master Chancellor.

THE CHANCELLOR, *legs apart like an old sea-dog riding the motion of pitch and toss.* Too long, Don Rodrigo, have you withdrawn yourself from the appreciation of your Sovereign and the expectation of your comrades in arms.

And if it is but too true, as is natural in human affairs, that the envy and wrath of the weak and foolish have taken free rein against you,

Still it was not a charitable or just or pious deed on your part to make no head against it and to give ground in silence.

To-day Spain and the world confess they can no longer do without your help.

It is not true that we need counsel more in adversity, for then necessity lays its law upon us.

It is when prosperity, as to-day, overwhelms us,

When an enterprise, as to-day, succeeds beyond our expectation, when incalculable responsibilities come knocking, and when all around us, in every sense, open avenues full of interest and peril ;

Then can be recognised the truly magnanimous heart, then, if it is any support to this overladen empire,

Let it come forward and say, "I can," and fly to support its Sovereign, who is creaking and groaning!

And like the three women of old who went seeking Coriolanus,

To-day not only England has come to throw herself at our feet, Mary whom the harlot's daughter deprived of her inheritance,

But Spain, but Christendom, but the Church, begging that Rodrigo no longer play them false!

(*Silence, sensation.*)

DON RODRIGO. I do not ask for troops or money. I ask that the King as soon as possible

Withdraw his soldiers and his ships. I will suffice.

THE CHANCELLOR. You anticipate the desires of His Majesty, who has need of all his forces in Germany,

THE MINISTER OF FINANCE.   And how will you do all alone without soldiers or ships to get the money out of the British? Who will refund us the costs of our expedition?

DON RODRIGO.   The good Christian wine of Spain and Portugal, my lord minister,
Which in our fogs we shall drink to your health,
That will undertake your payment.
Peace for evermore. The road to the Indies secure.

THE CHANCELLOR.   No troops nor money, that is understood. But do not be alarmed, we will provide you plentifully with helpers and advisers.

DON RODRIGO, *putting on his glasses and taking a paper from his pocket.*   I see here written on a paper which I amused myself with scribbling last night
That Rodrigo is worth a ha'penny whole and sound, and worth nothing at all once he is cut in two.

THE MINISTER OF JUSTICE.   What, no men of law to go with you?

DON RODRIGO.   That's down on my paper.

THE CHANCELLOR.   You want us to have absolute confidence in you?

DON RODRIGO.   It is down on my paper that it is necessary.
It is easier to have confidence in one man than in two.

THE MINISTER OF WAR.   And what obligations do you undertake in return?
What are you ready to do in the matter of military contingent and contribution?

DON RODRIGO.   The military contingent will be those troops which heretofore you devoted to our injury,
And as for the contribution, I may seek but I shall not find that expression in my book of words.

THE MINISTER OF WAR.   Is it in the interests of England and Spain that the King sends you over there to advise and govern?

DON RODRIGO.   I should be a very ill tutor if I did not take in hand the interests of my pupil.

THE MINISTER OF WAR. Must you sacrifice to them the interests of your mandatory?

DON RODRIGO. God forbid, I want to spare the Minister of Finance the expense of a new Armada.

Yes, while we are there let us make full profit of our victory! I want England and Spain after so many combats to bless forever the day they had the happy thought to shake hands!

Ah, we have fought well, but not more than we had to; we have got out of each other all that could be got.

The embrace would not have such savour if it were not a vanquished enemy that we had in our arms in the person of that fainting nation.

THE MINISTER OF PUBLIC INSTRUCTION. I beg Your Majesty to mark the unsettling proposals of Don Rodrigo.

THE KING, *who just now occupies a perilously slanting position while the courtiers on the other ship affect the opposite slant.* What he says is not without sense. I myself do not look upon England with other than peaceful and matrimonial intent.

I believe in love! What politics cannot do 'tis love's business to achieve.

What instance of the dainty give and take of Providence across so many battles, better

Than an arrangement making at once provision for universal peace and the establishment of my sons? Where could this forsaken queen be more comfortable than in the arms of Don Udolpho or Don Valentino?

DON RODRIGO. The problem of tolerance among the nations is already hard enough

Without adding to it that of agreement between husband and wife.

THE KING. Still I have noticed that Queen Mary looked on our Don Ernesto with a favourable eye.

DON RODRIGO. No, if anyone knows Queen Mary, I venture to say that I do. She is a reserved and touchy soul. She is hardly out of prison. 'Tis quite evident that she has passed her life in retirement far from the public gaze.

She needed the ingenuous admiration with which I inspired her before she would open her heart to me; I penetrated right to the bottom of that virgin heart, that blend of boldness and timidity.
I believe that if any man can influence her mind it is I.

THE KING. Then I put my son's cause in your hands.

DON RODRIGO. There must be no hurry.
Your Majesty will weigh and judge the whole question whether it be seemly to give later on to a stranger
A title to the Spanish succession.

THE KING. I will think it over.

THE MINISTER OF WAR. Don Rodrigo has omitted to tell us up to now the secret reason why he alone is sufficient, and how,
Without troops or money or marriage,
He will keep hold on England and make her forever the friend and ally of Spain.

DON RODRIGO. Give your enemies to eat, they will not come bothering you at your meal and snatching the bread from your mouth.

THE CHANCELLOR. I don't understand this parable.

DON RODRIGO. The Indies away there in the setting sun, I say they are beyond the appetite of a single man.

THE CHANCELLOR. I begin to understand.

DON RODRIGO. They have enough to provide for centuries a huge repast for all the world!
Why make such ado about this world when the other is over there merely for us to take, with His Catholic Majesty for evermore, thanks to me, holding the main artery?

THE KING. You want us, then, to give England the freedom and citizenship of our two Americas?

DON RODRIGO. Not England only! Not for nothing did God after Christopher invite us to cross the sea! I want all nations to celebrate the Pasch at this enormous table that He has laid for us between the two oceans!

When God gave America to that Ferdinand who is excellently called the Catholic, it was too big—it was not for him alone, but for all peoples to share.

Let England bless for ever the day of her reunion, when in exchange for that liberty of hers which was like the liberty of mutineers on a stolen ship, you gave her a new world!

Give all these little European peoples squeezed together and treading on one another room to move!

Unite all Europe in a single stream! And all those heresy-ridden peoples, since they cannot reunite at their sources, let them reunite by their river mouths!

THE KING. Am I to understand that before taking over this lieutenancy which I am ready to give you over England,

You demand that I open America to your new subjects, my recent enemies? Is that your condition?

DON RODRIGO.   I do not see what useful thing I can do there else.

(*Murmur of dissent among the bystanders in which the orchestra joins after taking time for reflection.*)

THE MINISTER OF WAR. What insolence!

THE MINISTER OF HYGIENE. What impudence!

THE MINISTER OF JUSTICE. What exorbitance!

THE MINISTER OF PUBLIC INSTRUCTION. What extravagance! Sir, we all beg you not to tem—

(*A heavy roll.*)

—not to temporise!
We all beg you not to temporise with the rash and insolent demands and extravagances of this exorbitant gentleman!

(*The orchestra adds peremptorily: That's it. And after a short pause sets to imitate the spasms of seasickness.*)

THE MINISTER OF OVERSEAS. All the same, we cannot turn America, which the genius and virtue of your never-to-be-forgotten grandfather brought forth from the bosom of the Indies, into

The common grazing-ground of all Europe!

THE MINISTER OF PUBLIC INSTRUCTION. We must not temporise! We must not temporise!

THE KING. And what do you say, my lord Chancellor?

THE CHANCELLOR. Excuse me. I do not know what to think. I am all upset and shaky, as you see.

THE KING. Do you see any way whatever of doing without Don Rodrigo in England?

THE CHANCELLOR, *bowing his head and knitting his brows as though he were making a great effort at reflection, then, with a gesture of desperate resignation.* Alas! Search as we may, we have no other choice!

THE KING, *to his Ministers.* Does any of you wish to receive England at my hand instead of Rodrigo?

THE MINISTER OF HYGIENE. So please Your Majesty, excuse me.

THE KING. Have you another name to suggest?

THE MINISTER OF PHYSICAL EXERCISES, *in loud desperation.* There are no others! There are no others! (*Hereupon a heavy roll forces him to regain his balance by a series of complicated figures.*)

THE CHANCELLOR, *pathetic and bleating.* Don Rodrigo, let me beg you to be conciliatory, listen to the advice of an old man.
You see the cruel dilemma in which our Sovereign is placed! Be magnanimous! Do not abuse the situation! You see that we cannot do without you!
I beg you not to ask more than it is possible to grant.

DON RODRIGO. I cannot ensure peace if you do not give me the whole world.

THE KING. The whole world is little to me, Don Rodrigo, if it but assures me your love and loyalty.
Go back to your ship. You shall know my decision presently. You have made yourself a sight for all men. Each has been able to gaze upon you in comfort.
Guards, accompany His Highness and watch his every step.

I cannot any longer keep you from the place which you yourself have chosen.

(*He goes out majestically, halting in time to the motion of the sea.* DON RODRIGO *goes out as he came in. All the great personages range themselves in three rows facing the audience, and at a hand-clap file out left and right, after indulging in certain displays of rhythmic gymnastics.*)

SCENE X

In the open sea under the full moon. DONA SEVENSWORDS *and the* BUTCHER'S DAUGHTER *swimming. No music, but some well-spaced thumps of the big drum. The cinema may be used.*

DONA SEVENSWORDS. Forward. Courage, Butchie!

THE BUTCHER'S DAUGHTER. Oh, it isn't goodwill I lack! Wherever you go, miss, I know well that I have no choice but to go with you.

DONA SEVENSWORDS. If you are tired you have only to turn on your back like this, crosswise, arms out.
There is only your mouth and nose out, and when you sink, a deep breath brings you back to the air at once.
A tiny movement like this with the feet and half the hands.
There is no danger of getting tired.

THE BUTCHER'S DAUGHTER. It isn't so much that I am tired, but someone told me he saw sharks. Oh, I am afraid of a shark coming and pulling me under by the feet!

DONA SEVENSWORDS. It isn't sharks, I have seen them! It's porpoises at play. Haven't they a right to play? Maybe it isn't fun to be a jolly porpoise. (*She kicks up the water noisily.*)

THE BUTCHER'S DAUGHTER. Oh, I am afraid they will jump on me!

DONA SEVENSWORDS. Don't be afraid, let 'em come; if there is one that tries to hurt you I will defend you against them, the bastards! (*She laughs uproariously.*)

THE BUTCHER'S DAUGHTER. Miss, I have been looking everywhere, and I can't see the red lantern any more.

DONA SEVENSWORDS.   Your friends in Majorca must have forgotten us, hurrah! Tra la la!

THE BUTCHER'S DAUGHTER.   Oh no, don't say that, I pray you, Miss, you make me so frightened!
Oh no, I am quite sure of Rosalie and Carmen and Dolores; they haven't forgotten me, and they are waiting for us somewhere with clothes all ready, as I told them.
Something must have frightened them.

DONA SEVENSWORDS.   You are frightened, they are frightened, they are frightening you! Fright! Fright! Fright! Fright! You have nothing but that word on your lips!
I cannot understand why you are in such a hurry to get there, it feels so good in the lovely sea!
Look at the moon in front of us in the water all flat like a gold plate! It looks as if I could catch it in my teeth.

THE BUTCHER'S DAUGHTER.   I say, Miss, shall we go back to your father's ship, we are not far from it yet?

DONA SEVENSWORDS.   We have left; it is done with; I don't want to go back.

THE BUTCHER'S DAUGHTER.   It will grieve him so to see you gone like that.

DONA SEVENSWORDS.   It won't grieve him at all. The King has given him England, behold him King of England. He already has thirty-six ideas about England, he isn't thinking of me any more.
He is going to paint all England sky-blue.

THE BUTCHER'S DAUGHTER.   If you explain everything to your father as you should, perhaps he would come with us.

DONA SEVENSWORDS.   No, he will not come, he has something else to do. They have given him the earth to enlarge.

THE BUTCHER'S DAUGHTER.   But doesn't it grieve you yourself to leave him?

DONA SEVENSWORDS.   Oh, yes, it grieves me, poor daddy! He is so stupid! It makes me cry just to think of it. He loves me well at bottom.

THE BUTCHER'S DAUGHTER. What would your mother say if she saw you leaving him like this?

DONA SEVENSWORDS. 'Tis she that is calling me.

THE BUTCHER'S DAUGHTER. What is she calling you to?

DONA SEVENSWORDS. What my father doesn't want to do I will do all by myself instead of him.

THE BUTCHER'S DAUGHTER. Don't say that your father doesn't want to do anything; look at all the things about him that he has done.

DONA SEVENSWORDS. There is only one thing necessary.

THE BUTCHER'S DAUGHTER. Is it to go with John of Austria?

DONA SEVENSWORDS. Yes, it is to go with John of Austria; you know we leave to-morrow; there is no time to lose. Forward!
My father has no need of me; he went off leaving me that little word; look at him like an old pike sinking in the water sending up from under, from behind him a few bubbles; he is no more to be seen.
And I too have left him a little word.

THE BUTCHER'S DAUGHTER. Oh, I wish I were a fish!

DONA SEVENSWORDS. Courage; there it is, there it is, I see it again! There is the red lantern again! I am sure they see us, it's as bright as mid-day. They must see our two heads quite well and the white we make with swimming!
There is only one thing necessary, that is the folk that we are necessary to. Forward!
Oh, if I could catch that sort of flat hat floating there in front of me, three feet before my mouth, and wave it over my head to signal them!

THE BUTCHER'S DAUGHTER. You were so enticing and it was so enjoyable to hear you talk, I came with you.
While you are there and talking, how jolly, I cease to exist, I don't feel it worth while existing.

DONA SEVENSWORDS. You will see if it is not worth while

existing, the nice husband that I will give you on board John of Austria's ship, all in steel and gold!

THE BUTCHER'S DAUGHTER. When you tell him about it, he will never be comforted for never having seen me.

DONA SEVENSWORDS. But it is nonsense, I tell you! The sea bears you up, it's delightful! There is hardly any effort to make, the water is warm. Who could get tired? There is nothing to be tired for. Don't go and tell me you are tired?

THE BUTCHER'S DAUGHTER. No, I am not tired.

DONA SEVENSWORDS. There is only one thing necessary, and blow all the rest.

What good is it to peer so much and walk about everlastingly like a connoisseur with a pot of colour in hand, retouching here and there?

And when a thing is finished to pack his little toucher-up outfit to go and tinker somewhere else?

There is only one thing necessary, and that is someone who asks everything of you and to whom you can give everything. Forward!

What would my wee John of Austria say to-night if he did not see me join the colours. I am wanted!

Since my father does not wish to fight I will fight in his place.

You know you heard how all Asia once more is beginning to rise against Jesus Christ; there is a smell of camel over all Europe.

There is a Turkish army round Vienna, there is a big fleet at Lepanto.

It is time for Christendom once more to fly bodily at Mahomet; he will see the medicine we will make him take, him and the King of France, his ally!

I hope you are not tired.

THE BUTCHER'S DAUGHTER, *almost spent*. No, no, I am not tired.

DONA SEVENSWORDS. If you are tired, it is all over, I shall never bring you out again with me.

THE BUTCHER'S DAUGHTER. Forgive me for being such a poor swimmer.

DONA SEVENSWORDS.　Let us go now quietly at our ease. It is delightful to soak in this kind of liquid light that makes us into hovering godlike beings, (*in thought*) glorified bodies.

No more need of hands to grasp with or feet to carry you.

You go on, like the sea-anemone's breathing, by the mere expansion of the body and the kick of the will.

The whole body is one sense, a planet watching the other planets in the air.

(*Aloud.*)

I feel immediately with my heart every beat of thy heart.

(*Here the* BUTCHER'S DAUGHTER *drowns.*)

The water bears up everything. It's delightful, your ear on a level with the water, to notice all those melting musics (*in thought*)—the dancers around the guitar,

Life, song, words of love, the incalculable crackle of all those whispered words!

And all that is no longer outside one, you are inside; there is something that unites you blissfully with everything, a drop of water mingling with the sea! The Communion of Saints!

(*Aloud.*)

How tiresome! I see that the boat has seen us, it is making for us!

Courage, Butchie, one more little stroke, you duffer! Forward! You have only to follow me.

(*She goes on swimming strongly.*)

SCENE XI

DON RODRIGO, BROTHER LEO, TWO SOLDIERS

The same night; the SOLDIERS, DON RODRIGO *in chains,* BROTHER LEO *on a boat steering for land. A great lantern fastened to the mast lights up the stage.*

The music is made up: first, of wind instruments (various flutes, very green and sharp, indefinitely keeping up the same note to the end of the scene; from time to time one of the instruments stops, uncovering the underlying notes which go on piping; secondly, three pizzicato notes in ascending scale on the strings; thirdly, a note from the bow; fourthly, a dry roll of drum-sticks on a little flat drum; fifthly, two little metal gongs; sixthly, ground-tone of bursts on a huge drum).

DON RODRIGO, *to one of the soldiers who is holding a letter in his hand.* I beg you give me that letter which belongs to me.

BROTHER LEO. Give him that letter, Manuelito.

THE SOLDIER. I will give it him if I like. I don't fancy anyone doing the King of England with me.

DON RODRIGO. That letter belongs to me.

THE SOLDIER. It's you, old Rodrigo, that belongs to me. The King, in his great mercy having thought good to pardon a traitor,
Gave you over lock, stock and barrel to his Chamberlain, who gave you in turn to his valet, in payment of ten gold pieces that son of a bitch had lent him,
And he in his turn, not knowing what to do with this old Peg-Leg,
Gave you for service rendered to me; it's a fine catch; to-morrow I am going to have you drummed through all Majorca; I shall get a good five penn'orth out of you at the present price of traitor's skin.

DON RODRIGO. Please consider, Sir, that that letter is from my daughter.

THE SOLDIER.   Well, if you like we will throw for it at dice. If you win it's yours.

(*He shakes the dice in a box which he offers him.*)

DON RODRIGO.   Brother Leo, I cannot take hold of this box because of my chains. I beg you play instead of me.

(*The* FRIAR *shakes the box and throws the dice on the floor.*)

THE SOLDIER, *looking at the dice*.   Three aces! that's not bad!

(*He throws the dice in his turn.*)

Four aces, I win!

BROTHER LEO.   Give him the letter all the same, son!

THE SOLDIER.   I won't give him the letter, but I will jolly well read it to him. Who knows if there isn't some plotting in it against His Majesty?

(*He opens the letter and going near the lantern, sets about reading it.*)

Ha! Ha! (*He laughs uproariously.*)

SECOND SOLDIER.   What's making you laugh?

FIRST SOLDIER.   "My dear Papa," she says.

SECOND SOLDIER.   What's funny in that?

FIRST SOLDIER.   He's got her to believe that he was her papa! Her papa is Devil-hunter, as they called him, Don Camillo, another renegade in his time, just like him, who did piracy on the coast of Morocco,
And who had for mistress the widow of an old captain-general of garrisons; wait a bit, she had a funny name, something like Ogress, or Buggress—Prouheze.

BROTHER LEO.   She was not his mistress but his wife. I know, because it is I that married them both long ago when I was at Mogador.

DON RODRIGO.   What, Father, did you know Prouheze?

FIRST SOLDIER. Looks as if Rodrigo was the papa all the same. "My dear Papa," she writes. Ha! Ha!

SECOND SOLDIER. Wait a bit, he has something to say—my lord has something to say?

DON RODRIGO. Not at all. I join in your simple merriment. Is it forbidden to laugh? Your comrade has a catchy laugh, sign of a happy disposition.

SECOND SOLDIER. And it doesn't matter to you that you were called a traitor?

DON RODRIGO. It would matter something if I were one.

SECOND SOLDIER. But it is true that you are one!

DON RODRIGO. Then they have been able to fix me so that I do no harm to anyone.

SECOND SOLDIER, *to the* FIRST. Read us the rest.

FIRST SOLDIER, *reading*. "The King has given you England. You have no more need of me." Ha! Ha! Ha! (*He laughs uproariously.*)

SECOND SOLDIER. The King has given him England, that's funny! He has only to go and take it!

FIRST SOLDIER. Old chap, there is an actress called—called something—she made believe to him that she was Mary, Queen of England.
She went and threw herself at his feet to ask him to fly to her rescue and accept a kingdom at her hand.

SECOND SOLDIER. That's funny!

FIRST SOLDIER. It's then they made every sort of little arrangement together against the King of Spain. She has told everything.

SECOND SOLDIER. I should like to have been there when he laid down his conditions to the King for taking over England! Everyone is laughing about it at sea!

DON RODRIGO. You see there an instance, Father, of the absurd situations that a man of fancy can get himself into. Nothing seems surprising to him.

How refuse to believe a pretty woman who took in with lips and eyes everything that I said, a charming person who drew so well and gathered my least intention with the end of her brush?

FIRST SOLDIER, *bringing the letter near the lantern.*   Where was I—"England, you have no more need of me."

BROTHER LEO.   Manuel, I have here in my sleeve four silver pieces that charitable souls have given me for my convent.

I will give them you if you give me that letter.

FIRST SOLDIER.   I will give it you when I have read it.

DON RODRIGO.   Let him read it, Brother Leo.

FIRST SOLDIER.   "I am setting off to join John of Austria;" that is a bit of news, you hear, old fellow? She is setting off to join John of Austria.

SECOND SOLDIER.   John of Austria is going to marry her for sure. Then he won't have to bother about settling himself.

FIRST SOLDIER.   She knew they were going to arrest her father. There was nothing for it but quit, double quick. This old bandy-leg that's going to jail, nothing for it but to drop him. It isn't for nothing you are daughter of two traitors.

SECOND SOLDIER.   It's the right time to join John of Austria.

FIRST SOLDIER.   Only has she rejoined him? Just now I heard tell that the fishermen had just taken out of the water a girl who died on their hands.

BROTHER LEO.   How can you both be so wicked and cruel?

FIRST SOLDIER.   It's he that's defying us and making game of us with his superior easy-going airs.

You could say that it's milord invited us, and feels sincerely satisfied with the joy he gives us in receiving us to the number of his domestics.

BROTHER LEO *to* DON RODRIGO, *putting a hand on his.*   Don Rodrigo, it isn't true, or else it is another girl.

DON RODRIGO. I am sure. What evil could happen to me on a night so lovely?

SECOND SOLDIER. It's a lovely night for you when they are either bringing you to jail or to sell you for a slave?

DON RODRIGO. I have never seen anything so magnificent! You might say that I am seeing Heaven for the first time. Yes, it is a lovely night for me is this, when I celebrate at last my betrothal unto freedom.

SECOND SOLDIER. Did you hear what he said? He's mad.

FIRST SOLDIER. Let's finish our reading. "I am going to join John of Austria, farewell. I put my arms round you. We shall meet again."—I can't make it out.

BROTHER LEO. Give me the letter.

FIRST SOLDIER.—"in Heaven, we shall meet again in Heaven."

SECOND SOLDIER. In Heaven or in quite another place, Amen.

BROTHER LEO. There is nothing else?

FIRST SOLDIER. "Your loving daughter, Mary of the Seven Swords."

SECOND SOLDIER. That's a good ending to the letter.

FIRST SOLDIER. There's another line. "When I am come to John of Austria, I will tell them to fire a gun. Look out."

(*A woman calling through the night, at sea.*)

Barque ahoy!

FIRST SOLDIER. We are hailed. There is a boat over there signalling us with a lantern.

(*Both go to another part of the boat.*)

DON RODRIGO, *softly*. Is it true, Brother Leo? Do you think it is really my daughter that the fishermen took out of the sea?

BROTHER LEO. No, my son. I am sure it isn't true.

DON RODRIGO. Brave Sevenswords, no, no, neither you nor

your father is of the sort that the sea takes down! He who has a strong arm and breathes God's air with full lungs is in no danger of drowning! He gaily tops this big and splendid wave that wishes us no harm!

BROTHER LEO. You must forgive her.

DON RODRIGO. Forgive her, say you? There is nothing to forgive. Ah, would that she were here, the dear child, that I might hug her in these fettered arms!
Go to thy destiny, my child, go fight for Jesus Christ, my lamb, beside John of Austria,
The lamb they see in the paintings with his little banner on his shoulder.

BROTHER LEO. Brother Rodrigo, wouldn't this be just the time to unburden your heart to me?

DON RODRIGO. It is laden with sins and with the glory of God, and it all comes pell-mell to my lips when I try to free my soul!

BROTHER LEO. Tell me it, then, altogether.

DON RODRIGO. What comes first is my own night, deep down in me, like a torrent of sorrow and joy at the touch of this night of splendour.
Look!—
You might call it a whole population, round us, living by the eyes alone.

BROTHER LEO, *pointing heavenwards*. It is there beyond, Rodrigo, that you will celebrate your betrothal unto freedom!

DON RODRIGO, *softly*. Brother Leo, give me your hand, try to remember. Is it true that you have seen her?

BROTHER LEO. Whom do you mean?

DON RODRIGO. That woman you gave in marriage long ago at Mogador to somebody. And so you have seen her? Is it true that you have seen her? What did she say to you? How did she look that day? Tell me if there has ever been in the world a more beautiful woman.

BROTHER LEO. Yes, she was very beautiful.

DON RODRIGO.   Ah, ah, cruel she! Ah, what dreadful courage! Ah, how could she betray me and marry that other man? And I never had her lovely hand but one moment against my cheek! Ah, after so many years the wound is still there, and nothing can heal it!

BROTHER LEO.   All that will be made clear to you some day.

DON RODRIGO.   You must remember. The day you married her, did she look happy beside that blackamoor? Did she give him her fair hand willingly, the finger of her hand for the ring?

BROTHER LEO.   It's so long ago. I no longer remember.

DON RODRIGO.   You no longer remember; what, not even those lovely eyes?

BROTHER LEO.   My son, we must not look now save at the stars.

DON RODRIGO.   You no longer remember?
Ah, that radiant smile and those eyes full of faith looking on me! Eyes that God never made to see what is vile and dead in me.

BROTHER LEO.   Leave these heart-rending thoughts.

DON RODRIGO.   She is dead, dead, dead! She is dead, father, and I shall never see her any more; she is dead and never will be mine; she is dead and 'tis I that killed her.

BROTHER LEO.   She is not so dead as that this sky about us and this sea beneath us be more everlasting.

DON RODRIGO.   I know, that is what she came to bring me with the sight of her!
The sea and the stars, I feel them under me and gaze at them and cannot have my fill!
Yes, I feel we cannot get away from them and that it is impossible to die!

BROTHER LEO.   Seek inwardly to your heart's content! You will never get to the end of those inexhaustible treasures! There is now no way of escape from them or being without them! All else but God has been withdrawn! The task-master is chained up! All in you that wretchedly fastened on things one by one and pertinaciously! We are done with servile works! Your limbs, those tyrants, are in chains, and you have but to draw breath to be full of God!

DON RODRIGO. You understand what I meant when just now I darkly felt that I was free?

(*A shock, the boat is boarded by another.*)

A WOMAN'S VOICE. Help! Help me!

(*An old nun helped by another comes on board.*)

FIRST SOLDIER. Welcome to the gleaning-sister.

THE NUN. Good morrow, little soldier, is there nothing for me on your boat?

FIRST SOLDIER. Yes, there is a heap of old odds and ends of every kind, old arms, old hats, old flags, old iron, broken pots, cracked boilers, they gave me to sell at Majorca.

THE NUN. Let us see, little soldier.

FIRST SOLDIER. It's too dirty and ugly for you.

THE NUN. There is nothing too dirty or ugly for the old rag-picker nun. All is fish to her net—waste, scrapings, sweepings, what you throw out, what nobody wants, that's what she spends her time hunting and gathering.

FIRST SOLDIER. And you make money out of that?

THE NUN. Enough money to feed a lot of poor and old folk and build convents for Mother Teresa.

DON RODRIGO. Is it Mother Teresa of Jesus that sends you like this to glean the sea?

THE NUN. Yes, my lad, I glean for her and every convent in Spain.

(*The* SOLDIER *has gone to get an armful of old clothes and heterogeneous objects, which he throws on the bridge. The* NUN *examines and moves them about with the end of her stick by the light of the lantern.*)

THE NUN. What do you want for all that?

FIRST SOLDIER. Three gold pieces.

THE NUN. Three gold pieces? I will jolly well give you two.

DON RODRIGO. Mother gleaner, mother gleaner, since you are a connoisseur why don't you take me too, with the old flags and the broken pots?

THE NUN, *to the* SOLDIER. Who is that man?

FIRST SOLDIER. It's a traitor that the King gave me to sell in the market.

THE NUN, *to* DON RODRIGO. Well, my lad, you hear? You are a traitor; what do you want me to do with a traitor? Even if you had your full allowance of legs—

DON RODRIGO. You will get me very cheap.

THE NUN, *to the* SOLDIER. Is he really for sale?

FIRST SOLDIER. He is for sale, why not?

THE NUN. And what can you do?

DON RODRIGO. I can read and write.

THE NUN. And do you know how to cook or sew and cut out clothes?

DON RODRIGO. I know perfectly well.

THE NUN. Or mend shoes?

DON RODRIGO. I can do that, too.

FIRST SOLDIER. Don't mind him, Sister, he is telling lies.

THE NUN. It isn't nice to tell lies, my lad.

DON RODRIGO. At least I can wash up the dishes.

FIRST SOLDIER. If you give 'em to him, he will smash everything.

DON RODRIGO. I want to live in the shadow of Mother Teresa. God made me to be her poor servant.

I want to shell the beans at the convent gate, I want to wipe her sandals all covered with the dust of Heaven!

BROTHER LEO.　Take him, Mother gleaner.

THE NUN.　To please you, Father. I will take him, but I won't pay anything for him.

FIRST SOLDIER.　It isn't that I am set on him, but you must give me a little tip. A silver ha'penny for the sake of saying that I got something out of him.

THE NUN.　You can keep him then.

BROTHER LEO.　Give him, soldier, you will be safe; no one knows what might yet come out of this queer old Rodrigo.

FIRST SOLDIER.　Then you can take him.

THE NUN.　And can I also have that sort of iron cauldron that I see over there and that is no use to you? Or else I won't have him.

FIRST SOLDIER.　Take it, take everything, take my shirt.

THE NUN.　Pack up all that, Sister, and you come with me, my lad. Look out for the ladder with that poor leg.

DON RODRIGO.　Hark!

(*A trumpet in the distance pealing triumphantly.*)

THE NUN.　That comes from John of Austria's ship.

DON RODRIGO.　She is safe! My child is safe!

(*Sound of a cannon shot in the distance.*)

BROTHER LEO.　Deliverance to souls in prison!

(*The instruments of the orchestra are silent one by one.*)

(Paris, May, 1919—
Tokio, December, 1924.)

EXPLICIT
OPVS MIRANDVM